Psalms 42–89

A CHRISTIAN UNION BIBLE STUDY

A CHRISTIAN UNION RESOURCE
PUBLISHED BY TYNDALE HOUSE PUBLISHERS

**CHRISTIAN
UNION**

Tyndale House Publishers
Carol Stream, Illinois

Visit Tyndale online at tyndale.com.

Visit Christian Union online at christianunion.org.

Christian Union Bible Studies: Psalms 42–89

Copyright © 2022 by Christian Union. All rights reserved.

A Christian Union resource published by Tyndale House Publishers, Carol Stream, Illinois 60188

Christian Union and Christian Union's logo featuring the cross and the "MAIOR AUTEM HIS EST CARITAS" text are registered trademarks of Christian Union, Inc.

Tyndale and Tyndale's quill logo are registered trademarks of Tyndale House Ministries.

Cover photograph of clouds by Eberhard Grossgasteiger on Unsplash.

Designed by Jennifer Phelps

Published in association with the literary agency of The Gates Group, www.the-gates-group.com.

For information about special discounts for bulk purchases, please contact Tyndale House Publishers at csresponse@tyndale.com, or call 1-855-277-9400.

ISBN 978-1-4964-6012-7   Softcover

Printed in the United States of America

28	27	26	25	24	23	22
7	6	5	4	3	2	1

CONTENTS

Series Introduction

It is written: "Man shall not live on bread alone,
but on every word that proceeds from the mouth of God."
(MATT 4:4, QUOTING DEUT 8:3)

You know the story. Jesus had been baptized in the Jordan River, God the Father had called Him "my beloved Son," and the Holy Spirit had visibly descended upon Him. And then He was tested. You have opened this book because, in one way or another, God has impressed upon you the value of knowing and feeding on His Word—of being able to meet life's trials as Jesus met His in the wilderness, with a sure declaration: "It is written . . ."

A NEW BIBLE STUDY SERIES

Following Jesus' example means knowing God's Word and acting on it. Christian Union's aim in publishing these Bible studies is therefore twofold: that through daily reading and rigorous study you will grow in your knowledge and understanding of what God says in the Scriptures; and that in so doing you will come to more deeply know, trust, love, and walk in step with the One whose words are life (John 6:63). Throughout each lesson, we seek to offer relevant insight from our own engagement with the Word and the best available biblical scholarship, and to stretch you in considering the implications of that insight as you endeavor to live a life that honors God—and to help you lead others in doing the same.

BACKGROUND TO CHRISTIAN UNION BIBLE STUDIES

From our beginnings in 2002 on the campus of Princeton University—and from there to several other of America's most secular, academically intense, and influential universities, and then to our ministries in key cities, online, and now in print—our mission as an organization has been, and continues to be, to develop Christian leaders who will bring the truth and power of the gospel to bear on every sphere of culture. Our vision is to see national revival and reformation so that every aspect of society brings praise and honor to Jesus Christ.

In keeping with our focus on training Christians as leaders, these studies assume that you have already confessed Jesus as your Savior and King, and that you still love learning. Building on the model we have developed in working with university students, we aim to facilitate a robust engagement of your heart and mind with the texts of Scripture. We do not assume you have received formal training in theology, nor that you have any prior knowledge of biblical languages, but we will introduce you to key terms along the way.

HOW TO USE THIS BOOK

Each book in this series is laid out as a ten-to-twelve-week study, with each week's lesson divided into five parts. This gives you a portion for five days of the week, with two days free for other study. You can make use of this book on your own, or it can be used as a guide for small-group Bible study. In either case, the intention is that you would set aside time on your own each day to pray, read through one part of this study (beginning with that day's Scripture), and answer the questions for that day. On most days, working through the lesson should take roughly fifteen minutes (the introductory lessons may take a bit longer)—though, of course, you may work at your own pace.

If using this for a group study, each member of the group should have a copy of this guide and work through it before meeting with the rest of the group. The leader can then draw on a week's worth of content and questions to facilitate discussion when the group comes together. Some groups may wish to work at a different pace than is implied by the weekly format of these study guides; this can be achieved without much difficulty, as each "day" is presented as a self-contained unit. Leaders can thus assign as many "days" as they wish to cover at the next group meeting.

EYES ON THE PRIZE

Foremost among our values at Christian Union is what we call a Seeking-God Lifestyle. (For more on this topic, see Appendix B in this volume.) The psalmist says: "Seek Yahweh and his strength. Seek his face continually" (Ps 105:4). We want to live in God's presence, and we need His power to walk in His ways and heal what is broken. As we seek a greater outpouring of God's holy and healing presence in our land, we aim to do as the Lord instructed Solomon: "If my people . . . will humble themselves, and pray, and seek my face, and turn from their wicked ways . . ." (2 Chr 7:14). So as you study the contents of these lessons, we will also encourage you to develop such ongoing habits as have marked the lives of the faithful throughout the ages.

Here is a promise worth remembering: "Be subject to God. Take a stand against the devil, and he will flee from you. Draw near to God, and he will draw near to you" (Jas 4:7-8). As you work your way through this study, may the Holy Spirit fill you and empower you to follow hard after the Lord Jesus and bring honor to our Father in heaven. Amen.

Acknowledgments

First, Christian Union wishes to honor and thank God for giving us His Word as a lamp for our feet and a light for our path (Ps 119:105).

This Bible study series is an outgrowth of the excellent Bible Course Manuals that a number of Christian Union faculty have produced over the years for our work on college campuses. They stem from the vision of our founder and CEO, Matt Bennett, who has supervised the writing process and edited each chapter before submission to the publisher. Thanks also go to Liz Green for her role in inspiring Matt to write Christian Union's first Bible Course and in shaping what has become a central feature of our ministry.

This study was written by Michael Racine, who, prior to working full-time on this project, served as a ministry fellow with Christian Union Lux, our ministry to undergraduates at Yale University.

Grateful acknowledgment is given to the Christian Union faculty and staff who improved this study by reviewing the drafts and giving feedback along the way: David Farrow, AVP of Christian Union Universities; Qwynn Gross, ministry fellow with Christian Union Nova (Princeton); Dr. Chuck Hetzler, director of Christian Union Day and Night; Michael Lee, our COO; and Dr. Ben Pascut, ministry director of Christian Union Lux.

We also wish to thank Don Gates, our literary agent, who brought us together with the good people at Tyndale House Publishers. And to Jon Bryant, our editor, and everyone at Tyndale who helped this vision become a reality—it was evident from our first meeting that you would make great partners, and we pray that the Lord would honor your every faithful step as you seek to make God's Word known and understood. From all of us at Christian Union: Thank you.

Finally, Christian Union wishes to thank all of our Cornerstone Partners, whose financial generosity has changed many lives to the glory of God. If you would like to accelerate the transformation that God is bringing among America's current and future leaders, please see ChristianUnion.org/Cornerstone.

A Note on Translation

Unless otherwise noted, all translations found in this book are the author's own work. We offer our own translation of the text under consideration for a few reasons. First, we do not presume to know which Bible version(s) you may be using regularly, or whether you and the other members of your small group all have the same version, so this keeps us all on the same page. Second, it will save you from juggling continually back and forth between this book and your Bible (though we will include a number of Scripture references along the way, which we encourage you to look up). Finally, we offer the supplied translation as a complement to whatever you already have. Every attempt to translate a Hebrew or Greek composition into understandable and readable English involves many different considerations; using our own translation allows us to preserve some idiosyncrasies of the original composition that we will then unpack in the discussion that follows.

One noteworthy feature of the biblical text that may cause modern readers some discomfort is the common use of a masculine singular pronoun where humanity in general seems to be in view. While some translations, for obvious reasons, substitute gender-neutral plurals (*they/them*) in place of the ancient authors' masculine language, we have specific reasons for retaining the singular pronouns of the original texts. As chief among these, we observe that all of Scripture points ultimately to Jesus (see Luke 24:27, 44), who fulfilled what the Psalms and Prophets foretold of that (masculine singular) figure. So when, for instance, the Psalms reference an unnamed "him," we can understand that pronoun as indicating (a) the psalmist himself—usually David; (b) the Son of David, Jesus the Messiah; and/or (c) each of us (male or female) whose identities are wrapped up in Christ Jesus. The same words can, and often do, operate at multiple levels of fulfillment, and we wish to preserve the ambiguity while allowing messianic prophecy to come through as transparently as possible. In Christ, of course, female and male are equally welcome and equally dignified (Gal 3:28), and all readers of this study are highly encouraged to root their identities in Him.

Because the same pronoun can refer to the psalmist, a generic human figure, or the Messiah, we use the lowercase pronouns *he/him/his* whenever translating a biblical passage that employs masculine pronouns. In our commentary, however, we use capitalized pronouns when referring unambiguously to Jesus, the Father, or the Holy Spirit.

1

LESSON ONE:

Psalms 42–47

As we enter Book 2 (Pss 42–72) of the Psalms' five books,[1] we come across a set of psalms associated with the "sons of Korah" (Pss 42–49), about whom we'll say more on Day 2 of this lesson. These first psalms of Book 2 are striking for how they cover the extremes of dejection and exultation: Psalms 42–44 lament the apparent absence of God in some of the most anguished terms one will find anywhere, while Psalms 45–47 celebrate God's presence and look forward prophetically to the consummate union of Christ and His people in God's eternal Kingdom.

DAY 1: PSALMS 42–43

We will take Psalms 42 and 43 together, as commentators have done since antiquity. While the Septuagint[2] gives a separate heading for Psalm 43, and the Hebrew Masoretic Text places both on their own,[3] they are unmistakably connected by the common refrain "Why do you sink down, my soul . . . ? Wait for God . . ." (42:5, 11; 43:5), as well as the repetition of 42:9b in 43:2b. Through a cycle of lament, refrain, lament, refrain, prayer, and refrain, the psalmist confronts his feelings of depression and abandonment by God. By the end of Psalm 43, his external circumstances have not yet changed, but his thinking has, and we see the first rays of hope.

PSALM 42

FOR THE DIRECTOR. A MASKIL FOR THE SONS OF KORAH.

> *¹ As a deer longs for streams of water,*
> *so my soul longs for you, God.*

---

[1] Volume 1 of this study series (*Psalms 1–41: A Christian Union Bible Study* [Carol Stream, IL: Tyndale House Publishers, 2022]) covers Book 1 (Pss 1–41). For a discussion of the five books of Psalms, see Lesson 1 in that volume.

[2] The Septuagint is an ancient Greek translation of the Old Testament that dates to the second and third centuries BC. Its name comes from the Latin word for "seventy," referring to the seventy Jewish elders said to have undertaken the project of translating the Hebrew Scriptures. It is often abbreviated with the Roman numerals LXX. (For more on the Septuagint, see *Psalms 1–41: A Christian Union Bible Study*, Lesson 1.)

[3] As discussed in Lesson 1 of the first volume in this series, Masoretic Text (hereafter MT) refers to the medieval manuscripts which constitute the oldest surviving complete Hebrew Bible and upon which modern translations of the Old Testament are based. Some other Hebrew manuscripts do set Psalms 42–43 as a single psalm.

2   *My soul thirsts for God, for the living God;*
     when shall I come and see the face of God?

3   *My tears have been my food by day and by night,*
     while they say to me all day, "Where is your God?"

4   *Let me remember these things and pour out my soul,*
     that I may pass into the shelter;[4]
  I shall lead them into God's house,
     with the sound of shouting and thanksgiving,
     the clamor of a festival.

5   *Why do you sink down, my soul,*
     and groan over me?
  Wait for God, for I shall yet acknowledge him,
     my salvation.

6   *My God, my soul sinks down within me;*
     therefore, I remember you
  from the land of Jordan and the Hermon range,
     from Mount Mizar.

7   *Deep calls to deep at the sound of your waterfalls;*
     all your breakers and waves have swept over me.

8   *By day Yahweh commands his loyalty,*
     and by night his song is with me,
     a prayer to my living God.

9   *I say to God, my rock:*
     "Why have you forgotten me?
  Why do I go about in darkness,
     oppressed by an enemy?

10   *With a shattering in my bones my foes have reproached me,*
     while saying to me all day long, 'Where is your God?'"

11   *Why do you sink down, my soul?*
     And why do you groan over me?
  Wait for God, for I shall yet acknowledge him,
     my salvation and my God.

PSALM 43

1   *Judge me, God,*
     and defend my case against a disloyal nation;
     from a deceitful and wicked man, rescue me.

---

4 Many translations render the Hebrew word here (*sak*) as "multitude" or "throng." Our translation follows John Goldingay (*Psalms: Volume 2: Psalms 42–89*, BCOTWP [Grand Rapids: Baker Academic, 2007], 20), who notes: "*Sak* comes only here. BDB takes it to mean a throng (an interwoven mass), but LXX and Jerome more plausibly take it as a variant for *sukkâ* referring to Yhwh's shelter or tent."

> ² *For you are God of my stronghold;*
>   *why have you rejected me?*
>   *Why do I go about in darkness,*
>   *oppressed by an enemy?*
> ³ *Send your light and your truth;*
>   *they shall guide me.*
>   *They shall bring me to your holy mountain,*
>   *to your dwelling place.*
> ⁴ *Let me come to the altar of God—*
>   *to God, the joy of my rejoicing—*
>   *and I will thank you with the lyre,*
>   *God, my God.*
> ⁵ *Why do you sink down, my soul?*
>   *And why do you groan over me?*
>   *Wait for God, for I shall yet acknowledge him,*
>   *my salvation and my God.*

STAYING HERE IS NOT AN OPTION

> *As a deer longs for streams of water,*
>   *so my soul longs for you, God. (42:1)*

Why would a deer long for streams of water? Because its very life depends on them. Like all grazing animals, a deer's daily and seasonal movements are governed by the need for fresh water and for the green plants that also require a water supply to stay alive and provide nutrients. A dehydrated animal is not a happy creature; this is how our psalmist describes the state of his own soul, anxiously searching for that on which its life depends.

We do not know who exactly has been pestering the psalmist with the question "Where is your God?" (42:3), but the question itself expresses the core problem: God's seeming absence is putting the psalmist's faith to the test. If you are struggling with the sense that God is far away and not responding to your prayers, you should know that many saints before you have had to wrestle through the same thing. The way the psalmist handles himself in the meantime is most instructive.

TAKING CHARGE OVER YOUR OWN MIND

The psalmist does not "follow his heart," as we are often encouraged to do, but leads it. He first interrogates his own soul—his mind, will, and emotions—and then commands it to walk in the obedience of faith (see Rom 1:5; 16:26):

> *Why do you sink down, my soul?*
>   *And why do you groan over me?*

Wait for God, for I shall yet acknowledge him,
my salvation and my God. (42:11; 43:5; see also 42:5)

This refrain is spoken three times (with very slight variations), giving form and definition to Psalms 42–43. It is also a living example of what it means to grab hold of our spiritual weaponry and "lead every thought captive into the obedience of Christ" (2 Cor 10:5). No matter how strongly we may feel something, if it is out of alignment with God's promises, it is not the truth. God's word is truth, even if our heart says otherwise. In the same passage of Scripture in which Jeremiah famously declares that "the human heart is the most deceitful of all things" (Jer 17:9, NLT), God likens the person whose heart turns away from Him to a shrub in the desert, parched and without hope (Jer 17:6). This image brings us back to Psalm 42 with its governing metaphor of water and thirst.

When the psalmist asks "Why do you sink down, my soul?" he speaks to how water flows toward the lowest point in a landscape—how it literally sinks into a depression or hole in the ground. Now, let's face it: Depression is devouring many people these days, in the church as well as in the outside world. And most people don't have a clue how to deal with it. One common response is to ignore one's feelings and pretend everything is all right; another is to try altering the chemistry of one's brain with psychiatric drugs.[5] The psalmist models a different response.

First, we see that he does not ignore his feelings. On the contrary, he readily acknowledges the sunken state of his soul, and he admits to weeping profusely (42:3) and feeling forgotten and rejected by God (42:9; 43:2). From that place, the psalmist fights the good fight of faith: He challenges his own feelings ("Why do you . . . ?" [42:5]), speaks truth over himself ("I shall yet . . ." [42:5]), and turns to God for the grace he needs to overcome ("Send your light and your truth; they shall guide me" [43:3]).[6]

Have you or someone close to you been caught in a cycle of depression? How might you invite God's light to penetrate the darkness and His truth to disarm patterns of unsound thinking? What specific truths need to be affirmed (cite Scripture verses as you are able)?

① Yes.

② I stay in the Word every day, memorize scriptures, use those scriptures as spoken affirmations for as long as it takes to defeat the black clouds when they appear.

③ Psalm 23: "The Lord is my Shepherd, I shall not want."

---

[5] For a sober assessment of pharmaceutical remedies, see Robert Whitaker, *Anatomy of an Epidemic: Magic Bullets, Psychiatric Drugs, and the Astonishing Rise of Mental Illness in America* (New York: Crown, 2010).

[6] It is also always helpful, of course, to build relationships with godly people who can give you wise counsel. If you are struggling with depression, you will want to open up to someone you trust who can walk with you in love and speak truth to your troubled mind.

"O Lord of Hosts, blessed is the man that trusts in thee." (Psalm

THIRSTY AMID A TORRENT OF WATER

My God, my soul sinks down within me;
therefore, I remember you
from the land of Jordan and the Hermon range,
from Mount Mizar.
Deep calls to deep at the sound of your waterfalls;
all your breakers and waves have swept over me. (42:6-7)

The peaks of Mount Hermon along Israel's northern frontier (between modern-day Lebanon and Syria) are the highest in the Promised Land. They are usually snowcapped, and the runoff of meltwater and mountain springs constitutes the source of the Jordan River. As the psalmist stands there, he hears the streams of water rushing down from the mountains toward the deeper waters they will eventually join (42:7a). He longs to run south himself, to join the roaring of worshipers in the Temple at Jerusalem (42:4); meanwhile, he feels like Jonah, out of place and tossed into the sea (42:7b).[7]

But he remembers (42:6). He remembers that Yahweh lives and that He is loyal to His people (42:8). Remembering this, the psalmist asks himself again, "Why do you sink down, my soul?" Again he exhorts himself, "Wait for God." God will bring salvation (42:11).

OUR DAY IN COURT

Judge me, God,
and defend my case against a disloyal nation. (43:1)

The psalmist's struggle is not limited to what is going on in his own mind; he also faces oppression from hostile parties (42:3, 9). Now, he takes these oppressors to court before the Judge of all, appealing to his loyal God (42:8) to save him from a disloyal nation (43:1). Remarkably, he calls upon God as both the judge and the advocate who will argue his side of the dispute. Of course, if you filed a lawsuit and your own attorney were the judge, one might suggest that the proceedings were severely biased in your favor. But in Christ, this is precisely the advantage you enjoy—God is the Judge of all, and the New Testament explicitly names both Jesus and the Holy Spirit as your Advocates.[8] Because Jesus has paid all your debt, God, who is both faithful and just, will absolve you of guilt (1 John 1:9) and defend your cause against the enemy of your soul.

There is, of course, much more that could be said about all of this. For now, we will close with an observation on the faith expressed in Psalm 43. The psalmist is still wrestling—in the same breath, he speaks of God as a stronghold and then asks, "Why have you rejected

7 The words of Psalm 42:7b are identical to those at the end of Jonah 2:3. See Derek Kidner, *Psalms 1–72: An Introduction and Commentary*, TOTC 15 (London: Inter-Varsity Press, 1973), 184.
8 John 14:16-17; Heb 12:22-24; 1 John 2:1.

me?" (43:2)—but he prays to God for light and truth, and he confesses, "They shall guide me. They shall bring me to your holy mountain" (43:3). He names God as "the joy of my rejoicing" and "God, my God," and declares by faith, "I will thank you with the lyre" (43:4). So when we come to the final refrain—"Why do you sink down, my soul?" (43:5)—we have a clearer sense that faith is indeed winning the battle. The accent falls decidedly on the refrain's second half:

> Wait for God, for I shall yet acknowledge him,
> my salvation and my God.

Can you recall a time from your own past when you struggled to maintain hope as you waited for God to send help? How did you make it through?

Yes. Every day of those 16 years I did not do what I wanted to do. I asked God what he wanted me to do (wait). That's what I did. I asked every day and I obeyed every day. In the process I became stronger, lost lifelong triggers, and everything ended up better than ever.

DAY 2: PSALM 44

Psalm 44 is a communal lament of God's people as they find themselves buffeted by enemies and losing their battles. Strikingly, though they acknowledge that God would justly allow Israel to experience defeat as a means of discipline if they had gone astray, the people here maintain that they have been faithful to God. This raises serious questions about suffering, and the psalm itself only hints at an answer. Further revelation would come in the New Testament in light of Jesus' death and the persecution of the church. But even here in this psalm, note how confusion does not lead to unbelief but to the type of fervent prayer in which a person lays hold of God's altar and refuses to walk away until His help comes.

Love this!

FOR THE DIRECTOR. FOR THE SONS OF KORAH. A MASKIL.

> 1   *God, with our ears we have heard—*
> *our fathers have told us—*
> *the deed you did in their days,*
> *in the days of old.*
> 2   *You, with your hand, you took possession of nations and planted them;*
> *you brought calamity on peoples and sent them away.*
> 3   *For not by their sword did they inherit the land,*
> *nor did their arm bring them victory,*

but it was your right hand and your arm,
and the light of your face,
for you favored them.

4 You yourself are my king, God;
command Jacob's victories.[9]

5 In you we shall charge through our adversaries;
in your name we shall trample those who stand against us.

6 For I do not trust in my bow,
and my sword will not give me victory.

7 But you have saved us from our adversaries,
and you have put our haters to shame.

8 In God we have boasted all day long,
and your name we shall acknowledge forever. Selah

9 Yet you have rejected and humiliated us,
and you do not go out with our armies.

10 You turn us back from the enemy,
and our haters have plundered for themselves.

11 You give us like sheep for food
and have scattered us among the nations.

12 You sell your people for a pittance
and have not profited from their sale.

13 You make us an object of reproach for our neighbors,
of mocking and ridicule for those around us.

14 You make us a proverb among the nations,
a cause for shaking the head among the peoples.

15 All day long my dishonor is before me,
and the shame of my face has covered me,

16 from the sound of reproach and reviling,
from the face of the enemy and the avenger.

17 All this has come upon us, but we have not forgotten you
and have not been false to your covenant.

18 Our heart has not turned back,
nor have our steps turned aside from your path,

19 that you should crush us in a place of jackals
and cover us with the shadow of death.

20 If we had forgotten the name of our God
and stretched out our hands to a foreign god,

[9] Here we have rendered the Hebrew as in MT. LXX implies that the final *mem* of *'elohim* ("God") belongs at the beginning of the next word ("command"), which changes the imperative into a participle and produces "You yourself are my king, my God, who commands Jacob's victories."

21 *would not God find this out?*
      For he knows the secrets of the heart.
22 *Yet because of you we have been killed all day long;*
      we have been regarded as sheep for the slaughter.
23 *Wake up! Why do you sleep, my Lord?*
      Awake! Do not reject us forever.
24 *Why do you hide your face,*
      ignore our lowliness and our oppression?
25 *For our soul has sunk down to the dust;*
      our belly clings to the earth.
26 *Arise! Come to our help!*
      And redeem us for the sake of your loyalty.

HOPE IN THE HEADING

It is worth noting at the outset that this psalm, which goes deeply into confusion and lament, actually begins with a testimony of redemption. Before the first verse, the psalm's heading flags this prayer as belonging to "the sons of Korah." Korah, as we know from Numbers 16, was judged by God and swallowed up alive into the pit[10] for leading a rebellion against Moses and Aaron. But in God's sovereign mercy, Korah's descendants are listed first among the Levites who are specifically appointed by David to lead the singing in the Tabernacle and subsequently in the Temple (1 Chr 6:31-38).

The Hebrew headings of Psalms 42–49 are grammatically ambiguous as to whether these psalms were written *by* the Korahites or rather assigned *to* them for singing. Given that the Septuagint attributes Psalm 43 to David and that Psalm 72 marks the close of Book 2 and "the prayers of David son of Jesse" (72:20), it would seem that David composed these psalms and gave them to his appointed song leaders. In any case, settling the question of authorship is immaterial to our understanding of the text; what is significant is that these sons of Korah, though descended from an infamous rebel, were nonetheless able to sing about God's faithfulness to their forefathers. Though God may visit the iniquity of fathers on their children to the third or fourth generation, He desires to forgive, and He is loyal for a thousand generations to those who love Him and walk in His ways (see Exod 34:6-7).

THE PROBLEM

The first eight verses testify that God has been, and will be, the One responsible for all of Israel's military victories. The shocking turn comes at verse 9: Though the people have boasted in God and sworn to acknowledge His Name forever (v. 8), they now find themselves humiliated in defeat before their enemies, seemingly rejected by the very God in whom they had trusted, and

---

10 Hebrew *She'ol* (Num 16:33).

left in disgrace. Had Yahweh not sworn to His people that He would cause their enemies to be defeated as long as they remained faithful (Deut 28:1-7)? How then can this be?

The psalm does not answer the question but only intensifies it: "Our heart has not turned back," the people cry to God (v. 18). "Yet because of you we have been killed all day long; we have been regarded as sheep for the slaughter" (v. 22). To further our understanding, let us turn to the apostle Paul, who quotes this very statement from verse 22 in his letter to the Romans.

NEW-COVENANT INSIGHT

What shall separate us from the love of Christ? Oppression, or confinement, or persecution, or hunger, or nakedness, or danger, or sword? As it is written, "For your sake we are put to death all day long; we are reckoned as sheep for slaughter." But in all these things we win overwhelmingly through him who loved us. For I am convinced that neither death nor life, nor angels, nor rulers, nor things present, nor things future, nor powers, nor height, nor depth, nor any other creation can separate us from the love of God that is in Christ Jesus our Lord. (Rom 8:35-39)

The first point to recognize here is that death is not the end. Far from being able to separate us from God's love, death actually reveals the love of Jesus who is "the resurrection and the life" (John 11:25). We know, moreover, that Jesus promised His followers the same kind of persecution He Himself faced. Hebrews 11 lists among the faithful those who conquered kingdoms and also those who were beaten, mocked, imprisoned, and stoned—all of which happened to Paul himself—as well as those who were sawn in two and slain with swords, martyrs "of whom the world was not worthy" (Heb 11:32-38). These martyrs live now and forever in the presence of God (see Rev 6:9-11). We must not mistake battle scars as marks of the Lord's rejection.

Further light is shed on this psalm by an incident that occurred while Jesus was in a boat with His disciples (Matt 8:23-27; Mark 4:35-41; Luke 8:22-25). Just as the people in our psalm found themselves in mortal danger and cried out to God, "Wake up! Why do you sleep, my Lord?" (v. 23), so the disciples, in peril as their boat was being tossed about in a storm and taking on water, were indignant at Jesus, who—can you imagine it?—was taking a nap. The disciples shook Him awake and said, "Teacher, don't you care that we are perishing?" (Mark 4:38), to which Jesus responded by commanding the storm to desist and interrogating the disciples' fear and lack of trust.

Have you ever accused God of abandoning you? If so, how has He given you grace to return to a place of trusting Him?

No. Never. He adopted me. He has sworn never to leave me.

If you have harbored thoughts that God has been unfaithful or uncaring but have repressed those thoughts (because you knew you shouldn't think such things), come clean with God. The Psalms teach us to be honest with Him, and He knows your thoughts anyway. Just as He heals the lame and cleanses the lepers, so He can restore your emotional health, removing any lingering root of bitterness and the fruit that comes of it.

THE LAST WORD

> *Arise! Come to our help!*
> *And redeem us for the sake of your loyalty. (v. 26)*

The psalm singers may be perplexed, but they are not giving up. And it is no accident that the last word of the psalm is *khesed*—God's loyalty to those with whom He has made covenant. The Faithful One will redeem His people, no matter what present circumstances suggest; indeed, He has already redeemed us through His own suffering and death so that we might have everlasting life. And this life is not only life after death; it is the new life that begins the moment we are born again by the Spirit of God, as Jesus declared to the Father: "This is eternal life: that they know you, the only true God, and the one you sent, Jesus Christ" (John 17:3; see also 1 John 3:14).

Do you have a living relationship with God now, or are you merely hoping to know Him after you die and go to heaven?

I have a very close relationship with God. We talk every day. All day. Nothing gives me more pleasure than listening and talking to My Father.

It is common in the church today for people to know and believe many things about God without personally knowing Him. If you are in that position, seek the Lord in prayer. He eagerly desires a relationship with you, and He bids you to ask, seek, and knock at His door (Matt 7:7-8).

DAY 3: PSALM 45

We jump now from the lament of the previous psalms to a rapturous celebration of the King in His majesty. As will be evident, Psalm 45—"a love song"—anticipates the vision of Jesus at the end of Revelation. There, we witness the King riding out in glory to bring an end to His enemies, and we see the nations bringing their gifts to the wedding of Jesus and His bride, the church.

FOR THE DIRECTOR. ACCORDING TO "LILIES." FOR THE SONS OF KORAH.
A MASKIL. A LOVE SONG.

1 *My heart stirs with a good word;*
I am speaking my verses to the king;
my tongue is the pen of a skillful scribe.

2 *You are more beautiful than the sons of Adam;*
grace is poured out on your lips;
thus God has blessed you forever.

3 *Fasten your sword upon your thigh, mighty one,*
your majesty and your splendor,

4 *and let your splendor advance!*
Ride for the cause of truth and humility and righteousness,
and may your right hand show you awesome things.

5 *Your arrows are sharpened—*
peoples are beneath you—
they fall in the heart of the king's enemies.

6 *Your throne, God, is forever and ever.*
A scepter of uprightness is the scepter of your kingdom.

7 *You have loved righteousness and hated wickedness;*
therefore, God, your God, has anointed you
with the oil of joy beyond your companions.

8 *Myrrh, aloes, and cassia anoint all your garments;*
from ivory palaces, strings delight you.

9 *Daughters of kings are among your nobles;*
a queen stands at your right hand in gold of Ophir.

10 *Hear, daughter, and see, and incline your ear;*
forget your people and your father's house,

11 *and let the king covet your beauty;*
since he is your lord, bow down to him.

12 *And the daughter of Tyre will bring you a gift,*
the richest of people entreat your favor.

13 *All glorious is the princess within;*
of gold filigree is her garment.

14 *In embroidered clothes she shall be led to the king;*
maidens behind her, her attendants, brought to you.

15 *They shall be led in the joy of rejoicing;*
they shall come into the king's palace.

16 *In place of your fathers shall be your sons;*
you shall make them princes in all the land.

me.
we are the
bride
Jesus is the
bridegroom

¹⁷ I will commemorate your name throughout all generations;
therefore, peoples shall acknowledge you forever and ever.

THE GREAT WEDDING CELEBRATION

And I heard what sounded like a vast crowd, like the roar of many waters and like the sound of a mighty thunder, saying:

> Praise Yahweh!
>   For the Lord, God, Ruler of all, is king.
> Let us rejoice and exult
>   and give him glory,
> for the wedding of the Lamb is come,
>   and his bride has made herself ready;
> it has been given her to clothe herself
>   in fine linen, radiant and clean. (Rev 19:6-8)

"My heart stirs with a good word." So the psalmist begins this delightful "love song" for the King at His wedding. A number of features indicate that this psalm is a messianic prophecy and not simply a wedding song for one of ancient Israel's kings. Perhaps the most obvious of these features comes in verse 6, where the King is addressed directly as God. As the quote above suggests and as we shall see presently, there are many parallels between Psalm 45 and the final chapters of Revelation.

The psalm moves immediately from extolling the beauty of grace on the King's *lips* (v. 2) to noting the *sword* with which He is to ride out in majesty and splendor "for the cause of truth and humility and righteousness" and the arrows with which He will pierce the heart of the *nations* that are His enemies (vv. 3-5). In Revelation 19, the vision of the Lamb's wedding quoted above yields immediately to the vision of Jesus charging out on a white horse at the head of the armies of heaven with a sharp *sword* (i.e., God's word) coming out of His *mouth* to strike down the *nations* (Rev 19:11-16). He is "called Faithful and True, and in righteousness he judges and wages war" (Rev 19:11).

In Revelation, once the Lord's wrath has been satisfied and the final judgment of God's enemies has been executed, the Lamb's bride, the New Jerusalem, appears (Rev 21:9-10). So, too, in this psalm, once it has been established that the Warrior-King has "loved righteousness and hated wickedness" (v. 7), the scene shifts to the palace, where the Bridegroom, anointed with "myrrh, aloes, and cassia" (v. 8), awaits His "glorious" princess (v. 13).

What is it that makes this princess—the King's bride—glorious? Verses 13-14 speak of her garments as embroidered with golden thread. In Revelation 19:8, the bride is similarly arrayed in "radiant" linen, and we are told that "the fine linen is the righteous deeds of the saints." And just as the bride in Psalm 45 is called to "bow down" to her Lord (v. 11), Psalms 29:2 and 96:9

call us to "bow down to Yahweh" in "holy array" or "adorned in holiness." Furthermore, we may understand Peter's instruction regarding wives' adornment in 1 Peter 3:3-6 as applying not only to married women in the literal sense but to all of us who are members of the church, the bride of Christ. We must take care to put ourselves together, not in terms of a fine hairstyle or clothing or gold ornaments, but in terms of "the hidden person of the heart, in the imperishable beauty of a gentle and peaceful spirit, which is precious in God's sight" (1 Pet 3:4).

me

So, then, the glory of the church consists of righteous deeds that proceed from a gracious and holy spirit. This is possible as we "put on the Lord Jesus Christ" (Rom 13:14), our "garment of salvation and robe of righteousness" (Isa 61:10), and are filled with *the* Holy Spirit, by whom we "are transformed from glory to glory" in reflection of our Lord (2 Cor 3:18).

Righteousness is the gift of God, and He gives it to those who want it. How deeply do you "hunger and thirst for righteousness" (Matt 5:6)? What steps are you willing to take in order to "throw off your old sinful nature," "let the Spirit renew your thoughts and attitudes," and "put on your new nature, created to be like God—truly righteous and holy" (Eph 4:22-24, NLT)?

① Every day
② my words - I want them to always reflect the love of God - I'm working on it. Also the make God my primary goal and focus every day. I want my eyes to always be on Him.

FORSAKING ALL OTHERS

Hear, daughter, and see . . .
forget your people and your father's house,
and let the king covet your beauty. (vv. 10-11)

You were made to be beautiful in the eyes of your King. To be His bride does mean forsaking all others, as the standard wedding vow puts it; but He is so worth it! Truly, He is "more beautiful than the sons of Adam" (v. 2), is anointed with joy (v. 7), and will welcome you into His palace "in the joy of rejoicing" (v. 15).

In asking you for your undivided loyalty, the Lord is asking no more than He has already given you. The King does covet your beauty; He sees past the dirty rags in which you first encountered Him and foreknows the excellence of what He has made you to become. He has given His very life to redeem you out of the muck and mire of sin and to clothe you in fine, embroidered garments (v. 14), "radiant and clean" (Rev 19:8). He makes you a child of God and gives you authority on the earth (v. 16).

Take some time now to compose your own love song for King Jesus, our glorious Bridegroom. What aspects of His nature most capture your heart?

Everything about Jesus is glorious.

But lately I have been working on getting to know God as my "Father."
- loving Father
- protective Father
- healing Father
- encouraging Father
- supportive Father
- Ever-present Father
- Rescue Father
- Refuge Father

DAY 4: PSALM 46

If Psalm 44 spoke in perplexity and anguish about God's seeming abandonment of Israel to the nation's enemies, Psalm 46 is a resounding cry of confidence that "Yahweh of Hosts is with us" (vv. 7, 11). He is "readily available" and helping us, providing refuge and strength (v. 1) to face even the most unimaginable turmoil (v. 2) and emerge into His victorious peace.

FOR THE DIRECTOR. FOR THE SONS OF KORAH. SET TO TREBLE VOICES. A SONG.

1 *God is for us refuge and strength,*
     help in times of trouble, readily available.
2 *Therefore we shall not fear, though the earth shifts,*
     though the mountains stagger into the heart of the seas,
3 *though its waters roar and foam,*
     the mountains quake as it swells. Selah
4 *A river—its streams gladden the city of God,*
     the holy dwelling of the Most High.
5 *God is in her midst; she will not be shaken.*
     God will help her at the dawning of the day.
6 *Nations were in tumult,*
          kingdoms staggered;
     he gave his voice—
          the earth melts.
7 *Yahweh of Hosts is with us.*
     Our stronghold is the God of Jacob. Selah
8 *Come, see the works of Yahweh,*
     how he has brought desolations on the earth,
9 *putting a stop to wars to the end of the earth.*
     The bow he breaks, and he cuts the spear in pieces;
     shields he burns in the fire.
10 *"Desist, and know that I am God.*
     I shall be exalted among the nations, exalted on the earth."
11 *Yahweh of Hosts is with us.*
     Our stronghold is the God of Jacob. Selah

God has all this election chaos under control. He determines the outcome.

THE CHILDREN SING

There is something profoundly beautiful in the fact that this song of confidence and praise is to be sung by "treble voices," not tenors or basses. For as celebrated as Israel's mighty men of valor may have been, the servants of God know that it is not their own swords that give them victory (44:6) but God alone who commands Jacob's victories (44:4). He is "Yahweh, strong and mighty; Yahweh, mighty in battle" (24:8). And as David testified to the Lord in Psalm 8, "From the mouth of children and infants you have established strength because of your foes, to bring a stop to the enemy and the avenger" (8:2). So now, the soprano voices of children[11] proclaim the strength of God (v. 1), who puts a stop to wars in all the earth (v. 9).

FEAR AND FEARLESSNESS

> God is for us refuge and strength,
>   help in times of trouble, readily available.
> Therefore we shall not fear. (vv. 1-2)

Fear of the living God is the beginning of knowledge and wisdom (Prov 1:7; 9:10). Having recognized the awesome, unstoppable power of the almighty God, if we then know that He is "for us" (v. 1) and "with us" (vv. 7, 11), it follows naturally that we should be utterly fearless in the face of whomever and whatever stands opposed. As Proverbs 28:1 states, "A wicked person flees though no one is chasing him, but the righteous are confident as a lion."

Psalm 46 speaks of confidence not only before warring nations (v. 6) but also in facing the end of the world as we know it: "though the earth shifts, though the mountains stagger into the heart of the seas . . ." (v. 2). As one commentator remarks, "I know of no more radical profession of faith anywhere in the Scriptures."[12] And such faith is well grounded. It is God who has set the earth immovably on its foundations (104:5) and barred the sea from swelling up over the land (Job 38:8-11). And when Jesus decrees an end to the present age, He declares to us that "heaven and earth shall pass away, but my words shall not pass away" (Matt 24:35).

How assured are you that you are well ensconced in the Lord's protection and favor? Are you walking closely with Him, or is there some area of shame in your life drawing you away from your Father's gaze? Allow Him to speak with you, then set right anything that needs to be set right and put on the "robe of righteousness" (Isa 61:10) He offers you in Christ Jesus.

① Yes. 100%

② No shame. Yes walking closely

---

[11] The Hebrew word ʾalamoth in the heading can refer literally to young women or, by extension, to the soprano voice or boys' falsetto (*Brown-Driver-Briggs Hebrew and English Lexicon* [BDB], s.v. "עֲלָמָה").
[12] Mark D. Futato, "The Book of Psalms," in *The Book of Psalms, The Book of Proverbs*, vol. 7 of *The Cornerstone Biblical Commentary* (Carol Stream, IL: Tyndale House Publishers, 2009), 168.

GAME OVER

Come, see the works of Yahweh,
*   how he has brought desolations on the earth,*
putting a stop to wars to the end of the earth.
*   The bow he breaks, and he cuts the spear in pieces;*
*   shields he burns in the fire. (vv. 8-9)*

In Psalm 2, the kings of the earth took their stand against Yahweh and His Anointed, and the Lord laughed. Now it's time to put this rebellion to bed. "Desist," He says, "and know that I am God" (v. 10). The call to "be still and know" is often quoted out of context, such that many people don't realize that "Be still" is actually God's command to the rebellious to give up their fight. The nations have tried to break away from Him (2:3), but they have inevitably failed. It's over. "Desist, and know that I am God. I shall be exalted among the nations" (v. 10).

These verses are full of encouragement for us as we engage in the battles to which the Lord has called us. Whatever weapons and armor the enemy may have, God can break them, chop them in half, and burn them.

As an aside, we note that while many English Bibles read "chariots" in the latter part of verse 9, the Hebrew word used here nowhere else refers to a war chariot; it is commonly used to denote a flatbed wagon or ox-drawn cart, and the ancient Greek translators identified it here as a *thyreos*, a large, oblong shield in the shape of a door (or upturned wagon).[13] We mention this because the same Greek word appears in Ephesians 6:16, where Paul instructs us to take up the "shield of faith, with which you are able to quell all of the evil one's flaming arrows." So we observe that while the shield of faith can withstand the enemy's fire, these rebels' shields cannot withstand God's fire. Yahweh of Hosts, the Commander of Heaven's Armies, has equipped us with superior armaments.

What sorts of arrows have been launched at you recently? How have you quelled them—or how might you do so—with faith?

Hurricane Helene:
① Root canal crown that took 2 months because of Hurricane Helene. X-rated texts that turned sexual predator. Chaotic thoughts from demons.
② Scripture affirmations. Stay in Word 24/7. Stay close to God in prayer and focus.

As a follower of King Jesus, you have been summoned to do battle—not "against flesh-and-blood enemies, but against evil rulers and authorities of the unseen world, against mighty powers in this dark world, and against evil spirits in the heavenly places" (Eph 6:12, NLT).

---

13 See Timothy Friberg, Barbara Friberg, and Neva F. Miller, *Analytical Lexicon of the Greek New Testament* (Grand Rapids: Baker Books, 2000), s.v. "θυρεός."

To believe all the promises in the Bible (healing, Psalm 91) are true and belong to me.

So "be strong and courageous," and do not waver from what God has assigned for you to do (Josh 1:6-7). Keep feeding continually on His Word, and let His Spirit breathe life into you as you abide in the love of Jesus. Then face adversity with confidence, declaring with God's people:

> Yahweh of Hosts is with us.
> Our stronghold is the God of Jacob. (v. 11)

DAY 5: PSALM 47

Psalm 47 follows very naturally on the heels of Psalm 46. The rebellious nations have been subdued, and now they are called to join Israel in honoring Yahweh as their King. But this is no mere humiliation of the conquered; it is a celebration for all who have joined "the people of the God of Abraham" (v. 9), through whom all peoples are blessed (Gen 12:3; 18:18; 22:18).

FOR THE DIRECTOR. FOR THE SONS OF KORAH. A PSALM.

> 1 All you peoples, clap your hands!
>   Raise a shout to God with a resounding voice!
> 2 For Yahweh Most High is awesome,
>   Great King over all the earth.
> 3 He subjugates peoples under us,
>   nations under our feet.
> 4 He chooses our inheritance for us,
>   the pride of Jacob, whom he loves. Selah
> 5 God has gone up with a shout,
>   Yahweh with the sound of the horn.
> 6 Make music to God, make music!
>   Make music for our king, make music!
> 7 For God is king of all the earth;
>   sing a maskil!
> 8 God reigns over the nations;
>   God sits on his holy throne.
> 9 The nobles of the peoples are assembled,
>   the people of the God of Abraham;
>   for to God belong the kings[14] of earth;
>   he is highly exalted!

---

14 Here the Hebrew word for "shields" represents "kings" in the same way "the crown" stands for the monarchy in English (Futato, "Book of Psalms," 171); see also Pss 84:9; 89:18.

SONG STRUCTURE

Commentators generally describe Psalm 47 as a praise song, or hymn, having two verses—the first verse comprising what our Bibles label as verses 1-5, and the second comprising verses 6-9. The following diagram plainly shows the pattern of repetition in the psalm:[15]

Theme	Verses
Call to praise God	vv. 1, 6
"For" He is King of all the earth	vv. 2, 7
He has asserted power over the nations	vv. 3-4, 8-9b
He has gone up on high	vv. 5, 9c-d

HISTORICAL CONTEXT

To understand Psalm 47 as its original audience would have, we should consider it in terms of sovereign-vassal relationships between nations. By virtue of the covenant made at Mount Sinai, Yahweh is King of Israel. Just as the various nations Rome later conquered came under the authority of Caesar, so the nations Israel conquered came under the authority of Yahweh, the King of kings. Noting the context of Israel's early military victories—including David's conquest of Jerusalem and the subjugation of surrounding peoples—we can imagine a literal event in which "the nobles of the [conquered] peoples are assembled" with the people of Israel (v. 9) and summoned to honor Yahweh with applause, shouting, and music making (vv. 1, 6).[16]

In this context, "our inheritance" and "the pride of Jacob" (v. 4) refer to the land of Canaan, which Yahweh promised to Abraham's descendants as a permanent possession (Gen 13:14-15). The subjugation of peoples under Israel's feet (v. 3) applies plainly to the conquest of that land, carried out largely in the days of Joshua but ongoing in the time of David.[17] And the language of God going up "with a shout" and "with the sound of the horn" (v. 5) recalls the day David and the people brought up the Ark, on which God's presence rested, to Jerusalem and installed it (see 2 Sam 6:15).

At the same time, we recognize that this psalm is not merely testifying to what God has already done in the history of Israel; it also prophesies the final exaltation of God as King over all the earth. Now, in one sense, it is of course true that God has always been King over all creation. But in another sense, the peoples of the earth have not been living under God's rule. As Paul explained to the Romans, "Knowing God, they did not honor him as God" (Rom 1:21). God consequently "gave them over" in enslavement to their passions (Rom 1:24), to faulty thinking (Rom 1:28), death (Rom 5:14), and sin (Rom 5:21; 6:6-14). Through fear, people have unwittingly given authority to the devil (Heb 2:14-15).

---

[15] Adapted from Goldingay, *Psalms 42–89*, 75.
[16] Peter C. Craigie, *Psalms 1–50*, WBC 19, 2nd ed. (Nashville: Thomas Nelson, 2004), 348.
[17] See Craigie, *Psalms 1–50*, 349; Futato, "Book of Psalms," 170.

In what areas of your life does sin have hooks in you? Name them clearly, then declare before God that you renounce those (and all) ties to the kingdom of darkness and that you yield all these aspects of your life to God's righteous rule.

① My words when I am triggered. I want to speak in love but not as often as I wish. ② Dear Lord, I denounce evil speaking and all ties to the kingdom of Darkness and I yield my tongue to you Lord and your righteous rule.

THE LORD ASSUMES HIS RIGHTFUL THRONE

Having "given over" rebellious peoples into the hands of sin and Satan, God has set a limit on the reign of darkness. Jesus appeared on the earth "to undo the works of the devil" (1 John 3:8). He came declaring, "The time is fulfilled, and the kingdom of God is at hand" (Mark 1:15). The only thing delaying the final devastation of the enemy's kingdom is that God wants people everywhere to hear the call of the gospel (Matt 24:14) and have an opportunity to turn from their rebellion and submit to God's reign willingly rather than perish with those who choose to remain in darkness (2 Pet 3:9).

When the last trumpet sounds, those in heaven will declare that "the kingdom of the world has become the kingdom of our Lord," and they will thank God for "taking up" His power and assuming His rightful role as King (Rev 11:15, 17).

> *God has gone up with a shout,*
> *Yahweh with the sound of the horn.*
> *Make music to God, make music!*
> *Make music for our king, make music!*
> *For God is king of all the earth;*
> *sing a maskil! (vv. 5-7)*

We are not exactly sure how to define the Hebrew word *maskil*, which appears in several psalm headings and evidently denotes a type of song. The root of this word, *skl*, deals generally with attentiveness, intelligence, and skill, and the Septuagint renders verse 7b as "sing intelligently." In any case, we certainly do well to tune our minds, hearts, souls, and strength to the key of God's praise.

ONE LORD, ONE FAITH

> *The nobles of the peoples are assembled,*
> *the people of the God of Abraham;*
> *for to God belong the kings of earth;*
> *he is highly exalted! (v. 9)*

While many translations, including the Septuagint, add the word *with* before "the people of the God of Abraham" in verse 9, the emphasis in this statement is that *all* the "noble" people belong to God. We need not have descended naturally from Abraham to be "people of the God of Abraham"—indeed, God's distinct and repeated promise to Abraham was that "all the families/nations of the earth" would be blessed through his offspring (Gen 12:3; 18:18; 22:18). Thus the New Testament begins with "the genealogy of Jesus Messiah, son of David, son of Abraham" (Matt 1:1), in whom that promise finds its ultimate fulfillment. Among those who have died to their former lives and "put on Christ," there is no longer a distinction between Jew and Gentile, for we are one people in Christ Jesus and we all share in the blessing of God's promise to Abraham (Gal 3:27-29).

Where do you see people within your reach whose lives have not yet been blessed with the knowledge of Abraham's God, your God? How might you encourage them to know God and learn to praise our awesome King?

I give them Bibles. I pray for them. I give them information on how to be born again. I encourage them to go to church.

Lesson Review

We began this week with a psalmist on the verge of utter despair. "Where is your God?" was a question that brought him to tears day and night (42:3) as he wrestled with his own depressed soul. But he persisted in fighting the good fight of faith (see 1 Tim 6:12), declaring to himself, "I shall yet acknowledge him, my salvation and my God" (42:11; 43:5). And acknowledge Him he has! Psalms 45–47 celebrate both the lived experience of God as the majestic Warrior who has come and subdued Israel's contentious neighbors and the prophetic hope of God as the Great King who will finally ordain peace over all the earth. And we have caught a glimpse of ourselves as the King's coveted bride, as we shall be presented to Jesus clothed in the righteousness He has bestowed upon us. All praise be to the One who has rescued us out of darkness and brought us into the Kingdom of Light (Col 1:13; 1 Pet 2:9)!

2

LESSON TWO:

Psalms 48–52

As the psalms of Lesson 1 moved from lament of God's apparent absence to joy in His presence, so too will this lesson's psalms explore opposing ends of a set of related dichotomies. Psalm 48 highlights how God's presence is a comfort to those abiding with Him and a terror to those standing against Him. Psalms 49 and 52 contrast the futility of selfish striving that leads to eternal death and the hope of the faithful for eternal life with God. Psalms 50 and 51 deal with sin and sacrifice, contrasting the true worship offered by a repentant heart that acknowledges God's mercy with the false worship that seeks to appease God without yielding one's heart.

DAY 1: PSALM 48

Psalm 48 continues in the strain of Psalms 45–47, celebrating the God who is present with His people and who grants them safety in the face of opposition. It focuses particularly on Zion, "the city of our God" (vv. 1, 8), which is exalted and secured by God's presence within it. Notice the difference between what hostile forces see as they approach (v. 5) and what God's people see (v. 8) within "the city of the Great King" (v. 2).

A SONG. A PSALM FOR THE SONS OF KORAH.

¹ *Great is Yahweh,*
      and exceedingly praiseworthy,
    in the city of our God,
      his holy mountain—
² *a beautiful height,*
      the joy of all the earth,
    Mount Zion her northern flanks,
      the city of the Great King.
³ *God, in her citadels,*
      has made himself known as a strong tower.
⁴ *For behold: The kings have assembled,*
      they have crossed over together.

⁵ *They saw, and thus they were astounded;*
they were dismayed, they panicked.
⁶ *Trembling seized them there,*
writhing like a woman giving birth.
⁷ *With an east wind you smash the ships of Tarshish.*
⁸ *As we have heard, so have we seen*
in the city of Yahweh of Hosts,
in the city of our God;
God will establish her forever. Selah
⁹ *We liken your loyalty, God,*
within your palace,
¹⁰ *to your name, God;*
therefore, we sing your praises to the ends of the earth.
Your right hand is full of righteousness.
¹¹ *Mount Zion shall be joyful,*
the daughters of Judah shall rejoice,
because of your judgments.
¹² *Go around Zion, go all around her;*
count her towers.
¹³ *Set your mind on her wall,*
pass through her citadels,
so that you may recount to a later generation
¹⁴ *that this is God,*
our God forever and ever.
He will lead us eternally.

PHYSICAL ZION AND SPIRITUAL ZION

In terms of its physical stature, Zion was a strong fortress on a hill. The Jebusites who built it certainly felt confident, boasting to David that he stood no chance of taking their stronghold—"Even the blind and lame could keep you out!" they taunted (2 Sam 5:6, NLT). But their confidence was misplaced as they did not know Yahweh, with whom David and his men would overcome their walls (see 18:29).

Psalm 48 describes the city as "a beautiful height, the joy of all the earth" (v. 2), not because Jerusalem sits atop an exceptionally tall mountain—many peaks in Israel surpass its relatively modest height of around 2,500 feet (760 meters)—but because God dwells there. Guarding her citadels, He "has made himself known as a strong tower" (v. 3). Commentators differ on whether to read "north" (*tsafon*) in verse 2 as a common or proper noun: The psalmist may be referring to the Temple Mount and the City of David on Jerusalem's northern flanks, or he may mean "Mount Zion, the heights of Zaphon" as a word of correction to Israel's neighbors regarding who dwells on this "holy mountain" (v. 1). As one advocate of the latter view explains, "Zaphon was to the Canaanites what Mount Olympus was to the Greeks,"[18] the dwelling of El and his viceroy, Baal. In either case, the psalmist is clearly articulating that Zion is, in fact, the mountain of God.

TERROR OR JOY

For those who are not in right relationship with God, the prospect of blundering into His holy and almighty presence is terrifying. So it is that the kings of the surrounding nations who had come together to defy Israel's claim on the land were "dismayed" and "panicked" when they came to Jerusalem and "saw" that the living God was present in her citadels (vv. 3-5). Indeed, the people of Israel had much the same reaction when they encountered God at Mount Sinai:

> And as all the people saw the thunderings and the lightnings, and the sound of the horn, and the mountain smoking, the people feared and trembled, and they stood far off. And they said to Moses, "You speak with us, and we will listen; but let not God speak with us, lest we die." (Exod 20:18-19)

But God, in His good and gracious purposes, had just called Israel to be "a kingdom of priests" (Exod 19:6), just as He calls His people, the church, today (1 Pet 2:9; Rev 5:10). And priests are those who stand in the presence of God, serving as conduits of communication and blessing between God's throne and the world of humanity.

Those who stand inside God's house see a very different picture from what the outside intruders see (v. 8). Their attention is drawn to God's loyalty (v. 9), which, like His Name (v. 10), is eternal. (As discussed in Volume 1 of this series, the name Yahweh means, essentially, "He who is, was, and shall be.")[19] Perceiving thus that Yahweh is forever committed to loving those with whom He has made covenant, the saints respond in the only way that makes sense: by singing His praises to the ends of the earth (v. 10).

If at one end of the spectrum are those who are frightened by the prospect of meeting their Maker, and at the other end are those who consistently, consciously, and joyfully dwell in His presence, where do you find yourself on that spectrum? What patterns of thinking or acting might be hindering you from experiencing more of God's living presence in your life?

---

[18] Willem A. VanGemeren, *Psalms*, vol. 5 of *The Expositor's Bible Commentary*, ed. Tremper Longman III and David E. Garland, rev. ed. (Grand Rapids: Zondervan, 2008), 416.
[19] See our "Note on the Divine Name (Yahweh)" in *Psalms 1–41: A Christian Union Bible Study*, Lesson 2.

SEE, AND TELL

> *Go around Zion, go all around her;*
>   *count her towers.*
> *Set your mind on her wall,*
>   *pass through her citadels,*
>   *so that you may recount to a later generation*
> *that this is God,*
>   *our God forever and ever.*
>   *He will lead us eternally. (vv. 12-14)*

The psalm ends with a commission for those who, by God's grace, have experienced the joys of His presence. To paraphrase: "Take stock of what you see here. Consider how securely God protects His people, such that no one could take them away from Him. Then tell your children and your children's children of the assurance that belongs to those who trust in God." There may be enemies all around, but your Father is pleased to provide deliverance.

Whom do you want to tell today about God's faithfulness? Ask the Holy Spirit for insight as to how you could best relate God's goodness to them. (Take notes below.) Make a plan, and ask the Lord to go before you in preparing the way.

_____

_____

_____

_____

DAY 2: PSALM 49

Psalm 49 is not so much a prayer as it is a sermon, an utterance of divine wisdom. Its subject is death, which comes to the wealthy and the wise just as it does to brute animals. While most of the psalm addresses the folly of those who think they can buy their way out of death, verse 15 stands out as one of the most hopeful "but God" statements in all of Scripture.

FOR THE DIRECTOR. FOR THE SONS OF KORAH. A PSALM.

> ¹ *Hear this, all peoples;*
>   *listen, all inhabitants of the age,*
> ² *sons of Adam and sons of man,*
>   *rich and poor together.*
> ³ *My mouth shall speak wisdom,*
>   *and the musing of my heart understanding.*

4   *I will extend my ear to a proverb,*
      let my riddle flow with a lyre.
5   *Why should I fear in evil days,*
      when the iniquity of my pursuers surrounds me,
6   *those who trust in their wealth*
      and boast in the abundance of their riches?
7   *A brother will not redeem a man,*
      will not give God his ransom,
8   *as the redemption of their soul is costly,*
      and he will come to an end forever,
9   *though he would live on everlastingly,*
      not see the pit.
10 *For he sees, the wise die,*
      the foolish and the brutish perish together,
      and they leave their wealth to others.
11 *Their inward thought is that their houses shall last forever,*[20]
      their dwelling places for all generations,
      though they called lands by their own names.
12 *But man with his honor will not remain overnight;*
      he is like the beasts that perish.
13 *This is their way, their folly,*
      and those after them approve their words. Selah
14 *Like sheep they are headed for Sheol;*
        Death shall shepherd them,
          and the upright shall rule over them in the morning;
      their image is for Sheol's consumption,
        rather than having an exalted dwelling.
15 *But God will redeem my soul out of Sheol's hand,*
      for he will take me. Selah
16 *Do not fear when a man becomes rich,*
      when the glory of his house abounds,
17 *for in death he shall take none of it;*
      his glory shall not go down after him.
18 *Though he blesses his soul while he is alive,*
      and they praise you when you do well for yourself,
19 *his soul shall come to the generation of his fathers,*
      who shall never again see light.
20 *Man has honor but does not understand;*
      he is like the beasts that perish.

---

20 Here LXX has "Graves shall be their houses forever," suggesting the Hebrew *qibram* ("their grave") in place of MT's *qirbam* (literally, "within them," understood here to mean their unspoken thoughts); see Goldingay, *Psalms 42–89*, 96, 102.

PRELUDE

Hear this, all peoples;
 listen, all inhabitants of the age,
sons of Adam and sons of man,
 rich and poor together.
My mouth shall speak wisdom,
 and the musing of my heart understanding.
I will extend my ear to a proverb,
 let my riddle flow with a lyre. (vv. 1-4)

The opening lines alert us that this psalm's themes concern all of us, irrespective of ethnicity or religion or socioeconomic status. Death is a subject with which we all must contend. And while the psalmist promises to share wisdom and understanding on the matter, verse 4 implies that we are about to hear more than just the thoughtful reflections of an old man or even the collective wisdom of our forebears; the speaker himself is listening ("I will extend my ear"), and the accompaniment of the lyre suggests the image of a prophet receiving and expounding divine revelation (see 2 Kgs 3:15). Though death is an enigma, as our natural senses and reason cannot fathom what it holds in store, the seer offers insight to the riddle.

THEME: THE FUTILITY OF WEALTH

The body of the psalm begins with a question: "Why should I fear . . . those who trust in their wealth?" (vv. 5-6). The words that follow recall the counsel of Psalm 37 that we shouldn't fret about those who do evil and seem to prosper, since they will wither and fall as quickly as the green grass that springs up before a hot summer (37:1-2). Here in Psalm 49, the focus is specifically on those who, like the rich fool in Jesus' parable, think stockpiles of earthly wealth will provide enduring comfort and have therefore failed to amass true riches in God (Luke 12:13-21).

While it has proven difficult to render a precise translation of verses 7-9, the obvious sense is that no amount of money will ever suffice to buy someone's way out of death. God already owns the whole earth and everything in it (24:1), so what earthly thing could you give Him in exchange for your soul (see Mark 8:37)?

Part of the difficulty of these verses for translators seems to stem from matters inherent in the unfolding of the "riddle" (v. 4): Though verse 7a reads "A brother will not [or cannot] redeem a man" in both the Hebrew and the Greek, scholars often seek to amend the text because it is "not the expected idiom."[21] But God does the unexpected: While the psalmist remarks in verse 7b that we cannot give God the price for a man's soul, it turns out that God Himself pays our ransom to Death (v. 15). We may add with the privilege of hindsight that it is, in fact,

---

[21] Futato, "Book of Psalms," 177. Futato goes on to state that "one would expect 'A brother cannot redeem a brother' or 'A man cannot redeem a man.'" Others, meanwhile, take "brother" (*'akh*) as a variant spelling of the interjection *'ak* ("ah!" or "surely"), understanding the line to mean "Surely a man cannot redeem *himself*" (Craigie, *Psalms 1–50*, 356 [emphasis added]; see also Goldingay, *Psalms 42–89*, 95).

a "brother" who redeems us; but this is no ordinary brother. We cannot work out the riddle until we know the man who was and is also God: Jesus, the unique Son of God through whom the world was created, who was yet "made like his brothers in every respect" (Heb 2:17), only without sin (Heb 4:15; see also Heb 1:2).

God is not impressed by a pile of money or by all the worldly power it can buy. He is impressed by the faith and obedience of His Son. Indeed, the redemption of our souls is costly, beyond what we could ever hope to pay (v. 8); but what money cannot buy, the life of Jesus, which He laid down in sacrifice, does.

It will likely come as no great revelation to you that money cannot buy eternal life, and anyone who has read the Gospels knows that a person cannot serve both God and money (Matt 6:24; Luke 16:13). Still, it is easy to slip into the subtle idolatry of placing our hopes in our financial planning rather than in God. Of course, there is a place for deliberate saving and investing, but not as a form of security over against the need to trust in God. Rather, the generation of wealth is the task of stewards who are about their Master's business and who readily yield everything back to Him for His purposes.

What are you currently saving for or investing money in? How do your investments reflect the priority of first seeking God's Kingdom and righteousness and trusting Him to provide for your ongoing material needs (see Matt 6:33)? Where might your priorities need to shift?

_____

_____

_____

_____

THIS WORLD IS NOT OUR HOME

Their inward thought is that their houses shall last forever.
_[. . .]_
But man with his honor will not remain overnight. (vv. 11-12)

Whether we translate verse 11 as above or follow the alternate reading "Graves shall be their houses forever," the point is the same: Relative to eternity, we pass through this life more briefly than an overnight lodger at a wayside inn. And then we go to our real, lasting home. For those outside of Christ, this thought may seem morbid. The psalm continues, "Death shall shepherd them" (v. 14b), which can imply not only ushering them to pasture but also using them for food, as it is then stated plainly that "their image is for Sheol's consumption" (v. 14d). Death and Sheol are presented in stark contrast to Yahweh, the Good Shepherd of Psalm 23.

In between the references to Death and Sheol, verse 14 contains the arresting statement that "the upright shall rule over them in the morning." Again we find ourselves anticipating the dawn of the Lord's great Day, whereupon those who prevail in righteousness will be given authority to rule over the nations (Rev 2:26-28; 5:10). Death and Sheol[22] will themselves be condemned, but not before giving up the dead who were in them to be judged before God's throne according to their deeds (Rev 20:13-14).

The contrast between the unredeemed masses and the favored of God is striking: "God will redeem my soul out of Sheol's hand," the psalmist testifies, "for he will take me" (v. 15). This language of God "taking" someone recalls the brief, enigmatic story of Enoch, who "walked with God, then wasn't there, because God took him" (Gen 5:24). Such language also appears when God "takes" Elijah up into heaven (2 Kgs 2:3, 5, 9-10).[23] God is not merely the passive recipient of the souls of the righteous; He actively steps in to extract them from the mortal realm and bring them to Himself (see Col 1:13).

RECAPITULATION

> Do not fear when a man becomes rich,
>   when the glory of his house abounds,
> for in death he shall take none of it;
>   his glory shall not go down after him. (vv. 16-17)

Just as a sonata introduces a theme, develops it, and finishes with a recapitulation of it, so here the psalmist and his lyre recapitulate the theme that we ought not to fear the wealthy in this world (see vv. 5-6). Even as he brings his "riddle" to a close (see v. 4), the final verses of the psalm still drip with wisdom. We note especially the warning against overvaluing the praises of mortals. Worldly people will indeed "praise you when you do well for yourself" (v. 18), but such regard is fleeting, as are those who give it (v. 19).

> Man has honor but does not understand;
>   he is like the beasts that perish. (v. 20)

Not only does this last verse recall verse 12 as a variation on a theme, but both verses recall Psalm 8 by way of contrast. We saw in that psalm the marvel that God crowned man with "glory and grandeur" and set all the animals under his feet (8:5-8). We also saw, with the help of Hebrews 2, how the life and dominion for which Adam and Eve were made fell prey, through sin, to death and decay, until redemption would be fully realized in Christ Jesus. So let us remember the honor for which we were created, as sons and daughters of God, and not be as those who "do not understand." We will all die, and fairly soon (unless Jesus returns before then); but if our treasure is in Him—if we entrust our lives to Him—He will raise us up to glory everlasting.

---

[22] In the Greek of the New Testament, as in LXX's rendering of the Psalms, the Hebrew word *She 'ol* is translated as "Hades."
[23] See Goldingay, *Psalms 42–89*, 104.

In the modern West, many people are strongly averse to thinking about death, and the separation of the terminally ill into hospital wards means most of us rarely, if ever, see it. How might you consider death more frequently, from the healthy standpoint of seeking to live out your days purposefully and in light of eternity, and help others to do the same?

_____

_____

_____

_____

DAY 3: PSALM 50

Psalm 50 connects to the previous psalm by way of the reminder that God cannot be bought with earthly goods. But while Psalm 49 dealt with the ungodly and the futility of their wealth, here the Lord speaks directly to His people about the kinds of sacrifices that do and do not please Him. God Himself instituted Israel's system of animal sacrifices[24] as a type of what was to come in Christ Jesus and to instruct His people concerning the connection between sin and death. But what He has always looked for is a heart that acknowledges Him for who He is (vv. 14, 23). To offer the mere formality of worship without a surrendered heart is repugnant.

A PSALM FOR ASAPH.

1　*God of gods, Yahweh,*
　　　has spoken and called the earth,
　　　from the rising of the sun to its setting.
2　*From Zion, the perfection of beauty, God has shone forth;*
3　*our God comes and will not be silent!*
　　Fire consumes before him,
　　　and round about him it is exceedingly stormy.
4　*He summons the heavens above,*
　　　and the earth, for the judging of his people.
5　*"Gather those loyal to me,*
　　　those who have made a covenant with me by sacrifice."
6　*And the heavens proclaimed his holiness,*
　　　for God himself is judge. Selah
7　*"Hear, my people, and I will speak,*
　　　Israel, and I will testify about you.
　　　I am God, your God.

---

[24] Israel's required offerings also included grain and oil, but animal sacrifices are the central focus here.

8   Not for your sacrifices will I reprove you,
        as your whole burnt offerings are before me continually.
9   I will not take a steer from your house,
        billy goats from your folds;
10 for to me belongs every animal of the forest,
        the beasts on a thousand hills;
11 I know every bird of the mountains;
        whatever moves in the field is with me.
12 If I were hungry, I would not tell you,
        for to me belong the world and what fills it.
13 Shall I eat the flesh of bulls,
        or drink the blood of billy goats?
14 Sacrifice to God acknowledgment,
        and fulfill to the Most High your vows,
15 then call me on the day of distress;
        I will pull you out, and you will honor me."
16 But to the wicked God has said:
        "What right have you to recount my ordinances
            or raise my covenant upon your lips,
17 when you have hated correction
        and thrown my words down behind you?
18 If you saw a thief, you were pleased with him,
        and you cast your lot with adulterers.
19 Your mouth you let loose in evil,
        and your tongue spins deceit.
20 You sit speaking against your brother;
        on your mother's son you lay blame.
21 These things you have done, while I kept silent;
        you thought I was like you.
        I will rebuke you and lay it out before your eyes.
22 Understand this, you who forget God,
        lest I tear you to pieces, and there be no one to rescue you.
23 The one who sacrifices acknowledgment honors me,
        and to the one who sets the path before him
            I will show the salvation of God."

WORSHIP IN SPIRIT AND TRUTH

Not for your sacrifices will I reprove you . . . (v. 8)

Psalm 50 gets at the heart of true and false religion. As the previous psalms were assigned to the sons of Korah, whom David had appointed to lead singing in the Tabernacle and the Temple, so this psalm is designated for Asaph, who is likewise listed among David's appointed music ministers (1 Chr 6:39). So the context for this psalm is the center of Israel's religious life in Jerusalem.

It is important that we understand what is being critiqued in this psalm. As verse 8 makes clear, the problem was not with the sacrifices that were being offered. God Himself instituted animal sacrifice for the covering of sin and shame when He killed an animal to clothe Adam and Eve (Gen 3:21), and He explicitly required in His covenant with Israel that the priests must offer a sacrificial lamb every morning and every evening (Exod 29:38-39). Failure to offer these animals, then, would have constituted blatant disobedience. The problem was that the people were failing to recognize that animal sacrifices were not all, or even primarily, what God wanted from His people. He didn't require burnt offerings because He was hungry (v. 12), but rather to instill in His people the understanding that sin leads to death and that forgiveness is costly—and to prepare them to understand the ultimate sacrifice He would make for their redemption in Christ Jesus.

WHAT'S MISSING?

Sacrifice to God acknowledgment,
and fulfill to the Most High your vows. (v. 14)

God's desire has always been that we should be *faithful*, in all senses of that word—that we should *trust* Him as our good and wise Father, that we should prove *dependable* in carrying out the tasks He has delegated to us, and that we should prove *true* to our word, following through on our commitments. After all, God put us on this earth to bear His image and govern His creation (Gen 1:26), and getting that project back on track means bringing us to where we thoroughly trust His wisdom and obey His authority.

So the first sacrifice God calls for is *acknowledgment*. Most translators render the Hebrew word here as "thanksgiving," which is not unreasonable; but we might say that at a more fundamental level the charge is simply to acknowledge what is true about God and about ourselves.[25] If we recognize just who it is we're dealing with here—how good and wise and faithful and patient and generous God has proven Himself to be—and how we have failed Him through sin, then that acknowledgment will take the form not only of gratitude for His mercy but also of joy and zeal in carrying out the purposes He has set before us. Thus, the second half of the line speaks of *doing* what we have said we would do, fulfilling our vows.

If we go through the motions of religious observance—as the immediate addressees of Psalm 50 were doing in offering their regular burnt offerings—without yielding our hearts

---

25 The Hebrew verb *yadah*, from which this noun in verse 14 derives, is variously translated in different contexts as "confess" (as in admitting that one has transgressed, e.g., Prov 28:13), "give thanks," or "praise." Thus the general sense is that of acknowledgment or recognition, whether the thing acknowledged be good or bad.

and minds to God for reshaping in accordance with His goodness and wisdom, that is false religion. It is an abomination. As God asks in verses 16-17, "What right have you to recount my ordinances . . . when you have hated correction and thrown my words down behind you?" If we do not respect Him enough to receive correction from Him or to honor His words as worthy of obedience, then He is not our God.

Of course, this problem is by no means unique to the old covenant. As Paul forewarned his protégé, Timothy:

> In the last days there will be troublesome times, for people will be lovers of self, lovers of money, pretentious, arrogant, insulting, disobedient to parents, ungrateful, unholy, loveless, irreconcilable, accusers, without self-control, brutal, not loving what is good, betrayers, falling headlong, puffed up, loving pleasure more than loving God, *having a form of religion but denying its power*. Steer away from them. (2 Tim 3:1-5)

Where have you seen or experienced the hollow shell of religious observance without the heart to seek after God? How did it leave you feeling?

_____

_____

_____

_____

THE BABY AND THE BATHWATER

Heartless, legalistic religion is repulsive. But we must also be careful not to overreact against the specter of legalism, as too many have, by jettisoning all forms of spiritual discipline and habit formation. Far too many Christians have perverted the gospel of salvation by grace into a license for lawlessness, which is sin (see 1 John 3:4-10). "Why do you call me Lord," Jesus asks, "and not do what I say?" (Luke 6:46). Elsewhere He says, "If you love me, you will keep my commandments" (John 14:15). Grace includes the divine empowerment to walk in God's ways, which we cannot do in our own strength (Rom 6; Titus 2:11-14; see also Ezek 36:27).

We are saved by grace through faith (Eph 2:8). Self-discipline and good habits—such as regular, morning-and-evening prayer and Scripture reading, or twice-weekly fasting—are commended to us by our Lord and His apostles as means of building up our faith.[26] While the hollow shell of legalistic religion is indeed sad to behold—that is, religion that treats spiritual disciplines as if they themselves merited God's favor and ceases to walk humbly with God in living relationship—we do need structure in our lives so as to foster the true religion that consists of walking in love and not conforming to the ways of the world (see Jas 1:22-27). So Psalm 50

---

[26] On morning-and-evening devotions, see *Psalms 1–41: A Christian Union Bible Study*, Lesson 2 (throughout, but especially the section on Psalm 1). On fasting, see Lesson 8, Day 4 of the same volume.

concludes with these words from the Lord: "To the one who sets the path before him I will show the salvation of God" (v. 23).

The most obvious way to "set the path before" yourself is, as Psalm 1 instructs us, to ruminate on God's Word day and night and eschew the counsel of the ungodly. While you will do well to incorporate practices such as regular, morning-and-evening devotions, Scripture memorization, and gathering frequently with other believers to stir up each other's love for God and zeal for His works (Heb 10:24-25), you may also need to curtail the amount of input coming from other sources (e.g., broadcast and social media). Pray about the path you are setting before yourself. What habits do you sense the Lord encouraging you either to take up or to let go of so that you can fix your eyes more consistently on Jesus (see Heb 12:1-2)?

DAY 4: PSALM 51

It is fitting that following Psalm 50, with its indictment of those whose devotion to God had grown hollow and who "hated correction" (50:17), we would have a prayer of acknowledgment (see 50:14, 23)—that is, an admission of sin and a plea for forgiveness, rooted in a sincere desire to walk in God's ways. This we find in Psalm 51. The story of David's adultery and cover-up, his murder of Uriah, and the prophet Nathan's rebuke is found in 2 Samuel 11–12. The consequences of David's sin would continue to trouble his household, but God did indeed honor David's repentance. All have sinned, but the broken spirit of one who acknowledges failure is a sacrifice God does not despise (v. 17). He is willing and able to wash the sinner clean (vv. 2, 7).

FOR THE DIRECTOR. A PSALM OF DAVID, WHEN NATHAN THE PROPHET CAME TO HIM BECAUSE HE HAD GONE IN TO BATHSHEBA.

1 *Be gracious to me, God, in accordance with your loyalty;*
      in accordance with your abundant mercy, wipe away my transgressions.
2 *Be magnanimous, wash me of my iniquity,*
      and cleanse me of my sin.
3 *For I know my transgressions,*
      and my sin is ever before me.
4 *Against you, you alone, have I sinned;*
         I have done evil in your sight,
      so you are right in what you speak,
         blameless in your judgment.

5   *Yes, in iniquity I was born,*
     and in sin my mother conceived me.
6   *Yes, you desired faithfulness in the womb,*
     and while I was hidden there you caused me to know wisdom.
7   *De-sin me*[27] *with hyssop, and I shall be clean;*
     wash me, and I shall become whiter than snow.
8   *Cause me to hear joy and exultation;*
     let the bones you have crushed rejoice.
9   *Hide your face from my sins,*
     and all my iniquities wipe away.
10   *Create in me a clean heart, God,*
     and renew a steadfast spirit in me.
11   *Do not cast me out of your presence,*
     and do not take your Holy Spirit from me.
12   *Bring back to me the joy of your salvation,*
     and with a willing spirit uphold me.
13   *Let me teach transgressors your ways,*
     and sinners shall return to you.
14   *Deliver me from bloodguilt, God,*
     God of my salvation;
     my tongue will loudly proclaim your righteousness.
15   *My Lord, open my lips,*
     and my mouth will declare your praise.
16   *For you do not desire a sacrifice,*
      or I would give it;
     with a whole burnt offering you would not be pleased.
17   *The sacrifices of God are a broken spirit,*
     a broken and crushed heart;
     these, God, you will not despise.
18   *Do good in your favor to Zion;*
     build up the walls of Jerusalem.
19   *Then you shall delight in right sacrifices,*
     burnt offerings whole and complete;
     then they will bring up bulls onto your altar.

---

[27] This Hebrew imperative is a form of the verb "to sin." The expression here, which we might render directly as "Sin me," denotes the removal of sin, as in English "to dust the furniture" is to remove the dust from it. For similar uses of this word, see Lev 8:15; 14:49; Num 19:19.

THE CRIME

The heading of Psalm 51 situates this prayer in a much more specific historical context than we have seen in most of the psalms thus far. So if that historical narrative is not fresh in your memory, it would be good to begin by reading the account that starts in 2 Samuel 11:1. We won't take the space here to analyze that story in detail, as our focus is on the psalm, but let us highlight a few points. First, it appears that in the wake of previous successes, David chose to stay comfortably at home while sending others to fight his battles for him (2 Sam 11:1). Then, when he was tempted by the sight of a beautiful woman, he inquired about her; after learning that she was married to one of his men, he summoned her to his bed anyway (2 Sam 11:2-4). After some interval—long enough for Bathsheba to realize she had become pregnant, but while the fighting men were still out on campaign—David compounded his sin, first by attempting to deceive Bathsheba's husband into thinking he was the child's father, and then, when that failed, by deliberately orchestrating the faithful soldier's death in battle (i.e., murder by proxy).

When the prophet Nathan recast this story—stripped of any personal identifiers—to David, the king was filled with the same righteous indignation you probably feel about it (2 Sam 12:5-6). He knew, just as well as we do, that the things he had done were atrocious; yet he was blind to the fact that he had done them until the prophet called him out (2 Sam 12:7-13). This is a sobering lesson, and it reminds us why we need to come before the Father continually and let the Holy Spirit address hidden waywardness in our hearts before it grows and wreaks havoc (see 19:7-14).

THE DEFENDANT PLEADS GUILTY

> *Be gracious to me, God, in accordance with your loyalty;*
> *   in accordance with your abundant mercy, wipe away my transgressions.*
> *Be magnanimous, wash me of my iniquity,*
> *   and cleanse me of my sin.*
> *For I know my transgressions,*
> *   and my sin is ever before me.*
> *Against you, you alone, have I sinned;*
> *   I have done evil in your sight,*
> *so you are right in what you speak,*
> *   blameless in your judgment. (vv. 1-4)*

Blessed David! It takes real courage to be this honest about one's own utter failure, and it takes real faith in God's character to address Him as David does. Notice the string of imperatives: "Be gracious," "Wipe away," "Be magnanimous," "Wash me," and "Cleanse me." On what basis does David give such bold directives? Nothing but God's "loyalty" and "abundant mercy" (v. 1). David knows that apart from these he has no recourse.

Loyalty (*khesed*) is, you may recall, a term of covenant commitment. Even though David has dishonored his Father through patently ungodly behavior, he still approaches Him as a son of the house. Unlike the prodigal, who was correct insofar as he said "Father . . . I am no longer *worthy* to be called your son" (Luke 15:18-19), David knows that it is not in the Father's heart to treat him as a hired hand.[28] And as Derek Kidner remarks concerning the opening line of verse 4:

> To say '*Against thee, thee only, have I sinned*' may invite the quibble that adultery and murder are hardly private wrongs. But it is a typically biblical way of going to the heart of the matter. Sin can be against oneself (1 Cor. 6:18) and against one's neighbour; but the flouting of God is always the length and breadth of it, as Joseph saw long before (Gen. 39:9). Our bodies are not our own; and our neighbours are made in God's image.[29]

Has it ever occurred to you that any mistreatment of yourself or others proceeds from an underlying disconnect with God? Consider some interpersonal dynamics in your life that stand in need of improvement, and invite God to show you His perspective on the root of the disorder. Agree with God about what you have done wrong, and seek His grace to set things right. Note here whatever comes to mind.

_____

_____

_____

_____

GOING DEEPER

> *Yes, in iniquity I was born,*
>   *and in sin my mother conceived me.*
> *Yes, you desired faithfulness in the womb,*
>   *and while I was hidden there you caused me to know wisdom. (vv. 5-6)*

While this psalm was occasioned by a particular set of gross misdeeds, David understands that the problem goes deeper. Sin has been a part of his life since before he was even born; in the startling words of verse 6, even while David was in the womb, God had a right to expect better. Of course, the point of these lines is not to condemn infants for their imperfections (still less to cast aspersions on David's mother) but rather to say that the psalmist's whole life, not just in these recent events, has been "conditioned by sin from its beginning."[30]

---

[28] Kidner, *Psalms 1–72*, 207.
[29] Kidner, *Psalms 1–72*, 208.
[30] James L. Mays, *Psalms*, IBC (Louisville: Westminster John Knox, 1994), 201.

But there is good news. God can remove our sin completely (v. 7); as the One who created us and breathed life into us, He can create in us new, clean hearts and breathe into us again a Spirit that will stay the course (v. 10). In so doing, He not only restores us to a place of joy (v. 12) but also positions us to share His grace with others (v. 13).

In Psalm 50, we learned that God desires *acknowledgment* as our essential "sacrifice." So here, when sin has been brought to light, "the sacrifices of God are a broken spirit, a broken and crushed heart" (v. 17). To acknowledge evil in ourselves is to be deeply grieved by it and to lay the broken pieces of ourselves before our loving Father, in whose tender mercies we are made whole again. As the beloved disciple affirms: "If we say we have no sin, we mislead ourselves, and the truth is not in us; but if we confess our sins, he is faithful and just to forgive us our sins and cleanse us from all unrighteousness" (1 John 1:8-9).

> *Then you shall delight in right sacrifices,*
> *burnt offerings whole and complete;*
> *then they will bring up bulls onto your altar. (v. 19)*

I implore you, brothers, by the mercies of God, to present your bodies as a living sacrifice, holy and pleasing to God, which is your reasonable service. (Rom 12:1)

In the space below, list some of the ways God has shown you His mercy (this will by no means be a complete list). As you do so, say "Thank you."

_____

_____

_____

_____

DAY 5: PSALM 52

Psalm 52 is primarily instructional in nature, contrasting the desolate fate of those who use evil means to advance in the world with the reward of those who trust in God's enduring loyalty. Like Psalm 49, it addresses the folly of trusting in one's wealth (v. 7), though it focuses more on the evils of violence committed in the pursuit of worldly advancement.[31] The background story for this psalm, as indicated by its heading, is found in 1 Samuel 21–22. Note how the psalm begins by calling out the foolish boasting of one who has done evil and ends not only with his mockery but also with the justified confidence of the faithful.

---

31 Futato, "Book of Psalms," 188.

FOR THE DIRECTOR. A MASKIL OF DAVID, WHEN DOEG THE EDOMITE CAME AND TOLD
SAUL, "DAVID HAS GONE TO THE HOUSE OF AHIMELECH."

1 *Why do you boast in evil, mighty one?*
God's loyalty continues all day long.
2 *Your tongue devises ruin,*
like a sharpened razor, you who practice deceit.
3 *You love evil more than good,*
falsehood more than speaking what is right. Selah
4 *You love all words that devour,*
and a deceitful tongue.
5 *God himself will demolish you forever,*
snatch you up and rip you out of your tent,
uproot you from the land of the living. Selah
6 *The righteous shall see and fear,*
and they shall mock him:
7 *"Behold, the man who did not make God his stronghold,*
but trusted in the abundance of his riches!
He is strong in ruin!"
8 *But I am like a luxuriant olive tree in God's house;*
I trust in God's loyalty forever and ever.
9 *I will acknowledge forever what you have done,*
and I will hope in your name, for it is good,
in the presence of those loyal to you.

THE CONTEXT

Psalm 52 takes us back to David's early days, when he was on the run from King Saul—indeed,
to "one of David's bitterest experiences."[32] Whereas in Psalm 51 David was responding to his
own moral failure, here David responds to a situation in which innocent men were slaughtered
because of their association with him—casualties of Saul's paranoia and Doeg's selfish ambition.

**Read through 1 Samuel 21–22. Imagine how you would feel if others were harmed because of
someone's unjustified hatred toward you. How would you respond? What would your prayer
sound like?**

_____

_____

_____

_____

---

32 Kidner, *Psalms 1–72*, 212.

A SMALL MAN DOES GREAT HARM

In the narrative of 1 Samuel, we see that Doeg's evildoing unfolds in two stages. First, when Saul is pursuing David and feeling that he lacks allies in carrying out his vendetta, Doeg seeks to ingratiate himself to the king by providing intelligence on where David had been and who had helped him (1 Sam 22:7-10).[33] We see that Ahimelech was a faithful priest who had no reason to suppose that Saul regarded David as anything other than a loyal servant, much less to think of it as treason when he provided food for David and his men. So Doeg's first "evil" (v. 1) is the slander of a blameless man. Second, when Saul's guards balk at the order to kill Ahimelech and all the other priests with him, Doeg—who is not one of the guards but the chief of Saul's herdsmen (1 Sam 21:7)—does the dirty deed and massacres eighty-five innocent men, priests of Yahweh, plus the women, children, and animals of their town (1 Sam 22:17-19).

The psalm, remarkably, does not focus on the massacre—though the ironic reference to the perpetrator as a "mighty one" in verse 1 does seem to take aim at the perversity of considering oneself a valiant warrior for butchering the innocent and defenseless. Instead, the psalm, particularly in verses 2-4, focuses on the first evil—Doeg's wickedly calculated speech—without which the slaying of innocents would not have taken place. This brings matters much closer to home for most of us; for while few of us (thank God) have been directly affected by mass murder, the use of words to cut others down and get oneself ahead in the world will not be a remote concept to any of us.

It is legitimate to manifest ambition when it leads us to accomplish our work with excellence, and it is fair to receive honor when we do so. But it is quite another thing to try to rise to the top by cutting others down, and the Bible condemns this as rivalry or selfish ambition (see Phil 2:3-8). In fact, we are called to just the opposite—to rejoice when our brothers and sisters have cause to rejoice and to outdo one another in giving honor rather than striving to receive it (Rom 12:10, 15).

Have you (perhaps in more subtle ways than Doeg the Edomite) used your words to put someone else down and help yourself get ahead? If so, write down the name(s) of anyone you have thus abused. Repent of your sin before God, and if possible, make a good-faith effort to restore honor to whomever you took it from. If you are carrying bitterness because of the way others have put you down, name who has hurt you, forgive them, and ask God to show them His mercy. Allow the Lord to heal your wounds.

---

33 Kidner, *Psalms 1–72*, 212-213.

LYING AND SELFISH AMBITION ARE SHORTSIGHTED

> *God himself will demolish you forever,*
> *snatch you up and rip you out of your tent,*
> *uproot you from the land of the living.*
> *The righteous shall see and fear. (vv. 5-6)*

Verse 5 serves as a reminder, both to those who would "devour" their neighbors (v. 4) and to the righteous who might be tempted to get justice by their own hands, of what our eternal God said long ago: "Vengeance is mine" (Deut 32:35). Any move intended to bring benefit to oneself that transgresses God's moral law is indeed poorly calculated. As the Psalms have reminded us again and again, the wicked may go humming along worry-free for a moment, but their time is short. All too soon they shall find themselves "snatched up" and "demolished."

The righteous, meanwhile, look upon the downfall of the wicked and have a proper fear of the Lord (v. 6). This does not mean that the people of God go about in anxiety, wondering whether God is going to smite them; if we have been reconciled to God through Christ Jesus and are walking in His ways, we need not fear punishment. But we recognize that God has established certain boundaries within which we are to live, and we are not glib about the fact that harm would come if we wandered astray. By analogy, we may observe that visitors to the Grand Canyon will not enjoy the majestic landscape properly if they are paralyzed by the fear of heights, but they also must be mindful of the cliff's edge and maintain steady footing. We know that no one can snatch us out of God's hand (John 10:28-29), so we are not afraid; but we are conscientious about not abusing the freedom God has given us and wandering away on our own two feet.

The mockery directed at the would-be strong man in verse 7 echoes God's response to rebellion in Psalm 2:4. And again, as Psalms 1 and 2 set out the diverging paths of faithfulness to God and rebellion against His authority, Psalm 52 closes by contrasting the selfish man's ruin with the hope of the faithful.

> *But I am like a luxuriant olive tree in God's house;*
> *I trust in God's loyalty forever and ever.*
> *I will acknowledge forever what you have done,*
> *and I will hope in your name, for it is good,*
> *in the presence of those loyal to you. (vv. 8-9)*

The olive tree is a fitting image here, both because it is one of the longest-living trees and because its fruit is filled with the oil of anointing. And a good tree in God's house is sure not to be uprooted (cf. v. 5). Twice in these closing verses, we are reminded of the great value of loyalty in our relationship with God: God's loyalty lasts forever (v. 8; see also v. 1), and those who are loyal to Him (v. 9c) will have eternity to share their gratitude (v. 9a).

How would you summarize the connection between the fear of God and the confidence we have in our Father's love?

Lesson Review

At the outset of the Psalter, we were told that "Yahweh knows the way of the just, but the way of the wicked will fail" (1:6). God's presence is either dreadful or wonderful, depending on the relationship one has with Him (see Ps 48). Trying to avoid God is foolishly shortsighted (Pss 49, 52), and there is no reason to do so. For even when we have acted in ways that we know are nowhere near acceptable, God is prepared to meet us with mercy. He asks only that we acknowledge our fault, truly repent of our wrongdoing, and come to Him trusting in His loyal love (Pss 50–51).

3

LESSON THREE:

Psalms 53–57

Psalms 53–57 remind us that because God is just, we must learn to be similarly just. Psalm 53 demonstrates that it is foolish to imagine we should avoid God's scrutiny, while assuring us that God will do good to those who belong to Him. All the psalms in this lesson deal with people who act violently and must face God's judgment. Meanwhile, the swelling declarations of trust in God's promises both buoy our hope for answers to prayer and challenge us to be steadfastly faithful, as God is.

DAY 1: PSALM 53

Psalm 53 is a variation on Psalm 14:[34] Most of that text is copied verbatim, though verse 5b-d is different; and whereas Psalm 14 refers to the Lord as both ʾelohim ("God") and Yhwh ("Yahweh"), Psalm 53 uses ʾelohim throughout. The repetition of what is mostly the same psalm suggests that its subject is worth revisiting, while the variations invite us to consider how the psalm may be adapted to speak in a particular context. Both psalms address the folly of living as if we should not have to answer to God.

FOR THE DIRECTOR. ON "MAKHALATH."[35] A MASKIL OF DAVID.

> [1] *The fool says in his heart, "There is no God."*
> *They are corrupt; they have acted abominably in wickedness;*
> *there is none who does good.*
> [2] *God from the heavens looks down upon the sons of man*
> *to see if there is any who understands, who seeks God.*
> [3] *Each has turned aside together; they are corrupt,*
> *there is none who does good; there is not even one.*
> [4] *Do they not know,*
> *all the evildoers consuming my people as they eat bread,*
> *and who do not call on God?*

---

[34] See *Psalms 1–41: A Christian Union Bible Study*, Lesson 4, Day 4.
[35] The meaning of this term is uncertain, but it is probably the name of a tune.

51

5   *There they tremble in dread,*
        where there had not been dread,
    for God scatters the bones of people pleasers;[36]
        you put them to shame, for God has rejected them.
6   *Who will give from Zion the salvation of Israel?*
        When God brings about a restoration of his people,
        Jacob will rejoice, Israel will be glad.

THE PRACTICAL ATHEISM OF CONFESSING BELIEVERS

When we discussed Psalm 14 in Volume 1 of this study, we noted that the psalmist is not merely—or even primarily—critiquing atheism as we understand the term today. Virtually no one in the ancient world would have defended the metaphysical claim that no supernatural beings exist. The more pertinent issue, as Paul draws out in the opening chapters of Romans, is that people suppress what they inevitably *do* know about God because they lack the humility to honor God *as* God and submit to His wise authority. The result of this willful blindness is a combination of idolatry and immorality.

We also noted that professing believers can still say *in their hearts*, "There is no God." That is, though we may recognize the reality of God and may wish to know Him, we still act all too often as though God were not involved in our affairs. For example, we might pray, and even take comfort in the act of praying, without any expectation that God will manifest an answer. Whereas Jesus' disciples were befuddled when they were unable to heal a sick child, asking Jesus what had gone amiss (Matt 17:19), we might be much more surprised if we prayed and someone did get healed. Our churches are filled with unbelieving believers.

In your recent Scripture reading, what biblical truths has God most remarkably drawn off the page and impressed upon you as living realities? What doubts in your life do you see Him presently dismantling (or hope to see Him dismantle)?

DIFFERENCES BETWEEN PSALMS 14 AND 53

The most significant difference between Psalms 14 and 53 appears in 14:5-6 and 53:5:

There they tremble in dread,
    for God is with a righteous generation.

---

[36] Here we follow LXX. Where MT has *khonak* (חֹנָךְ, "your besieger"), LXX (with *anthrōpareskos*) suggests *khanef* (חָנֵף, "profane/ungodly"), as in the RSV, NRSV, and JB.

The counsel of the afflicted you would put to shame,
but Yahweh is his refuge. (14:5-6)

There they tremble in dread,
where there had not been dread,
for God scatters the bones of people pleasers;
you put them to shame, for God has rejected them. (53:5)

It is uncertain from the ancient sources whether, in Psalm 53:5, God is scattering the bones of "people pleasers" or of "your besieger." The distinction hinges on one Hebrew letter (either a final *kaf* or a final *pe*, which appear very similar), and we will not presume to adjudicate which reading is original.[37] If a besieging enemy is in mind, then we are reminded (as in many other Scriptures) that God will deliver His people from those who seek to "consume" them (v. 4). If "people pleasers" are in view, we see that those who have "turned aside together" (v. 3) and do not "seek" or "call on" God (vv. 2, 4) but covet the approval of others will find themselves rejected by Him and ashamed (v. 5) if they do not repent. This accords with Jesus' words to the church in Laodicea: "I am about to spew you out of my mouth. For you say, 'I am wealthy, I have become rich, and I don't need anything,' and you do not recognize that you are wretched and pitiable and poor and blind and naked" (Rev 3:16-17). In fact, there is not such a great difference between the people pleaser who ignores God and the hostile adversary coming against God's people; at the end of the day, both are fools, and "friendship with the world is enmity with God" (Jas 4:4).

If you are feeling beleaguered by opposition, then call upon God, seek to abide in Him, and trust in His power and promises to break apart your opposition. If you find yourself tempted to resist God's leading in your life because you fear what other people may think of you or do to you, then let this be a warning: Do not resist God in an attempt to please people. (You cannot please everyone anyway.)

In what context(s) do you find yourself most strongly tempted to suppress the promptings of your conscience, or of the Holy Spirit within you, out of regard for the opinions or feelings of others? Confess this to God as sin (see 1 Sam 15:24), and ask for His grace to strengthen you in the obedience of faith.

---

37 The RSV and NRSV follow LXX's implied reading of *khanef*, which they translate as "ungodly." Most contemporary versions follow MT's *khonak*, "your besieger." For the use of the Greek term *anthrōpareskos* (the word used in LXX of Psalm 53:5) in the New Testament, see Eph 6:6; Col 3:22.

FINAL NOTE

The other commonly noted difference between Psalms 14 and 53 is the use of the general term "God" throughout Psalm 53, whereas Psalm 14 uses both "God" and "Yahweh." Commentators have observed that the proper name Yahweh appears far less frequently in Books 2 and 3 of the Psalms than in other portions of the Psalter; however, the name does still appear throughout this part of the collection, so we have opted not to draw any particular conclusions from this observation.

DAY 2: PSALM 54

Psalm 54 is a prayer for deliverance from enemies. That these enemies "do not set God before them" (v. 3) recalls the "fool" of the previous psalm. The heading connects this psalm to the events of 1 Samuel 23:19 (or possibly 1 Samuel 26:1), shortly after the episode with Doeg referenced in Psalm 52. In Psalm 54, we see not only that God sustains the psalmist's life (v. 4) but also that God's *Name* is used synonymously with His presence and power to save (vv. 1, 6-7).

FOR THE DIRECTOR. WITH STRINGS. A MASKIL OF DAVID, WHEN THE ZIPHITES WENT
AND SAID TO SAUL, "IS NOT DAVID HIDING AMONG US?"

1 *God, with your name save me,*
   and with your might give me justice.[38]
2 *God, hear my prayer;*
   give ear to the words of my mouth.
3 *For strangers have arisen against me,*
   and terrifying adversaries seek my life;
   they do not set God before them. Selah
4 *Behold, God is my helper;*
   my Lord sustains my soul.
5 *He will return the evil to those who stalk me.*
   In your faithfulness, put an end to them!
6 *Freely will I sacrifice to you;*
   I will acknowledge your name, Yahweh, for it is good,
7 *for it has delivered me from all distress,*
   and my eye looks on[39] *my enemies.*

---

[38] I.e., act as judge and give judgment.
[39] "Looking on" enemies seems to imply gloating over or otherwise looking triumphantly at them (as in Ps 22:17). See Marvin E. Tate, *Psalms 51–100*, WBC 20 (Dallas: Word Books, 1990), 44-45; Goldingay, *Psalms 42–89*, 158.

NARRATIVE CONTEXT

When the Ziphites went and said to Saul, "Is not David hiding among us?" (Ps 54 heading)

As King Saul, in his pursuit of David, had just ordered the slaughter of a whole village of innocents (1 Sam 22:6-19; see Ps 52), David remained on the run. In 1 Samuel 23, we find David hiding in the wilderness of Ziph (in the Negev region of southern Judah), with Saul hot on his trail. The Ziphites' words, quoted in the heading of Psalm 54, are copied verbatim from 1 Samuel 23:19.

The narrative provides no motive for the Ziphites to help Saul hunt David down. Presumably, like Doeg, they simply wanted to ingratiate themselves to the reigning king. But we feel the sting of unwarranted hostility as David lifts his grievance to God:

For strangers have arisen against me,
  and terrifying adversaries seek my life;
  they do not set God before them. (v. 3)

Psalm 53 described those who do not seek God as "consuming" God's people like bread (53:4); so here, those who "do not set God before them" become "terrifying adversaries"—not necessarily because they have any personal animosity against David but perhaps simply because sacrificing him to Saul might elevate their standing with the man in charge. Of course, history is replete with examples of crimes committed in deference to someone else in power, whether we think of Henry II's knights taking it upon themselves to murder Archbishop Thomas Becket or of the war criminals at Nuremberg who were "just following orders." If, on the other hand, we "set God before" us—that is, if we are mindful that He is truly in charge and that He will repay us according to our works (Rom 2:6-8)—we will not so easily appease the ill will of human authorities.

Has someone in a position of power over you ever asked you to do something to which your conscience objected? How did you respond?

SALVATION IN HIS NAME

God, with your name save me,
  and with your might give me justice.

[. . .]

I will acknowledge your name, Yahweh, for it is good,
for it has delivered me. (vv. 1, 6-7)

Observe that the psalmist speaks of God's Name as both a means of salvation (in parallel with God's "might" or power [v. 1]) and as the actual Savior (v. 7). This tells us something important about the reality that God's Name represents His person. In the Exodus narrative, Yahweh commands the people to respect His "angel" (or "messenger"), "because my name is in him" (Exod 23:20-21). This angel of Yahweh is so thoroughly identified with Yahweh Himself that they appear as practically one and the same: Both the angel and God Himself are said to be in the burning bush (Exod 3:2, 4) and to have brought the people out of Egypt (Exod 20:2; Judg 2:1). Indeed, we may say that the angel/messenger of Yahweh was not an angel like Michael or Gabriel but the visible "image of the invisible God" (Col 1:15)—that is, the preincarnate Christ (note that the New Testament explicitly says *Jesus* led Israel out of Egypt [Jude 1:5]).[40]

As Christians, it is important that we understand the inseparability of God's Name and His person. We proclaim salvation in the *name* of Jesus, and He promises to be present with us as we go and do His works in His name (Matt 28:18-20). In one of Jesus' most extraordinary promises, He assures us that He will do whatever we ask in His name (John 14:13-14)! Clearly, this does not mean that every prayer will get answered as long as we conclude with the phrase "in Jesus' name, amen." Rather, it is an invitation to be so identified with Him, so filled with His indwelling presence, that our prayers represent His will. In that same passage from John, Jesus says of Himself, "The words that I speak to you I do not speak of myself, but the Father dwelling in me does his works" (John 14:10). And He goes on to speak of Himself likewise dwelling in us (John 14:20; 15:4; 17:23).

If you desire to pray truly *in Jesus' name*, and not simply to invoke His name over your own soul's requests, make sure you are continually feeding on and delighting in His Word (see Ps 1). As Jesus restates the promise of answered prayers asked in His name, "If you abide in me, and my words abide in you, ask whatever you desire, and it shall be done for you" (John 15:7).

How have you understood what it means to pray (or otherwise act) "in Jesus' name"? How might that change as you see God's Name identified with His presence, His will, and His power?

_____

_____

_____

_____

---

[40] For a more extensive discussion of Yahweh, His angel, and His Name, see Michael S. Heiser, *The Unseen Realm: Recovering the Supernatural Worldview of the Bible* (Bellingham, WA: Lexham Press, 2015), 141-148.

DAY 3: PSALM 55

As in the previous psalm, here we find a prayer for deliverance from enemies and a call that justice be done to them. But whereas Psalm 54 spoke of the enemies as "strangers" (54:3), Psalm 55 speaks of a close friend (vv. 12-14) and of those bearing a grudge (v. 3). This betrayal is personal, and it hurts. But though the psalmist is "restless" and "agitated" (v. 2), he testifies that God hears him (v. 17) and will save (v. 16), redeem (v. 18), and sustain him, so that ultimately he is not shaken (v. 22). This psalm shows us a way to hate evil and love justice without taking retribution into our own hands.

FOR THE DIRECTOR. WITH STRINGS. A MASKIL OF DAVID.

1   *Give ear, God, to my prayer,*
     and do not hide yourself from my plea for grace.
2   *Give attention to me and answer me;*
     I am restless in my musing and agitated
3   *from the sound of my enemy,*
       in the face of pressure from the wicked;
     for they loose trouble upon me,
       and in anger they bear a grudge against me.
4   *My heart squirms within me,*
     and terrors of death fall upon me.
5   *Fear and trembling enters in me,*
     and shuddering envelops me.
6   *And I say,*
       "Who will give me wings like the dove?
       I would fly away and settle down.
7   *Yes, I would flee far away;*
       I would lodge in the wilderness. Selah
8   *I would hurry to a shelter for myself*
       from the wind of a storm, from a tempest."
9   *Confound them, my Lord, divide their tongue,*
     for I see violence and strife in the city.
10 *By day and by night they encircle her, upon her walls,*
     and sorrow and trouble are within her.
11 *Ruin is within her;*
     injury and deceit do not leave her square.
12 *For it is not an enemy who reproaches me, which I could bear—*
     it is not my hater who magnifies himself against me, from whom
       I could hide—

¹³ but you, a man of my rank,
  my friend whom I know.
¹⁴ We had sweet conversation together;
  in the house of God we walked among the crowd.
¹⁵ Devastations be upon them!
  Let them go down to Sheol alive,
  for evils make their home within them.
¹⁶ As for me, I call to God,
  and Yahweh will save me.
¹⁷ Evening, morning, and midday
  I muse and murmur,
  and he hears my voice.
¹⁸ He redeems my soul in peace
  from the battle against me,
  though many are against me.
¹⁹ God will hear and answer them—
  God who sits enthroned of old, Selah
  in whom there are no changes—
  while they do not fear God.
²⁰ He stretches out his hands against those at peace with him;
  he has profaned his covenant.
²¹ His mouth is smoother than curds,
  but his heart is war!
His words are softer than oil,
  but they are drawn swords!
²² Cast your care upon Yahweh,
  and he will sustain you.
  He will never let the righteous be shaken.
²³ And you, God, will make them go down
  to the deepest pit,
those men of bloodshed and treachery;
  they will not live out half their days.
But as for me, I trust in you.

AS EVIL CLOSES IN

My heart squirms within me,
  and terrors of death fall upon me.
Fear and trembling enters in me,
  and shuddering envelops me.

And I say,
　"Who will give me wings like the dove?
　I would fly away and settle down.
Yes, I would flee far away;
　I would lodge in the wilderness." (vv. 4-7)

Psalm 55 deals with evil that is much too close for comfort and is also pervasive in the city (vv. 9-11). Its themes are not new to us: Psalm 12 focused on betrayal from those thought to be loyal, and in Psalm 11, David sought a way to remain faithful when a whole society had succumbed to moral ruin. And yet, we experience the same sorts of trials differently at different times.

In Psalm 11, an unnamed interlocutor had advised David to escape the evil surrounding him in the city, saying, "Fly, bird, to your mountain" (11:1). David's response was, essentially, "How can you say that?" He knew he must trust in Yahweh alone for safety. But now, filled with fear and trembling, David admits to entertaining the very thought he had once rebuked.

We observe that the enemy of our souls is not terribly creative—he will keep poking to see if he can find a weak spot in our defenses. Therefore, we must remain alert. At the same time, we note that having a desire which runs counter to God's purposes and admitting to it is not the same as acting on it. In the garden of Gethsemane, Jesus admitted plainly to the Father that in His human weakness He wished to avoid the painful sacrifice for which He had come to the earth. But He did not sin; rather, in expressing His desire, Jesus also submitted to the Father's purposes: "Not my will, but yours be done" (Luke 22:42). Similarly here, David acknowledges the turmoil in his squirming heart, but he chooses to act in faith: "As for me, I call to God, and Yahweh will save me" (v. 16).

If you find thoughts coming into your head that you are not proud of, do not try to hide them from God in shame. In the first place, you could not hide your thoughts from God even if you wanted to (see Ps 139). But more to the point, as Jesus and David both teach us, there is no shame in laying bare the desires of our flesh before God; indeed, such transparency is part of what it means to "walk in the light" (1 John 1:7). Generally, we sin not in merely having thoughts and desires but in yielding to them against God's instructions. Holiness comes from turning to God with our faces uncovered, letting ungodly thoughts dissolve before His wondrous majesty (2 Cor 3:18).

David testifies: "Evening, morning, and midday I muse and murmur, and he hears my voice" (v. 17). How regularly do you consciously share your "musings"—including your unpleasant "murmurings"—with God? Is anything weighing on you now?

_____

_____

_____

_____

RIGHTEOUS INDIGNATION

A remarkable feature of Psalm 55 is that its most memorable declaration of faith—"Cast your care upon Yahweh, and he will sustain you. He will never let the righteous be shaken" (v. 22)—is sandwiched between two denunciations of the ungodly:

> *His mouth is smoother than curds,*
> > *but his heart is war!*
> *His words are softer than oil,*
> > *but they are drawn swords!*
> *[. . .]*
> *And you, God, will make them go down*
> > *to the deepest pit,*
> *those men of bloodshed and treachery;*
> > *they will not live out half their days. (vv. 21, 23)*

While we can certainly appreciate how the sting of betrayal gave rise to verse 21, we also cannot forget that Christ tells us to love and pray *for* our enemies (Matt 5:44). So, then, one might question the appropriateness of David's pronouncement in verse 23, or the more explicit cursing in verse 15: "Devastations be upon them! Let them go down to Sheol alive." Let us make a few observations here. First, as we have already suggested, it is better to be honest with God and vent anger in prayer than to pretend you aren't angry and go on simmering. When you have the grace to do so, it is good to pray sincerely for God's mercy on your persecutors; meanwhile, God can relieve you of your anger if you bring it to Him. Second, Jesus affirms in many places that God will indeed inflict sore punishment on those who act wickedly and do not turn to Him in humble repentance and faith (e.g., Matt 7:13, 23; 8:12; 11:20-24; 12:41; 18:7-9). David's assertion that "men of bloodshed and treachery" will be brought "down to the deepest pit" will prove accurate unless they repent. Thank God that He gives us so many opportunities to come around! A third observation we can make, based on verses 12-15 as well as verses 21-23, is that David grieves over his betrayer (singular) and then calls for judgment on those (plural) who act treacherously.[41] His grief is personal, but justice is no respecter of persons. Finally, we must not forget that David admitted to his own guilt of betrayal and sought mercy with repentance (Ps 51).

JUDGMENT AND PREMATURE DEATH

Further comment is warranted on the pronouncement "They will not live out half their days" (v. 23). While it is true that sinful activity can lead to premature death, we are neither to presume that we are morally superior to those who meet an untimely death (Luke 13:1-5) nor to assume that illness or premature death always indicates punishment from God (see John 9:1-3). The Lord is indeed merciful, but this does not preclude the possibility of illness or death as a

---

[41] See Kidner, *Psalms 1–72*, 218.

punishment for sin (see Acts 5:1-11; 1 Cor 11:29-30). However, Jesus expresses that the primary purpose of His incarnation is to give abundant life, while the *thief* comes "to steal and kill and destroy" (John 10:10). Peter likewise describes Jesus' earthly ministry as marked by "doing good and healing all who were oppressed by the devil" (Acts 10:38).

Moreover, the notion that "they will not live out half their days" implies an expected duration that one normally ought to live. In Genesis 6:3, God sets a cap on human life at 120 years (which corresponds closely with the longest lives known in recent history), while in Psalm 90 Moses suggests a typical life expectancy of between 70 and 80 years (90:10). If you or a loved one is facing a potentially mortal illness at a younger age than this, you have biblical grounds for appealing to the throne of God for healing and sustaining grace until you have lived out the full measure of your days. That the one who comes to "kill and destroy" is called the "thief" means he will try to take that which he has no right to take; therefore, we must fight for what is rightfully ours.

> *They will not live out half their days.*
> *But as for me, I trust in you. (v. 23)*

Many beloved saints have died prematurely, but this ought not to keep us from contending for life—not out of a fear of death, for we know that we shall live on forever, but out of a desire to fulfill what God has purposed for us to accomplish during our sojourn on the earth. We may not know why some are taken early, but we can join David in trusting God to sustain us until the day He has ordained to call us home.

Psalm 55 has dealt with a number of heavy issues: betrayal, pervasive violence, inner turmoil, retribution, and premature death. Which of these do you find most difficult to grapple with? What lessons can you take from David's example to help you contend faithfully?

_____

_____

_____

_____

DAY 4: PSALM 56

Psalm 56 could be read as a lament or as a psalm of confidence. In actuality, it is a lament, as the opening line shows, prayed in a spirit of great confidence. There is clear movement in the poem as lamentation and confidence alternate until confidence prevails.[42]

---

42 Futato, "Book of Psalms," 196.

FOR THE DIRECTOR. UPON "THE SILENT DOVE FAR AWAY." OF DAVID, INSCRIBED, WHEN THE PHILISTINES LAID HOLD OF HIM AT GATH.

1 *Be gracious to me, God, for a man hounds me;*
    fighting all day long, he presses me.
2 *My stalkers hound me all day long;*
    indeed, many fight against me on high.
3 *The day I am afraid,*
    I trust in you.
4 *In God, whose word I praise,*
    in God I trust; I shall not fear.
    What can flesh do to me?
5 *All day long they twist my words;*
    all their plans are against me for evil.
6 *They band together, they hide;*
    they watch my steps
    as they lie in wait for my soul.
7 *For their iniquity, carry them off;*
    in anger bring the peoples down, God.
8 *You must have recorded my agitation;*
    put my tears in your flask.
    Is it not in your scroll?
9 *Then my enemies shall turn back*
    on the day I call;
    this I know, because[43] *God is for me.*
10 *In God, whose word I praise,*
    in Yahweh, whose word I praise,
11 *in God I trust; I shall not fear.*
    What can man do to me?
12 *Upon me, God, are my vows to you;*
    I will fulfill them with thank offerings to you.
13 *For you have delivered my soul from death—*
        have you not kept my feet from stumbling?—
    to go about before God
        in the light of life.

---

[43] Or "that."

THE CONTEXT

Of David . . . when the Philistines laid hold of him at Gath. (Ps 56 heading)

The heading of Psalm 56 takes us to the story recounted in 1 Samuel 21:10-15, when David sought refuge among Israel's enemies while fleeing Saul's maniacal manhunt only to have to feign lunacy to escape those to whom he had fled. Alert readers will recall that this is the same episode which gave rise to Psalm 34 (with its famous line "Taste and see how good Yahweh is!" [34:8]).

Notice how the first verse of Psalm 56 speaks of a single pursuer, while the second verse switches to the plural and speaks of "many":

Be gracious to me, God, for a man hounds me;
  fighting all day long, he presses me.
My stalkers hound me all day long;
  indeed, many fight against me on high. (vv. 1-2)

Given the context, we may suppose that the singular "man" refers to Saul. While the subsequent plurality of the opposition may include supernatural forces (with fighting "on high" suggesting angelic warfare), it certainly includes the men Saul commanded, and potentially also the Philistines surrounding David after his flight to Gath.[44] It is particularly regrettable when the personal quarrel of one man or woman with another in God's family comes to involve a multitude in conflict. Unity within the body of Christ requires that we learn to address interpersonal grievances without unnecessarily involving other parties, as Jesus instructs us.

Read Matthew 18:15-17. How consistently do you handle conflict in this way? Can you think of examples from your own life of when this practice was not followed, causing what might have been settled between two people to escalate into a much larger dispute?

FEAR AND TRUST

While verse 3 displays David's ready admission that he experienced fear, verses 3-4 together artfully show us—by way of a chiasm—how he moved from fear to confidence:[45]

---

44 See Futato, "Book of Psalms," 195. Commentators have interpreted "on high" in several different ways, suggesting that it indicates the haughtiness of the (human) aggressors or that it repeats the address to God ("Many fight against me, O Most High"); see Tate, *Psalms 51–100*, 66.
45 Futato, "Book of Psalms," 196.

> The day I am afraid,
>
> > I trust in you.
> >
> > > In God, whose word I praise,
> >
> > in God I trust;
>
> I shall not fear.

The first move upon acknowledging fear is choosing to trust God. But this choice hinges on the esteem one has for God's word. Biblical faith is not blind, baseless belief; it comes by hearing what God has spoken (Rom 10:17) and respecting God as someone who means what He says. It is because faith is established on God's word that it can undergird hope and convince us of realities we do not see (see Heb 11:1). By knowing and treasuring what God has promised ("whose word I praise" [v. 4]) and respecting the character of the One who made the promises ("I trust in you. . . . In God I trust" [vv. 3-4]), we move from "I am afraid" (v. 3) to "I shall not fear" (v. 4).

If faith comes by hearing and treasuring what God has said, then we want to keep an ear open to what God is saying and would do well to commit His Word to memory. (We ultimately want to be *doers* of the Word [Jas 1:22-25], but first we need to know what the Word actually says.) In earlier lessons, we discussed the biblical pattern of praying and reading Scripture every morning and evening, and we encouraged you to make Scripture memorization a regular part of your devotional life.[46] How is that going? What new verses have you learned recently? (Try to recite them without looking.) Psalm 55:22, from yesterday's reading, would be an excellent promise to commit to memory if you haven't already done so.

A TIME TO GRIEVE

The profession of faith in verse 4 is such a gem that it becomes a motif, echoed with subtle variation in verses 10-11 as well as Psalm 118:6 (which is quoted in Hebrews 13:6). But between verse 4 and verse 10, David restates and elaborates on the case he laid out before God in the opening verses: God should intervene on his behalf because people are plotting evil against him (v. 5), "hounding" him (vv. 1-2) by continually watching at his heels and waiting for an opportunity to seize him (v. 6). (Consider the parallel situation Jesus faced with the Pharisees; see Luke 11:53-54.)

---

[46] See Lesson 2, Day 3 in this volume, as well as Lessons 2 and 4 in *Psalms 1–41: A Christian Union Bible Study.*

You must have recorded my agitation;
  put my tears in your flask.
  Is it not in your scroll? (v. 8)

When people around us pursue evil, grief is an appropriate response, and one that God does not fail to notice. In fact, Ezekiel reports that when the people in Jerusalem had turned to idolatry, God commanded His angel to put a mark on the foreheads of those individuals who groaned in lament over the abominations done in their city, and a death sentence was pronounced upon all who did not bear the mark (Ezek 9:3-6). Likewise, Malachi sees God paying attention to the conversations of His people and having a "scroll of remembrance" written for those who honor Him (Mal 3:16). God does indeed "record our agitation" (see also Zeph 3:18).

Therefore, if you are not complacent about the brokenness in your midst but sincerely yearn for God's Name to be honored and His will to be done on earth as in heaven, you may be assured, as David expresses in the next line, that "God is for [you]," and He will respond on the day you call on Him (v. 9).

DAY 5: PSALM 57

The heading of Psalm 57 places it in the narrative context immediately following that of Psalm 56: After David escaped from Gath, he went to the cave of Adullam (1 Sam 22:1). Like the previous psalm, its first word (in Hebrew) is "Be gracious to me," a plea for refuge; and as in the previous psalm, David responds to acute and severe danger (v. 4) with declarations of trust in the Lord (vv. 2-3, 7-11). David's God is no divine watchmaker who ceased to intervene after setting the creation in motion; He is the God who hears His servant's cries and intervenes on his behalf (v. 2).

FOR THE DIRECTOR. "DO NOT DESTROY."[47] OF DAVID, INSCRIBED, WHEN HE FLED FROM SAUL INTO THE CAVE.

1   *Be gracious to me, God, be gracious to me,*
      for in you my soul seeks refuge;
      in the shadow of your wings I seek refuge
        until ruin passes.
2   *I call to God Most High,*
      to the God who accomplishes for me.
3   *He will send from the heavens and save me;*
      he reproaches the one who hounds me; Selah
        God will send his loyalty and his faithfulness.
4   *My soul! In the midst of lions I must lie down,*
      man-eaters,

---

47 This is probably the name of a tune to which the psalm would be sung.

> their teeth a spear and arrows
> > and their tongue a sharp sword.
> 5 Be exalted above the heavens, God;
> > over all the earth be your glory.
> 6 They set a net for my feet;
> > my soul is bowed down;
> > they dig a pit in front of me;
> > > they fall into the middle of it. Selah
> 7 My heart is set, God,
> > my heart is set:
> > I will sing and make music.
> 8 Awake, my glory!
> > Awake, lute and harp!
> > I will awaken the dawn!
> 9 I will acknowledge you among the peoples, my Lord;
> > I will make music for you among the nations.
> 10 For great as the heavens is your loyalty,
> > as the skies your faithfulness.
> 11 Be exalted above the heavens, God;
> > over all the earth be your glory.

GOD BE GLORIFIED

While Psalm 56 made a refrain of declaring trust in "God, whose word I praise" (56:4, 10), the refrain of Psalm 57 is a God-honoring imperative:

> Be exalted above the heavens, God;
> > over all the earth be your glory. (vv. 5, 11)

While this refrain divides the psalm into two verses of a single song, it also serves as the hinge of a chiasm encompassing the whole psalm, doubly marking its importance to the overall theme:[48]

> A. Trust in God's loyalty and faithfulness (vv. 1-3)
> > B. The enemies (v. 4)
> > > C. Refrain: God be glorified (v. 5)
> > B′. The enemies (v. 6)
> A′. Trust in God's loyalty and faithfulness (vv. 7-10)
> > > (Repeat refrain, v. 11)

---

48 See Futato, "Book of Psalms," 199; VanGemeren, Psalms, 461.

This prayer of trust, centered around a concern for God's glory, is very much like the prayer Jesus taught His disciples to pray: "Father, hallowed be your name" (Luke 11:2). *Father* is a relational term implying trust and protection, and "hallowed be your name" sounds like a concise restatement of the psalm's refrain. (Note also how the parallel in the refrain between "above the heavens" and "over all the earth" [vv. 5, 11] resonates with the "on earth as in heaven" language of the Lord's Prayer.)

Now, if you found yourself surrounded by enemies as dangerous as man-eating lions (v. 4), you might be forgiven for thinking more in that moment about preserving your life than about glorifying God—though we are warned that seeking to preserve our lives will backfire (Luke 17:33). How do you suppose David was able to make God's glory the heart of his prayer in this moment?

REMEMBER THE FUNDAMENTALS

Psalm 57 begins with a cry for help that sets its hope on God's "loyalty" and "faithfulness" (v. 3). These are words we have seen again and again in the Psalms, and we cannot draw attention to them too often. We expect salvation for no other reason than that God has promised it ("Faith comes by hearing" [Rom 10:17]), and we are confident that God will fulfill His promises because He is loyal and faithful.

Loyalty here means that God is committed to the covenant relationship He has established with His people. He calls us sons and daughters, and though the Father will discipline His children as necessary for correction and growth, His underlying motive is always unfailing love. As His image bearers, we are likewise called to demonstrate loyalty in our covenant relationships, particularly in marriage, which serves as a symbol of the everlasting union between Christ and the church (see Eph 5:25-33). God hates divorce (Mal 2:16) because it is antithetical to His deep desire that we practice undying loyalty.

Faithfulness means that God stands by His word and makes it reliable; His word is truth (John 17:17). Again, God desires that we, as His image bearers, likewise stand by our words. As Jesus teaches, we should have no need for swearing oaths but should consistently let our "yes" mean yes and our "no" mean no, such that nothing further is necessary to guarantee the truth of what we say (Matt 5:33-37).

Has your life been marked by any broken covenants? Can others report that you consistently follow through on what you say you'll do? If you are feeling convicted over failures in this regard, ask the Lord for grace; then give Him time to speak to you about what needs to change so that your word may prove true going forward. Use the space below to note what comes to mind.

_____

_____

_____

_____

Lesson Review

The defining place of loyalty and faithfulness in God's revelation forms the bedrock on which our faith is built, and it calls us to learn how to embody these same virtues. If we live in ignorance of who God is, Psalm 53 calls us fools; and if we actively betray our brothers and sisters, Psalm 55 calls down curses upon us. But if we look to God when we need help, and if we let His Word be our hope and our guide, we shall gain proper confidence, saying:

> *In God, whose word I praise,*
> *in Yahweh, whose word I praise,*
> *in God I trust; I shall not fear.*
> *What can man do to me? (56:10-11)*

4

LESSON FOUR:

Psalms 58–62

These five psalms confront the forces of opposition David encountered while endeavoring along the way of the just. This lesson begins with Psalm 58 calling out the spiritual forces which stand behind corrupt human behavior, and the lesson closes in Psalm 62 with the peace of mind that comes from a proper perspective and trust in God, our tower of unassailable strength.

DAY 1: PSALM 58

Psalm 58 opens with an indictment of the divine beings assigned by Yahweh long ago to exercise authority over the nations (see Deut 32:8-9; Ps 82)—beings Paul would later call "rulers" or "principalities" (Eph 3:10; 6:12)—and the human rulers in league with them. The injustices conceived by these overseers (v. 2) unfold in wicked acts of violence on the earth (vv. 4, 7), and the psalmist pulls no punches in his prayer against them. Though extremely violent in its imagery, the psalm ends on a note of confident assurance that the righteous shall delight to see justice carried out in due course.

FOR THE DIRECTOR. "DO NOT DESTROY." OF DAVID, INSCRIBED.

1. *Do you truly speak in righteousness, gods?*
    Do you judge uprightly, sons of Adam?
2. *No, in your heart you commit injustices;*
    on the earth your hands weigh out violence.
3. *The wicked go astray from the womb;*
    those who speak lies are wayward from birth.
4. *They have venom like serpent's venom;*
    like a deaf cobra that stops its ear
5. *so that it will not hear the whisper of the charmers,*
    the skilled weaver of spells.
6. *God, smash their teeth in their mouth;*
    rip out the lions' fangs, Yahweh!

> [7] *Let them melt away like waters that run off;*
> *when he aims his arrows, let them be like withered branches,*
> [8] *like a slug that goes away trailing slime,*
> *like a woman's stillbirth which doesn't see the sun.*
> [9] *Before your pots can feel the flame of a thornbush,*
> *he will sweep it away, the green branches as well as the burning.*
> [10] *The righteous will rejoice when he sees vengeance;*
> *he will wash his feet in the blood of the wicked.*
> [11] *Man will say,*
> *"Indeed, there is fruit for the righteous;*
> *indeed, there are gods exercising judgment on the earth."*

WHO ARE THESE "GODS"?

Many readers will be perplexed at seeing the Bible address "gods" the way it does here—not as the mere inventions of pagan myths but as real entities "exercising judgment on the earth" (v. 11). Even some professional scholars interpret "gods" (Hebrew *'elim*) as an ironic reference to human tyrants. But there are good reasons to believe that Psalm 58 has spiritual authorities in mind. (As discussed in our study of Psalm 8 in Volume 1 of this series, the Hebrew terms *'el, 'elim,* and *'elohim* can apply broadly to spiritual, immortal beings, including but not limited to God with a capital *G.*) The Scriptures are abundantly clear, of course, that Yahweh is the one true God, Creator of everything and everyone else who exists in heaven and earth; that He knows no equal (Exod 9:14; Deut 32:39; Ps 18:31; Isa 43:10; John 17:3); and that we are to worship only Him (Exod 20:3). But the Scriptures also speak plainly about a multitude of spiritual beings created by and subordinate to Yahweh—for example, the holy angels, the seraphim, and the cherubim, among whom are the "living creatures" around God's throne (Ezek 10; Rev 4:6-11)—as well as the fallen angels, the demons, and the "unclean spirits" who are in rebellion against the One whom Moses rightly called the God of gods (Deut 10:17).

In Deuteronomy 32:8-9, we are told that God assigned each member of a group of divine beings called "sons of God" to exercise authority over each nation of fallen humanity, reserving Israel for Himself as a witness to the rest. (Note that the term "sons of God" does not challenge the uniqueness of Jesus as *the* Son of God any more than our being called "children of God" does; they, like we, were created *by* Him and *for* Him [Col 1:15-20; cf. John 1:12].) We also see that these spiritual "princes" over the nations have joined in Satan's rebellion against God (Dan 10:13; John 12:31); they have sown injustice on the earth, and God has declared judgment on them (Ps 82).

This reality that nations operate under the sway of corrupt authorities in the heavens has been ignored by much of the church in our age, though it is a through line in Scripture. We are plainly called to wrestle the control of our land from these wicked spirits by prayer and proclamation of God's word, armed with truth, faith, righteousness, and salvation, and walking in the peace of the gospel (Eph 6:10-19). There is much more to say about this, of course, than we could possibly cover in today's lesson,[49] but we cannot read Psalm 58 intelligently without at least a basic understanding of the worldview articulated in Deuteronomy 32—that the nations of the earth have been given into the hands of spiritual powers.

DAVID TAKES ON THE GIANTS

> *Do you truly speak in righteousness, gods?*
> *Do you judge uprightly, sons of Adam?*
> *No, in your heart you commit injustices;*
> *on the earth your hands weigh out violence. (vv. 1-2)*

From the outset, David takes aim at those who are responsible for injustices on the earth. And it is difficult to separate divine and human culpability—the spiritual powers ("gods") and human beings ("sons of Adam") exercising decision-making authority are set in parallel, and all are accused of injustice and violence.

> *They have venom like serpent's venom;*
> *like a deaf cobra that stops its ear*
> *so that it will not hear the whisper of the charmers. (vv. 4-5)*

Not only are these persons deadly, they are incorrigible. Though a skilled snake charmer may be able to subdue a cobra, these perpetrators of violence stop their ears to any pacifying words one might hope to say to them. The image of the serpent is, of course, rich in allusion. It recalls not only the divine being who tempted Eve to sin in the garden (Gen 3) but also the instruments of judgment God sent upon rebellious Israel after their deliverance from Egypt (Num 21:4-9) and the prophecy that Jacob spoke prior to his death regarding one of his sons: "Dan shall be a serpent on the road, a viper on the path" (Gen 49:17). The tribe of Dan fell deeply into idolatry and wickedness, as evidenced in Judges 18 (and later 1 Kings 12:28-30), and it is surely no accident that they do not appear among the redeemed of Israel in Revelation 7.

So, then, we are dealing with incorrigibly rebellious and violent entities who have turned from God and are harming His people. This explains the forcefulness of David's prayer in response: He calls on God to defang these predators (v. 6) and let their arrows fall limply to the ground (vv. 7-8). But he goes beyond simply wanting to stop their attack; justice demands that these purveyors of violence reap what they have sown, so the psalmist declares unashamedly that "the righteous will rejoice when he sees vengeance; he will wash his feet in the blood of the wicked" (v. 10). On the gruesome imagery of this statement, Derek Kidner writes:

---

49 For a much more thorough treatment of this subject, see Heiser, *Unseen Realm.* By way of introduction, Derek Prince gives an excellent one-hour teaching on our war with the kingdom of Satan in a talk called "Casting Down Strongholds," available on YouTube at the time of writing: https://www.youtube.com/watch?v=-Q2XsucBAIA.

What might appear as ghoulishness in 10b takes on a different aspect against the rebuke of Isaiah 63:1–6, where God is appalled that none will march with him to judgment. These are warriors, not camp-followers. The New Testament will, if anything, outdo this language in speaking of the day of reckoning (e.g. Rev. 14:19f.; 19:11ff.), while repudiating carnal weapons for the spiritual war (Rev. 12:11).[50]

In Matthew 23, Jesus pronounces woes over a group of leaders He calls "serpents" and "vipers" about to be sentenced to hell (Matt 23:33). His judgment is decisive, and yet He laments the fact that He would have gathered them to Himself if only they had been willing (Matt 23:37). At this point in your study of the Psalms, how do you understand the relationship between punishment and lament in God's response to unrepentant evil? Are there any people you have written off as incorrigible who might yet be moved to repentance?

A VIEW TO THE END

The final verse of Psalm 58 reaffirms the psalmist's hope that justice shall prevail:

> *Man will say,*
> *"Indeed, there is fruit for the righteous;*
> *indeed, there are gods exercising judgment on the earth." (v. 11)*

One commentator aptly paraphrases this final line by saying, "The designated agents of God's will in the world take action for the sake of justice."[51] But the question remains: Who are these "designated agents"—these "gods"—executing God's will on the earth?

Whom did God originally assign to represent Him on the earth? To whom did He entrust dominion over every living creature on earth (see Gen 1:26-28)? Us! Though our forebears failed in their assignment, God's purpose has always been redemption through Christ Jesus, leading to our restoration as God's image bearers and vice-regents. So Paul asked the Corinthian church: "Do you not know that the saints shall judge the world?" And again, "Don't you know that we shall judge angels?" (1 Cor 6:2-3). Obviously, a thorough sanctification of our hearts and our understanding needs to happen before we are fit to exercise such authority. But our destiny is indeed to be "sons of God," members of God's divine council, as John also testified: "He came to his own, and his own did not receive him. But to all who received him, he gave the

---

50 Kidner, *Psalms 1–72*, 228.
51 Goldingay, *Psalms 42–89*, 209.

right to become children of God—to those trusting in his name, who were born not by blood nor by the will of the flesh nor by the will of man but of God" (John 1:11-13).

We know that before we can rightly judge anyone else, we must remove all impediments to our own clear vision—i.e., get the proverbial planks out of our eyes (Matt 7:5)—and have our minds renewed by the Word and Spirit of God. To do this thoroughly requires deep connections with others in Christian community. In addition to daily and weekly involvement in the life of your church, one of the best ways to renew your mind is by taking time off for a multiday Christian conference or retreat. As the Israelites of the Old Testament were profoundly blessed by coming together for extended periods of time at events such as Passover and the Feast of Booths (see especially 2 Chr 30; Neh 8), so too when believers today set aside longer periods of time for worship, fellowship, prayer, and hearing God's Word, the Holy Spirit often does great works in their lives.

When was the last time you gathered with other believers for multiple days of seeking God? How did He meet you then? Are you looking forward to another such gathering in the near future?

DAY 2: PSALM 59

Like so many of the psalms, Psalm 59 is a prayer for deliverance from unwarranted hostility. The heading sets it early in David's career, amid the first violent outbursts of Saul's jealous rage, specifically at the moment David had to flee from his home within Saul's own house (see 1 Sam 19:11). The protest against this injustice gains intensity as the psalm builds momentum, but the last word is a vow of confidence in God's loyalty and strength to accomplish the rescue presently awaited.

FOR THE DIRECTOR. "DO NOT DESTROY." OF DAVID, INSCRIBED, WHEN SAUL SENT MEN AND THEY WATCHED THE HOUSE SO AS TO KILL HIM.

1. *Rescue me from my enemies, my God;*
   set me above the reach of those who rise up against me.
2. *Rescue me from evildoers,*
   and from men of bloodshed save me.
3. *For behold, they lie in wait for my soul;*
   strong men quarrel against me,
   though for no transgression of mine and no sin of mine, Yahweh.

⁴ *For no iniquity of mine, they run and prepare to attack.*
　　Rouse yourself to meet me and see!
⁵ *Yes, you! Yahweh, God of Hosts, God of Israel!*
　　Wake up to deal with all the nations;
　　show no mercy to all evil betrayers! Selah
⁶ *They come back in the evening and growl like dogs*
　　as they go around the city.
⁷ *See, they foam at the mouth,*
　　swords on their lips,
　　for "Who will hear?"
⁸ *But you, Yahweh, must laugh at them;*
　　you will ridicule all the nations.
⁹ *My strength, I watch for you,*
　　because God is my stronghold.
¹⁰ *My God in his loyalty will meet me;*
　　he will make me look in triumph upon my watchful foes.
¹¹ *Do not kill them, lest my people forget;*
　　shake them with your strength and bring them down,
　　my Shield, my Lord.
¹² *For the sin of their mouth, the word of their lips,*
　　let them be captured in their pride—
　　and because of the oath and the lie they tell.
¹³ *Put an end to them in wrath,*
　　　put an end to them so that none remain
　　and they know that God rules in Jacob,
　　　to the ends of the earth. Selah
¹⁴ *Meanwhile, they come back in the evening and growl like dogs*
　　as they go around the city.
¹⁵ *They stumble about for food;*
　　if they are not satisfied, they will remain through the night.
¹⁶ *But I will sing about your strength,*
　　　I will cry out in the morning about your loyalty;
　　for you have been a stronghold for me,
　　　a refuge on the day of my distress.
¹⁷ *My strength, to you I make music,*
　　for God is my stronghold, my loyal God.

MAD WITH ENVY

. . . when Saul sent men and they watched the house so as to kill him. (Ps 59 heading)

In 1 Samuel 17, David heroically took down a giant, the champion of the Philistine army. Because the people of Israel sang David's praises more highly than those of King Saul, Saul became viciously angry and jealous—to the point that the Lord released an evil spirit on him and he tried to kill David in a fit of rage (1 Sam 18:7-11). After that attempt failed and Saul had calmed down, he began to plot David's death more carefully: He first lured David into conflict with the Philistines again, hoping they could dispatch him; but that backfired, as by a second victory David won more renown, plus Saul's daughter Michal in marriage.

Next, Saul simply told his son Jonathan and his servants to kill David. But Jonathan protested David's innocence and argued against the sin of shedding innocent blood (1 Sam 19:1-5), anticipating David's prayer in verses 2-3 ("From men of bloodshed save me. . . . Men quarrel against me, though for no transgression of mine . . ."). Jonathan's plea succeeded initially, but after David won a third victory over the Philistines, Saul again flew into a demonic rage and tried to murder him, prompting David to flee from Saul's house (1 Sam 19:8-10). It is at that point we read: "And Saul sent deputies to David's house to watch over it and to kill him in the morning" (1 Sam 19:11). This time, Saul's daughter Michal alerted David and helped him escape.

We see in all this that David was plainly in the right and that Saul was wildly out of line; even his own children, Jonathan and Michal, sided with the man he madly took to be his nemesis. In context, then, the language of growling dogs foaming at the mouth (vv. 6-7) is not particularly hyperbolic. The real madness of these bloodthirsty hounds, however, is revealed in what they tell themselves while preparing to pounce: "Who will hear?" (v. 7).

Saul and his lackeys failed to comprehend that God most certainly hears—in fact, He knew what was in their hearts even before they moved to action (see 139:2-4). As for David, after an urgent prayer for God to "wake up" (v. 5) and pay attention to what is happening, he recalls and affirms the truth he articulated in Psalm 2, that "he who sits in the heavens laughs" and "mocks" those who presume to overthrow Yahweh and His anointed king (v. 8; see also 2:4).[52] (While Saul was still de facto king of Israel at this point, the Lord had already rejected Saul and anointed David to replace him [1 Sam 15–16].)

---

[52]The references to "the nations" here in verses 5 and 8 likely stem from the allusion to Psalm 2; Saul and his men are Israelites, but they are acting as the "kings of the earth" and "rulers" coming against Yahweh and His anointed (Ps 2:2). See Futato, "Book of Psalms," 203.

In your day-to-day life, how mindful are you of the fact that God perceives what you are thinking and knows what you are doing? How does that awareness either encourage you or trouble you?

If the previous question leaves you unsettled, you'll want to repent of whatever it is you'd rather God not see. But you will also do well to thank Him for His loyal love, demonstrated in Jesus' giving Himself for us even while we were sinners (Rom 5:8), and to receive the blessing that comes with making Jesus your refuge (2:12; see also 59:9-10).

MAKING AN EXAMPLE OF THE REPROBATE

> *Do not kill them, lest my people forget;*
> *shake them with your strength and bring them down,*
> *my Shield, my Lord.*
> *For the sin of their mouth, the word of their lips,*
> *let them be captured in their pride—*
> *and because of the oath and the lie they tell.*
> *Put an end to them in wrath,*
> *put an end to them so that none remain*
> *and they know that God rules in Jacob,*
> *to the ends of the earth. (vv. 11-13)*

It may seem strange that David would ask God *not* to kill his attackers only to follow up with a call to "put an end to them so that none remain." But the reasoning behind this threefold petition—"Do not kill them. . . . Let them be captured. . . . Put an end to them in wrath"—is readily discernible. Rather than simply bringing his persecutors to a quick end, which would solve his immediate problem, David wants God to put His wrath in judgment on display so "they know that God rules in Jacob" (v. 13).

This idea is by no means original to David. In Exodus 7:3-5, the Lord Himself told Moses that He would use the stubbornness of Pharaoh to bring mighty plagues upon Egypt until Pharaoh relented and let the Israelites go—as a means of making the Egyptians know who Yahweh is. Reflecting on that same passage, Paul asks: "What if God, desiring to show wrath and make known his power, bore with much long-suffering vessels of wrath prepared for destruction, so as also to make known the riches of his glory in vessels of mercy, which he has prepared in advance for glory?" (Rom 9:22-23). And in Revelation, the holy angels and saints give glory to God as they witness His righteous wrath on the unrepentant (e.g., Rev 15:1-4; 19:1-3).

So, then, we should not be squeamish when confronted with the ferocity of God's wrath, nor consider it incompatible with His mercy and love. Rather, as we come to comprehend just how wicked it is to spurn our good Creator and see how He has lavished grace on us by forgiving our wrongdoing and replacing our hard hearts with new, soft ones by His Spirit, our proper response is overflowing gratitude, praise, and willing obedience (see Rom 12:1).

How willing are you to agree that God's judgments—which include severe torment for the obstinate—"are true and just" (Rev 19:2)? Are you tempted to think that sin isn't that bad? (Since this would imply that you are more merciful than Jesus, consider just how accurate that assessment is likely to be.)

THE SONG OF THE REDEEMED

> *But I will sing about your strength,*
> *I will cry out in the morning about your loyalty;*
> *for you have been a stronghold for me,*
> *a refuge on the day of my distress.*
> *My strength, to you I make music,*
> *for God is my stronghold, my loyal God. (vv. 16-17)*

At precisely the moment when David was forced to flee from Saul's house, he had been in the act of making music—specifically, playing the lyre in an (ultimately unfruitful) attempt to soothe his troubled patron (1 Sam 19:9-10; see also 1 Sam 16:16). David vows that when all this is over, he will play for a much more gracious and worthy audience, whose strength is matched by His loyalty.

David's life was fraught with many problems, particularly as God's favor on him provoked jealousy in others. That this vow was made while David was fleeing for his life stands as a testament to his faith in the faithfulness and power of God, grounded in the foundational truths we can observe in the first two psalms of the Psalter. Mark Futato reflects on David's prayer here in Psalm 59:

> The truth of Psalm 2—all who take refuge in the Lord will be blessed—was a truth
> that the anointed king himself needed to rely on. It is a truth that we too can rely on,
> especially when we are falsely accused and attacked. God is our strength in the day of

distress, so we can sing his praise with confidence that he will rescue us from every evil attack (2 Tim 4:18).[53]

Are you afraid of being slandered as you navigate life in a society that is increasingly hostile toward God? How might God's demonstrated commitment to David encourage you?

_____

_____

_____

_____

DAY 3: PSALM 60

The heading of Psalm 60 alludes to a series of events described in 2 Samuel 8–10; 1 Kings 11:14-24; and 1 Chronicles 18:3–19:19. As Derek Kidner comments:

> But for this psalm and its title we should have had no inkling of the resilience of David's hostile neighbours at the peak of his power. His very success brought its dangers of alliances among his enemies (cf. 2 Sam. 8:5) and of battles far from home. At such a moment, when his main force was with him near the Euphrates (2 Sam. 8:3), Edom evidently took its chance to fall upon Judah from the south.
>
> The setting of the psalm, then, is the deflating news of havoc at home (1-3), and of a defeat, apparently, at the first attempt to avenge it (10). But the sad tale and the closing prayer are dominated by the startlingly boisterous rejoinder of God (6-8).[54]

FOR THE DIRECTOR. ACCORDING TO "LILY OF THE TESTIMONY." INSCRIBED, OF DAVID, FOR TEACHING. WHEN HE FOUGHT ARAM-NAHARAIM AND ARAM-ZOBAH, AND JOAB RETURNED AND STRUCK EDOM IN THE VALLEY OF SALT, TWELVE THOUSAND OF THEM.

> ¹ _God, you have spurned us, burst out against us;_
>   _you have been angry; may you restore for us._
> ² _You have shaken the land and split it open;_
>   _mend its fractures, for it totters._
> ³ _You have shown your people hardship;_
>   _you have made us drink wine that causes us to stagger._

---

[53] Futato, "Book of Psalms," 205.
[54] Kidner, _Psalms 1–72_, 232-233.

> ⁴ *You have given to those who fear you a standard*
>   *to rally around in the face of truth.*⁵⁵ Selah
> ⁵ *So that your beloved may be rescued,*
>   *save with your right hand and answer us.*
> ⁶ *God has spoken in his holiness:*
>   *"I will exultantly divide up Shechem*
>   *and measure out the valley of Succoth.*
> ⁷ *Gilead is mine, and Manasseh is mine,*
>   *and Ephraim is the helmet of my head,*
>   *Judah my scepter.*
> ⁸ *Moab is my washbasin;*
>   *upon Edom I will fling my sandal;*
>   *over Philistia I will raise a war cry."*⁵⁶
> ⁹ *Who will bring me into the fortified city?*
>   *Who will lead me to Edom?*
> ¹⁰ *Is it not you, God, who spurned us?*
>   *And will you not go out, God, with our armies?*
> ¹¹ *Give us help against the adversary,*
>   *as salvation by man is useless.*
> ¹² *With God we will do mightily,*
>   *as he will trample down our adversaries.*

GOD DISCIPLINES WHOM HE LOVES

God, you have spurned us, burst out against us;
    you have been angry; may you restore for us. (v. 1)

Psalm 60 begins much like Psalm 44, with the sense that God has allowed Israel's enemies to come and rain destruction on them (see especially 44:9). Verse 4 attests that God has raised a banner for His people to gather around, but it seems He is calling them to retreat rather than attack:[57]

You have given to those who fear you a standard
    to rally around in the face of truth.

As it happens, there seems to be a pun at work here in the Hebrew text. Hebrew has two consonants that sound like the letter *t*: *tet* and *taw*, with *tet* being more emphatic. Here, the word

---

55 LXX has "bow" instead of MT's "truth." The words are near homonyms in Hebrew, but "bow" (*qesheth*) is spelled with the letter *taw*, while "truth" (*qoshet*) is spelled with *tet*. See the commentary that follows for the possible pun at work here.

56 MT here reads "Against me, Philistia, raise a war cry!" which may be an ironic taunt, but it is likely a copyist's error. Our translation (like many others) follows the parallel statement in Psalm 108:9.

57 Cf. Jer 4:6; see also Kidner, *Psalms 1–72*, 234-235.

for "truth" (*qoshet*, with a *tet*) sounds like the word for "bow" (*qesheth*, with a *taw*). So we can imagine that while Israel is fleeing from the archers of an invading army, these invaders represent the hard reality ("truth") of God's judgment.

Yes, the Lord does punish His people at times, but always in love and with a good purpose in view: "Yahweh chastens whom he loves, as a father chastens a son whom he favors" (Prov 3:12). Knowing this, the psalmist appeals in verse 5 "that your *beloved* may be rescued," to which he receives the response:

> God has spoken in his holiness:
>   "I will exultantly divide up Shechem
>   and measure out the valley of Succoth.
> Gilead is mine, and Manasseh is mine,
>   and Ephraim is the helmet of my head,
>   Judah my scepter.
> Moab is my washbasin;
>   upon Edom I will fling my sandal;
>   over Philistia I will raise a war cry." (vv. 6-8)

Notice the union of correction and hope in this declaration. The places named in verses 6-7, from Shechem to Judah, encompass the land God promised to Israel; yet the Lord reminds them that the land is not theirs but His ("mine . . . the helmet of my head . . . my scepter"). We are stewards of His creation, appointed to govern it on His behalf, but we must not forget that "Yahweh's is the earth and what fills it, the world and those who dwell in it" (24:1). And as it pertains to the battles we wage here to secure what God has entrusted to us, we must not forget Joshua's encounter on first entering the Promised Land:

> When Joshua was near Jericho, he lifted his eyes and saw—and behold!—a man standing in front of him with his sword drawn and in hand. And Joshua went to him and said to him: "Are you for us, or for our adversaries?" And he said: "No. I am the commander of Yahweh's army." (Josh 5:13-14)

God is not the one who has to choose sides. He is the One who is, was, and ever shall be; *we* are the ones who had better be on *His* side. If we get that straight, we will be vessels of honor ("helmet" and "scepter" [v. 7]), while those who take the other side—in this case, Moab, Edom, and Philistia—will be put to shame. Choose well, and live (see Deut 30:19; Josh 24:15).

As a reader of this study, you have no doubt made the choice already to align yourself with God (as David and Israel had). But it remains possible, as you get caught up in doing the work God has given you to do, that you will lose track of His voice as He desires to interact with you in an ongoing relationship. When that happens, you may find yourself asking God to bless *your* ideas for how you can serve Him, when all the while He has been waiting to share *His* heart and His plans with you.

Has God ever interrupted you in a season of busy activity and called you to refocus your attention on what He wants to say (see Luke 10:38-42)? If so, what happened?

_____

_____

_____

_____

LET THE WEAK SAY, "I AM STRONG"

> *Salvation by man is useless.*
> *With God we will do mightily. (vv. 11-12)*

Surrendering to God is a wonderful thing. When we recognize that we are hopeless without Him, He gives us grace to find hope *in* Him. In the revelation of Christ Jesus, we recognize that God's saving work of "trampl[ing] down our adversaries" (v. 12) applies not only, or even primarily, to the people who manifestly oppose us. Better yet, God gives us victory over our greatest adversaries: sin, death, and the spiritual hosts of wickedness. Apart from God, fallen human beings are enslaved to sin and subject to death and darkness; but having died and been born again, "baptized into Christ Jesus," you are free to live victoriously in the power of the Holy Spirit (Rom 6:1-14; see also Rom 8:12-15; Col 1:13-14).

Ask the Holy Spirit to point out anything you have been trying to achieve in your own strength, and let Him bring you to victory by His means. Note whatever comes to mind, and thank Him for His grace.

_____

_____

_____

_____

DAY 4: PSALM 61

In Psalm 60, David wanted God to lead him victoriously into the "fortified" city of invading Edom (60:9); in Psalm 61, he now wants God to lead him to safety high on a "crag" (the word translated as "crag" comes from the same Hebrew root as "fortified"), which represents the protection found in God's presence (vv. 2-4).[58] Unlike the preceding psalms, which have headings that tag them to specific points in the narrative of David's life, Psalm 61 might have

---

[58] See Futato, "Book of Psalms," 208.

been written at any number of points when David felt fainthearted and far from home (v. 2). If you ever find yourself feeling that way, David's words here can help you step into a place of faith in the God who does draw near to those who honor His Name.

FOR THE DIRECTOR. WITH STRINGS. OF DAVID.

¹ *Hear, God, my cry;*
attend to my prayer.
² *From the end of the earth I call to you*
while my heart is faint;
may you lead me to a crag that rises high above me.
³ *For you have been my refuge,*
a strong tower against the enemy.
⁴ *Let me sojourn in your tent forever*
and take refuge under the covering of your wings. Selah
⁵ *For you, God, have heard my vow;*
you have given the inheritance of those who fear your name.
⁶ *May you add days to the days of the king;*
may his years extend from generation to generation.
⁷ *May he sit forever before God;*
assign loyalty and truth to watch over him.
⁸ *Thus I shall make music to your name forever,*
fulfilling my vows day by day.

NOT GIVING UP

From the end of the earth I call to you
while my heart is faint. (v. 2)

Whatever particular circumstances may have led the psalmist to utter these words, the feelings of distance from home, distance from God, and faintness of heart belong to everyone's experience at some point or another. There are many different reasons, of course, why you might find yourself in such a situation; the question is, what do you do while you are there?

Can you recall a time in the past when you felt fainthearted and far away? How did you seek God then? Or how did He seek you?

_____

_____

_____

_____

RUNNING TO GOD FOR HELP

David's course of action here during one such time should perhaps be obvious, as we have seen him do this time and again: He calls out to God (v. 2a). While we have already heard the beginnings of this response in verse 1—"Hear, God, my cry"—the substance of his prayer begins at the end of verse 2: "Lead me to a crag that rises high above me."

David often speaks of a "rock" (or "crag" or "cliff") because he had so often hidden in the rocky hills and caves of the Judean wilderness when hunted, first by Saul and later by Absalom. One commentator writes, "David knew every cranny, track, and hiding place in the vast rocky wilderness. So when he fled to the rocks he knew that he was safe in their protection."[59] While that may be, David clearly understood that his safety was not ultimately a question of physical terrain; rather, the rocky heights were a means and a symbol of God's protection, as he attests in the following verse:

> For you have been my refuge,
>   a strong tower against the enemy. (v. 3)

As David seeks to draw near to God ("Let me sojourn in your tent forever" [v. 4a]), he takes the posture of humility that is absolutely essential for doing so. His prayer is not "Set me on top of the world"; rather, his hope is in the Rock that "rises high above" himself (v. 2c) and in the "refuge under the covering of [God's] wings" (v. 4b). Though David was renowned as a great warrior, he gladly pictures himself in relation to God as a defenseless chick under a mama bird's protection. (Contrast this posture with the pride of the religious leaders Jesus lamented over in Jerusalem [Matt 23:37].)

Let us learn humility, then, from Israel's great warrior-king. David's humble, God-exalting heart was exactly the reason why the Lord chose him to be in charge of His people (1 Sam 16:7). And let us learn from "great David's greater Son,"[60] Jesus, who became—quite literally—humility incarnate (Phil 2:5-11). God indeed desires to gather those who are willing to come under His protective wings (Matt 23:37).

GRACE TO THE HUMBLE

Having called on the Lord as one lowly and in need, David is assured of a gracious response:

> For you, God, have heard my vow;
>   you have given the inheritance of those who fear your name. (v. 5)

The rest of the psalm overflows with hope, extending from here to eternity. Not only will David get out of his current predicament alive, he will abide in God's presence "forever" (vv. 7-8; see also v. 4). His life is secured by God's own loyalty and truth (v. 7), to which he responds in kind by offering God his unending fidelity and praise (v. 8).

---

59 James Montgomery Boice, *Psalms 42–106*, vol. 2 of *Psalms: An Expositional Commentary* (Grand Rapids: Baker Books, 2005), 503-504.
60 James Montgomery, "Hail to the Lord's Anointed" (1821).

Observe how the turn in this prayer from fainting to hope hinges on the remembrance of God's prior work in David's life (v. 3) and the inheritance God has promised for the future (v. 5). Take a moment now to reflect on where and how you have seen God show up in your times of need. David likens God to a rock or crag; what image would you use to describe what He has been to you? And what inheritance are you looking forward to?

DAY 5: PSALM 62

While Psalm 61 began with a "faint" heart, Psalm 62 begins with a "quiet" soul declaring calm assurance in God. God is again depicted as a "rock" (vv. 2, 6), and David speaks as one who has found the shelter he was seeking in the previous psalm. Note that six lines of this psalm begin with the Hebrew particle 'ak, the sense of which varies with context—it can be emphatic ("truly," "surely") or contrastive ("only," "howbeit"). We render it here with the similar-sounding (and similarly ambiguous) English interjection *ah*.

FOR THE DIRECTOR. ACCORDING TO JEDUTHUN.[61] A PSALM OF DAVID.

1 *Ah, before God my soul is quiet;*
    from him is my salvation.
2 *Ah, he is my rock and my salvation,*
    my stronghold: I shall not be greatly shaken.
3 *How long will you assault a man,*
    all of you striking down,
    like a leaning wall or a battered fence?
4 *Ah, from his exalted position they plan to thrust him down;*
        they are pleased with deceit;
    with his mouth they bless,
        while inwardly they curse. Selah
5 *Ah, be quiet in God, my soul,*
    for from him is my hope.
6 *Ah, he is my rock and my salvation,*
    my stronghold: I shall not be shaken.

---

61 Jeduthun was one of David's appointed music ministers (1 Chr 16:41-42). The preposition 'al ("according to") suggests a tune or musical style associated with him.

7 *On God depend my salvation and my honor;*
      my strong rock, my refuge is in God.
8 *Trust in him at all times, people;*[62]
      pour out your hearts before him;
      God is our refuge. Selah
9 *Ah, the sons of Adam are but vapor;*
         the sons of man are a deception.
      Weighed on a balance,
         they are less than a vapor all together.
10 *Do not trust in extortion,*
      and in robbery do not become worthless;
      when wealth bears fruit, do not set your heart on it.
11 *One thing has God spoken,*
         two things have I heard:
      that strength belongs to God,
12 *and to you, my Lord, belongs loyalty,*
      for you reward each man according to his deeds.

FREE TO BREATHE

Psalm 62 is rich with multivalent language, the immediate sense of which is often hard to pin down, inviting us to stop and sit with phrases for a while as we chew on the various possible meanings. And from the opening sigh ("Ah"), stopping and sitting is the name of the game:

Ah, before God my soul is quiet;
   from him is my salvation. (v. 1)

Commenting on this notion of "quiet," James Mays writes:

The Hebrew does not mean verbal silence, as some translations suggest; verse 8 commends pouring out one's heart in prayer as an act of trust. Nor is waiting implied; the state of soul described is already consummated. The [psalmist speaks] rather of a quietness of soul, an inner stillness that comes with yielding all fears and anxieties and insecurities to God in an act of trust.[63]

On the other hand, another commentator has observed that the psalmist is indeed "silent toward God" (which is another valid reading of the Hebrew phrase) until the very last verse, when he turns from the people he has been addressing and finally offers a statement of trust to God directly.[64] This certainly stands in contrast to the opening cry of "Hear, God!" in Psalm 61.

---

[62] LXX has "Trust in him, all the congregation of the people," implying *'edath* ("congregation") instead of *'eth* ("time").
[63] Mays, *Psalms*, 215-216.
[64] Goldingay, *Psalms 42–89*, 244, 246.

Psalm 62 does confront restlessness in verse 3 ("How long will you assault a man, all of you . . . ?"). The psalmist does not specify who is meant by "you" here (or "they" in the next verse); we see only that there is a coordinated effort to bring a man down (v. 4a) by people with no hesitation about using unscrupulous means to do so ("They are pleased with deceit" [v. 4b]). Thankfully, God is a mighty, unshakable rock wall (v. 2), because a person left to these devils would be "like a leaning wall or a battered fence" (v. 3), unable to withstand their onslaught.

We gave careful thought to using the word *devils* in the previous sentence, as we do not want to conflate flesh-and-blood persons—whom we are commanded to love no matter how they might wrong us (Matt 5:43-48)—with the real, spiritual enemies of our souls. But it seems possible here that the psalm is actually a rebuke against evil spirits that bring deception, such as the one that tormented Saul and set him violently against his faithful servant David. Lying and deceptive spirits generally prefer to remain hidden; they will lead people to speak blessings out of their mouths while the voices in their heads speak condemnation (v. 4c-d).[65]

If your soul is restless or your inner life is plagued with voices of accusation, come to the Lord for deliverance. Hear Jesus' invitation to "come" and "find rest for your soul" (Matt 11:28-30), and renounce any ways you may have agreed with the deceiver's accusations. The Gospels record that Jesus drove out evil spirits wherever He went, and He continues to do so today for and through those who come to Him (see Matt 4:23-24; 8:16; 10:8; 28:18-20; Luke 10:17; Acts 8:7). So silence the voice of the accuser (see Isa 54:17), speak peace over your soul (v. 5), and turn everything in you over to God (v. 8).

Are you carrying anxieties in your spirit today? Use the space below to note any thoughts that have been troubling you. Then reject anxiety as not belonging to your inheritance in Christ Jesus, and speak verses 5-7 over yourself.

_____

_____

_____

_____

FINDING PEACE IN A RIGHT PERSPECTIVE

Ah, the sons of Adam are but vapor . . . (v. 9)

A similar reflection appears in Psalm 39 (a psalm that also begins with a declaration of silence and is designated "for Jeduthun"), though the very different context here in Psalm 62 introduces the idea more unexpectedly. But as we begin to digest verses 9-12 together, the logic becomes clear.

---

[65] Most commentators and translators emend "his" to "their" in verse 4c so that the text reads more easily as a commentary on (human) conspirators: "With *their* mouth they bless, while inwardly they curse." This seems reasonable, but we want to remain open to the possibility that the apparent quirk in the original text is not without meaning.

Peace of mind comes from seeing through the mirage of physical and temporal things to what is real and eternal. If you fixate on the people lined up against you, your mind will be troubled (like Elisha's servant in 2 Kings 6:15-17). But you needn't be so troubled, because "strength belongs to God" (v. 11) and even the combined weight of every human being opposed to Him is "less than a vapor all together" (v. 9). Likewise, no amount of wealth will be of use in the end to those at odds with God (v. 10).

If you want true peace of mind, and if you seek to still the restlessness in your soul, fix your attention on the truth God has revealed. He is strong (v. 11), He stands faithfully with those who seek refuge in Him (v. 12a), and He will reward you for walking by faith (v. 12b).

What obstacles currently stand against the outworking of God's purposes in your life? Name them here, and then ask God to give you His vision to move past them.

Lesson Review

This lesson opened with the insight from Psalm 58 that the evils we encounter come via human cooperation with divine entities in rebellion against God. Without the renewal of the mind that comes by grace through faith in Jesus and by feeding on His Word, people are all too easily deceived and led into acts of violence. But God towers over all opposition as a mighty rock wall, and in turning to Him we find hope that does not disappoint. So even while opposition remains, we are able to operate from a place of steady confidence that God will come through rather than from a place of anxious worrying: "For God did not give us a spirit of cowardice, but of power and love and good judgment" (2 Tim 1:7).

5

LESSON FIVE:
Psalms 63–67

These five psalms move us from a "dry and weary land" (63:1) to flowing meadows that God has abundantly watered, even in the wilderness (65:9-13). God's praise runs throughout these psalms, beginning with David and moving out to "all the peoples" (67:3). Another through line is the justice of God's judgments, which cause His enemies to "wither" (66:3), the faithful to "rejoice" (63:11; 67:4), and all to learn a healthy respect for the One who is truly Lord (67:7).

DAY 1: PSALM 63

Likely composed while David was on the run from his son Absalom (see 2 Sam 15–17), at a point when David was literally faint with thirst (v. 1; see also 2 Sam 16:14),[66] this psalm expresses the abiding joy of one who loves and is loved by God. Verses 1-2 encapsulate the principle "Seek, and you shall find" (Matt 7:7), and the psalm as a whole testifies both to the psalmist's faithful pursuit of God throughout his life and to God's faithfulness to him in turn.

A PSALM OF DAVID, WHEN HE WAS IN THE WILDERNESS OF JUDAH.

1   God, you are my God; I search for you;
         my soul thirsts for you,
      my flesh faints for you,
         in a dry and weary land without water.
2   So in the sanctuary I have seen you,
         beholding your power and glory.
3   For better is your loyalty than life itself;
         my lips will praise you.
4   So I will bless you throughout my life;
         in your name I will lift up my hands.
5   My soul is satisfied as with fat and oil,
         and with shouts from my lips my mouth will praise you.

---

[66] See Goldingay, *Psalms 42–89*, 256.

6 *When I remember you on my bed,*
   in the night watches I ruminate on you.
7 *For you have been my help,*
   and in the shadow of your wings I give a resounding cry.
8 *My soul clings to you;*
   your right hand has laid hold of me.
9 *But they go to ruin who seek my life;*
   they enter the depths of the earth.
10 *Those who would fell him by the power of the sword*
   will become food for jackals,
11 *while the king rejoices in God.*
   Everyone who swears by him will exult,
   for the mouth of those who speak lies will be shut up.

SEEKING GOD WITH A WHOLE HEART

Blessed are those who hunger and thirst for righteousness,
    for they shall be satisfied.
[. . .]
Blessed are the pure in heart,
    for they shall see God. (Matt 5:6, 8)

Psalm 63 begins with yearning: "God . . . I search for you," David declares (v. 1). The verb he uses—from the same root as "daybreak"—suggests "the effort and commitment we show when we get up early to do something."[67] As Jesus instructs, "Seek *first* the kingdom of God and his righteousness" (Matt 6:33). The urgency of this search is expressed vividly in the rest of verse 1: "My soul thirsts for you, my flesh faints for you . . ."

While the language of thirsting and fainting may have been prompted by David's physical experience of these realities while he fled from Absalom in the wilderness, verse 2 makes plain that David is not just speaking about one moment of desperation. Seeking God as though his life depended on it was standard operating procedure throughout David's life—"So," he testifies, "in the sanctuary I have seen you, beholding your power and glory." (In the wilderness David is far from the sanctuary, but he testifies to what has been his experience.)

If you want to see God—if you want to behold His power and glory—be pure in heart. Do not waver between competing desires, but pursue Him with a singleness of purpose. Just as you would make it your priority to find a source of water if you were dropped into the middle of the desert, so make the pursuit of God your number one agenda item every day.

---

67 Goldingay, *Psalms 42–89*, 256.

How thirsty are you for God's living water? Will you be content to carry on according to the status quo, or do your life and purpose depend on the further outpouring of His Spirit?

THE PEARL OF SURPASSING VALUE

For better is your loyalty than life itself. (v. 3)

What could be of greater value than life? Without life, one cannot experience any other good in existence. And yet, Jesus teaches, "Whoever aims to save his life will lose it, but whoever loses his life for my sake will find it" (Matt 16:25). If you abide in God's loyalty, even death cannot separate you from what you hold dear; for you will have everlasting life on God's holy mountain, where there is fullness of joy in His presence (16:11; 24:3-4; see also John 11:25; Rom 8:38-39).

So I will bless you throughout my life;
in your name I will lift up my hands. (v. 4)

The Father seeks those who will worship Him in spirit and truth (John 4:23). And (blessed be His Name forever!) He has given us everything we need in order to do so and thus to become close to Him (2 Pet 1:3-11). He will satisfy your soul as a rich feast satisfies your body, so that shouts of praise will issue naturally from the upwelling of joy in your spirit (v. 5). And at the end of each day, you will have the opportunity to look back and reflect on His sustaining grace (v. 6).

From the psalmist's opening reference to a "search" performed first thing in the morning (v. 1) to his "ruminating" on God in bed at night (v. 6), we get the picture of a day that begins and ends with intentional focus on God. And we see the overflowing joy that comes with the continual remembrance of His faithfulness. The psalmist proclaims, "You have been my help, and in the shadow of your wings I give a resounding cry" (v. 7).

In this Psalms study, we have repeatedly encouraged you to dedicate time for fellowship with God every morning and evening. What could be better than entering God's presence at the beginning and end of the day! What does that currently look like for you? Is God your first thought when you wake up and your last thought as you drift into sleep? How has He been rewarding your seeking His face in the morning? And with what reflections have you been wrapping up the evening?

The Psalms never speak in ignorance of the brokenness that remains in this world because of sin, nor could David possibly have been oblivious to it as he was being hunted. But even as the final verses of Psalm 63 mention those seeking to kill the king, David's confident assertion is that these attackers will ultimately be swept away, while the king will live to rejoice in God. Justice shall prevail, and the faithful will exult.

DAY 2: PSALM 64

Psalm 64 begins, as so many psalms do, with a cry for help and a vivid account of enemies seeking the psalmist's downfall. As is often the case, the enemies' words are their weapons (v. 3). But God's response, told in just one verse (v. 7), is swift and decisive. The schemers reap what they have sown (v. 8), and those who witness God's judgment on them learn to respect Him as they ought (v. 9). As in Psalm 63, the final note is the joy of the righteous (v. 10).[68]

FOR THE DIRECTOR. A PSALM OF DAVID.

> ¹ *Hear, God, my voice as I muse.*
> *Keep my life from the terror of the enemy.*
> ² *Hide me from the plots of the wicked,*
> *from the throng of evildoers,*
> ³ *who whet their tongue like a sword;*
> *they aim their arrow, bitter words,*
> ⁴ *to shoot from hiding places at the person of integrity.*
> *They shoot suddenly and are not afraid.*
> ⁵ *They encourage themselves with an evil word;*
> *they recount it, hiding traps;*
> *they say, "Who will see them?"*

---

68 See Kidner, *Psalms 1–72*, 245-247.

⁶ *They plot injustices:*
  "We have perfected a well-plotted plot,
  and the heart and mind of man are deep."
⁷ *But God shot them with an arrow suddenly;*
  they are wounded.
⁸ *They brought it down upon themselves with their tongue;*
  all who look on them would recoil,
⁹ *and all mankind feared*
  and declared the work of God
  and considered his doing.
¹⁰ *The righteous rejoices in Yahweh*
  and takes refuge in him,
  and all the upright in heart exult.

TRANQUILITY COMES WITH TRUST IN GOD

In Psalm 63, the psalmist spoke from a place of having "seen" God (63:2) and of continually drawing close to Him ("My soul clings to you" [63:8]). Psalm 64 likewise speaks to God within the context of a close relationship. Its opening line ("Hear, God, my voice as I muse") might be expressed more idiomatically as "God, here's what's on my mind."[69] David opens up to God as his trusted friend—and a trusted friend is exactly what he needs, as liars and conspirators are what presently occupy his attention.

What David does not want on his mind is fear: He prays, "Keep my life from the terror of the enemy" (v. 1). The threat against him is real—many are seeking to sow division in his kingdom and thereby overthrow him (vv. 2-6)—but God is also real and immeasurably more powerful than they are. As long as David stands close to God, he need not be afraid (see 27:1).

WRONGDOERS ARE DECEIVED

The enemies David describes in this psalm think that they are being very clever. They "shoot suddenly" and do so "from hiding places" so they can take down their target before he can put up a fight; they "are not afraid" (v. 4). They think that no one will be able to detect the traps they have laid (v. 5), and they thoroughly congratulate themselves for their ingenuity: "We have perfected a well-plotted plot, and the heart and mind of man are deep" (v. 6). If only . . .

Of course, the irony here is palpable. David himself is well aware of what they are doing. But much more to the point, these "deep" thinkers are fools for forgetting about God (see Pss 14, 53), from whom no creature is hidden, before whose eyes all are naked and exposed, and to whom we must give an account (Heb 4:13). Unlike David, who is safe in God's protection, these people *should* be afraid as they plot evil against a person of integrity (v. 4). If only they

---

[69] Most translations have "my complaint" where we have "as I muse," but the Hebrew word *siakh* refers more generally to what occupies one's attention, whether positive or negative (cf. Pss 104:34; 119:97, 99).

had learned the lessons of Psalm 1: "Blessed is the man who does not walk in the counsel of the wicked" (1:1) and "Yahweh knows the way of the just, but the way of the wicked will fail" (1:6).

Sometimes ignorance leads people to do exactly the wrong thing while thinking they are doing good. So Paul the apostle, prior to his encounter with Jesus on the Damascus road, thought he was defending God's honor against blasphemers by persecuting Jesus' disciples. And while Jesus was on the cross, He prayed this extraordinary prayer over His killers: "Father, forgive them, for they do not know what they are doing" (Luke 23:34). But there is also the culpable ignorance of those who willfully suppress what God has made known to them (see Rom 1:18-23). And the Lord judges justly.

Has anyone been launching "bitter words" (v. 3) at you? Take such people before the Lord in prayer, and ask Him for discernment and wisdom in case a word of truth might shift the mindset from which they are operating. Regardless, do not respond in fleshly anger, but let the Holy Spirit guide you. Write down any names that come to mind and any action steps you feel the Lord leading you to take.

SWIFT JUSTICE

David's opponents here have no excuse for sharpening their tongues like swords and sniping at their God-appointed ruler with "bitter words" (v. 3). And as Jesus told His disciples, when God gives justice to His chosen ones, that justice comes swiftly (Luke 18:7-8). Hence, verse 7 of the psalm is succinct:

> But God shot them with an arrow suddenly;
>   they are wounded.

The psalm goes on immediately to say, "They brought it down upon themselves with their tongue" (v. 8). That is, these people are reaping exactly what they have sown—they who "suddenly" shot the arrow of their bitter words (vv. 3-4) have been suddenly shot by the One whose word is true.

The result of this outpouring of justice is that everyone who saw and considered it "feared" (v. 9). Faced with the reality that people reap what they sow, these onlookers cannot help but take stock of what they themselves have been sowing. For most of us, honest self-appraisal will reveal some things we would rather not see, much less have to present before the Judge—hence the fear—but the good news is that God forgives those who have the humility to acknowledge their wrongs freely (1 John 1:9).

So while the words of fools and evildoers may be "bitter" (v. 3), God's judgments are "sweet" to those who allow His word to shape their lives (19:9-10; 119:103). "The righteous rejoices in Yahweh and takes refuge in him, and all the upright in heart exult" (v. 10).

Sowing and reaping is an eternal principle in God's Kingdom (see Gal 6:7-10). What sorts of seed have you been sowing recently, and what sort of harvest are you looking forward to?

DAY 3: PSALM 65

This song of praise and thanksgiving immediately recalls Psalm 62 with its notion of "quiet"— which again indicates not verbal silence so much as tranquility of mind and heart, which is the fruit of faith in the Good Shepherd. Psalm 65 testifies to God's goodness as the One who hears our prayers, atones for our transgressions, provides for the nourishment of our bodies, and awes the world with His wondrous power in and over creation.

FOR THE DIRECTOR. A PSALM OF DAVID. A SONG.

1. *Quiet in you is praise, God in Zion,*
        and to you a vow shall be fulfilled.
2. *Hearer of prayer,*
        to you all flesh must come.
3. *Though iniquities are stronger than I,*
        you atone for our transgressions.
4. *Blessed is the one you choose and bring near,*
        who dwells in your courts.
        May we be sated with the goodness of your house,
        your holy palace.
5. *With awesome deeds in righteousness you answer us,*
        God of our salvation,
        Confidence of all the ends of the earth
        and the farthest sea,
6. *who set up the mountains by his strength,*
        girded with might;
7. *who stills the roar of the seas,*
        the roar of their waves and the clamor of the peoples,

⁸ *so that those who live at the ends of the earth are in awe of your signs;*
   east and west you make resound.
⁹ *You attend to the earth and water it,*
      abundantly enriching it;
   God's canal is full of water;
      you provide their grain, for so you have prepared the earth,
¹⁰ *saturating its furrows,*
      sinking its grooves;
   with showers you soften it,
      its growth you bless.
¹¹ *You have crowned the year of your goodness,*
   and your tracks flow with fatness.
¹² *Meadows flow in the wilderness,*
   and hills gird themselves with rejoicing.
¹³ *Pastures are clothed with flocks,*
   and valleys are covered with wheat;
   they shout—indeed, they sing.

TRANQUILITY TESTIFIES TO TRUST IN GOD

Quiet in you is praise, God in Zion. (v. 1)

This is a rather unusual statement for the Psalms, considering how often they tell us to shout, sing, and otherwise make a joyful noise to the Lord.[70] Of course, Psalm 65 is not denying the appropriateness of boisterous praise—its final statement is that the very meadows and valleys of God's creation "shout" and "sing" for joy (vv. 12-13). Rather, the point here seems to be that a calm assurance before the One on whom "all flesh" depends (v. 2) and to whom all must give an account can testify in its own way to our faith in Him—especially faith in His having atoned for our sins (v. 3). God is indeed worthy of our trust, and one of the ways we demonstrate that trust is by not being worried.

This is not a blissful ignorance of the things that might make one worry. David is well aware of "iniquities" that are beyond his capacity to deal with (v. 3a), but he knows his God can and does deal with them, both on David's behalf and on behalf of all God's people: "You atone for our transgressions" (v. 3b). So David is a happy man: "Blessed is the one you choose and bring near, who dwells in your courts" (v. 4).

Consider your own standing before God. No doubt you have made it through countless situations in which success or failure was far beyond your control, but here you are. And no doubt

---

[70] Various translations (including LXX) have something to the effect of "Praise to you is fitting" instead of "Quiet in you is praise." As John Goldingay remarks, that is "a true and good (though less striking) point that requires considerable stretching of the meaning of the root from which they are deriving the word" (Goldingay, *Psalms 42–89,* 272 [note]). We may also note several points in Scripture where, in the context of God's judgment, reverent silence is explicitly expressed or commanded (e.g., Hab 2:20; Zeph 1:7; Zech 2:13; Rev 8:1).

the Lord has met you with grace more than "seventy times seven" times (Matt 18:22) when your own heart was out of line. Thank Him (as loudly or softly as you like) for His extraordinary patience and faithfulness to forgive and sustain you in His grace, and for His demonstrated commitment to seeing you through life's challenges. If anything has been making you restless, let God's proven track record of faithfulness dissolve your worry. Let your thoughts find rest in Him, even as He leads you to engage actively in the work He has assigned to you in the world.

Now consider someone in your life who does not find him- or herself "blessed" and "near" to God. First, pray for that person, that he or she would have an encounter with the grace and love of God. As you do so, acknowledge that "there but for the grace of God go I." Then ask God to put on your heart how you might be His agent in bringing about that encounter. Write down any thoughts below, and make a plan to follow through on those thoughts.

FROM THE PERSONAL TO THE UNIVERSAL

Verses 3 and 4 both move from the singular ("Iniquities are stronger than *I*"; "Blessed is *the one you choose*") to the plural ("You atone for *our* transgressions"; "May *we* be sated"). This is not an uncommon gesture in the Scriptures, as the person praying recognizes himself as belonging to a people.[71] But the psalm also reminds us that God always intended His chosen people, the children of Abraham, to be His witnesses to the rest of the world. So verse 5 moves from Israel ("You answer *us*, God of our salvation") to all humanity, declaring that God in Zion is indeed the "Confidence of all the ends of the earth and the farthest sea."

Even apart from the witness of other people whom God has brought near, all of creation testifies to the majesty of its Creator and Ruler (vv. 6-8; see also Pss 8, 19, 24; Luke 19:40). And we are reminded that God gives blessings worthy of gratitude upon all the earth: He sends rain and gives growth to food crops (vv. 9-10)—for which He Himself has provided the seed (Gen 1:29)—and leaves a trail of abundance in His wake wherever He goes (v. 11). Even in the wilderness, where men have not labored to till the earth (see Gen 3:17-19), God provides pasture for flocks (vv. 12-13). All these gifts loudly proclaim the generosity of the Giver.

---

71 Goldingay, *Psalms 42–89*, 276; see Isa 6:5.

As you are mindful of the multitudes who, for various reasons, are not experiencing the same measure of abundance as you are, do not forget that you are blessed in order to bless others (see Gen 12:2)—and that this applies spiritually as well as materially. In what area(s) of your life are you experiencing particular abundance? How is that abundance spilling over and blessing others? Is there an area in which you are holding back where you feel the Lord prompting you to pour out for others what He has freely poured into you?

DAY 4: PSALM 66

Psalm 65 moved from "quiet" reverence (65:1) to a celebration of God's providence over all the earth and an acknowledgment that the hills and meadows "shout" and "sing" for joy (65:13); Psalm 66 picks up the theme that praise toward God resounds in all the earth. Stronger emphasis is placed here on the role of God's specific, historical actions on behalf of His chosen people—acts which serve as testimonies to the nations. While Psalm 65 moved from the personal to the universal, Psalm 66 moves conversely from "all the earth" (v. 1) to Israel (v. 6) to the psalmist (v. 13), who testifies that God has heard his prayer (v. 19; see also 65:2).

FOR THE DIRECTOR. A SONG. A PSALM.

¹ *Raise a shout to God, all the earth!*
² *Make music of the glory of his name;*
    make his praise glorious.
³ *Say to God, "How awesome are your deeds;*
    with your great strength, your enemies wither before you.
⁴ *All the earth shall bow down to you and make music to you,*
    make music to your name!" Selah
⁵ *Come and see the works of God,*
    awesome in action over the sons of Adam.
⁶ *He turned the sea into dry land;*
    they crossed the river on foot.
  So let us rejoice in him,
⁷ *who rules by his might forever,*
    whose eyes keep watch on the nations;
    let not the rebellious rise against him. Selah

8   *Bless our God, peoples,*
    and make the sound of his praise be heard,
9   *he who sets our soul among the living*
    and has not let our feet stagger.
10 *Indeed, you have tested us, God;*
    you have refined us as one refines silver.
11 *You brought us into a snare;*
    you put a constraint on our hips.
12 *You made a man ride at our head;*
    we went through the fire and through the water,
    and you brought us out into overflow.
13 *I will enter your house with burnt offerings;*
    I will fulfill to you my vows,
14 *which my lips uttered*
    and my mouth spoke when I was in trouble.
15 *As whole burnt offerings I will offer up fatlings to you*
    and the aroma of rams;
    I will prepare bulls and goats. Selah
16 *Come, listen, and I will recount, all who fear God,*
    what he has done for me.
17 *To him I called with my mouth,*
    with praise on my tongue.
18 *If I had seen iniquity in my heart,*
    my Lord would not have heard.
19 *But God did hear!*
    He listened to my voice in prayer.
20 *Blessed be God,*
    who has not cast aside my prayer
    or his loyalty from me.

PRAISE THE LORD!

Psalm 66 opens with a string of imperatives: "Raise a shout to God," "Make music of the glory of his name," "Make his praise glorious," and "Say to God." Since the Lord's blessing is on those who not only hear His word but also *do* as it says (Matt 7:24-27; Jas 1:22-25), take time now to underline these imperatives and do as the psalmist says before you proceed with the rest of your business for today. Give praise to God, who is worthy to receive it.

COME AND SEE

Having called "all the earth" to praise the glory of God's Name (v. 1), the psalmist turns to give testimony about what God has done to demonstrate just how glorious He is. Perhaps unsurprisingly, the testimony given here to explain why all people should praise God matches the rationale He gave Israel for why they should serve Him alone: He is the One who brought Israel up out of Egypt, out of slavery (Exod 20:2), and ultimately into the land He had designated as their inheritance. Verse 6 obviously refers to the parting of the sea when Israel escaped Pharaoh's army ("He turned the sea into dry land") but likely also refers to the crossing of the Jordan when the people entered the Promised Land ("They crossed the river on foot").[72]

Now, it is self-evident why Israel should be grateful for their deliverance from bondage—and for God's continuing vigilance over their wayward neighbors (v. 7). But how are these events a cause for the people of other nations to celebrate?

Here we note God's own statements that by demonstrating His power in bringing a people miraculously out of Egypt, word would get out from Egypt that Israel's God, Yahweh, is great and awesome beyond comparison with the gods of even the strongest nation (Exod 7:5; 9:16). While this would be cause for despair for people inescapably bound to their lesser gods, the invitation is extended to all who would come to leave those gods behind and serve Yahweh, the true God. Not only does God command Israel at many points to show hospitality to foreigners who come to live among them, but His display of power over Egypt's gods (see Exod 12:12) stands to assure potential converts that they need not fear the wrath of their old gods as a result of forsaking them and serving Yahweh.

This concern is still alive today, though not as much in the West as in other parts of the world. In places like India, where millions of people are actively striving to appease a host of deities that can be quite unfriendly (i.e., demonic powers and principalities), it is important to prove that the Lord is still able to deliver those who call on Him from the hand of every rival and pretender.

The testimony that God is present and active among His people is always an invitation to join the party. In a striking prophecy of coming revival, Zechariah writes:

Thus says Yahweh of Hosts: "Yet again, peoples and the inhabitants of many cities shall come, and the inhabitants of one city will go to another and say, 'Let us go without delay to entreat Yahweh, to seek Yahweh of Hosts. I myself am resolved to go.' And many peoples and great nations will come to seek Yahweh of Hosts in Jerusalem and to entreat him."

Thus says Yahweh of Hosts: "In those days ten men of all languages and nations will seize a Judean man by the hem of his garment, saying, 'Let us go with you, for we have heard that God is with you.'" (Zech 8:20-23)

---

[72] Some commentators take all of verse 6 as referring to the sea crossing; in any case, the people's emergence into "overflow" by the end of verse 12 certainly gets us into the Promised Land before the testimony is over.

How are God's presence and power most evident in the life of your church community? Where and how can you invite others to "come and see"?

_____

_____

_____

_____

After wrapping up the summary of Israel's emergence from trials into the promised land of abundance (v. 12), the psalmist proceeds to testify that he has personally experienced an answered prayer. We do not know the details of the story—only that he was "in trouble" (v. 14). The purpose, however, of this final portion of the psalm is not to give a specific account of one man's experience but to attest two realities: chiefly, that God does hear and faithfully answer the prayers of His people (vv. 19-20), but also that the iniquity in one's heart will keep Him from doing so (v. 18; see also Isa 59:1-2).

There are certain prayers that God has vowed always to answer. If you publicly acknowledge the lordship of Jesus and trust in His resurrection from the dead, you can expect to receive the same mercy He showed to the penitent evildoer on the cross next to Him (Luke 23:39-43; see also Rom 10:9). But as a rule, the principle still applies that sin must be removed before other prayers get answered. We see this principle applied positively as Jesus forgives a paralytic's sins before healing his paralysis (Mark 2:1-12) and in His instruction to be reconciled to one's brother before presenting an offering to God (Matt 5:21-24). And we see it applied negatively in Jesus' story of the unforgiving person who is handed over to the tormentors (Matt 18:23-35). Christian Union staff can personally testify—as can virtually all ministers who regularly see healing in answer to prayer—that breakthrough often comes after a person repents of unforgiveness. This is not to say, of course, that anyone who doesn't get healed must be guilty of unforgiveness or of any other particular sin; it is simply to say that when sin is at the root of the problem, prayer will not circumvent the need for repentance.

As you offer yourself before the Lord today, is the Holy Spirit revealing any iniquity in your heart? If so, know that He does not point anything out in order to condemn you. Rather, in His grace He wants to free you from it. If your conscience is clean, what other steps of faith is He prompting you to take today?

_____

_____

_____

_____

DAY 5: PSALM 67

Psalm 67 is a prayer for God's blessing on His people and land. It combines the themes of the two preceding psalms—that all the earth should recognize God's sovereignty over nature and its abundance (Ps 65) and that His saving work on Israel's behalf invites all the nations to seek Him and His favor (Ps 66).

FOR THE LEADER. WITH STRINGS. A PSALM. A SONG.

> *¹ God be gracious to us and bless us,*
>   *make his face shine among us. Selah*
> *² Knowing your way on the earth,*
>   *your salvation among all nations,*
> *³ let the peoples acknowledge you, God,*
>   *let all the peoples acknowledge you.*
> *⁴ Let the peoples rejoice and shout,*
>   *for you judge peoples with equity,*
>   *and you guide the peoples on the earth. Selah*
> *⁵ Let the peoples acknowledge you, God,*
>   *let all the peoples acknowledge you.*
> *⁶ The earth yields its produce;*
>   *God, our God, will bless us.*
> *⁷ God will bless us,*
>   *and all the ends of the earth will fear him.*

BLESSING AND BEING BLESSED

> Then Yahweh said to Moses: "Tell Aaron and his sons, 'Thus shall you bless the sons of Israel, saying to them:
>
> Yahweh bless you and keep you.
> Yahweh make his face shine upon you and be gracious to you.
> Yahweh lift up his face toward you and give you peace.'" (Num 6:22-26)

The opening verse of Psalm 67 is very clearly drawing on this high priestly blessing. What is particularly noteworthy here is that while Aaron's blessing is for God's face to shine "upon"—literally, *toward*—the people of Israel, Psalm 67 asks that God's face shine "with" (or "among") them. The preposition *'eth* can be used variably to mean "together with," "with the help of," or "by means of," or it can simply denote proximity ("beside," "among"). In context, the change in wording from the well-known Aaronic blessing in Numbers 6 seems to underscore the theme that God's favor doesn't simply come *at* us but bears witness *through* us. The psalm carries this theme through to the finish: "God will bless us, and all the ends of the earth will fear him" (v. 7).

This wording also recalls the description of God's people in Psalm 34:5: "They look at him and shine, and their faces shall not be ashamed." In our comments on that psalm,[73] we likened God's people to the moon, which reflects the sun's radiance back to the earth in dark of night. The same idea is present here. Jesus, the Light of the World, has made His dwelling with you and in you, with the intention that His face should also shine forth from you and give light to others "that they might see your good works and glorify your Father who is in heaven" (Matt 5:16).

While the Scriptures exhort us to "stir each other up to love and good works" (Heb 10:24), Christians are sometimes (understandably) wary of mistaking the fruit God wishes to bear through us as some sort of work we must do to initially earn God's favor. If you catch yourself thinking that God will love you *if* you are an effective witness, check yourself. He loved you enough to die for you while you were still mired in sin (Rom 5:8). Jesus called the Twelve to Himself first "that they might be with him" and second "that he might send them out to preach" (Mark 3:14). Likewise, He chose you and called you foremost because He values you and desires a living relationship with you. He will call to others through you because He loves them also.

So to paraphrase verses 2-3: "Let all the peoples recognize God's goodness by the ways He has shown Himself kind to you and by the saving grace that He has given to you—the grace He offers to all who call on Him."

When you think of God's kindness toward you, what comes to mind first? Write that thought down, and seek to articulate it in such a way that you can share with someone else how God has been gracious to you.

AS WITH THE PEOPLE, SO WITH THE LAND

> *The earth yields its produce;*
> *God, our God, will bless us. (v. 6)*

In 2 Chronicles 7:14, God promises to heal His people's land of famine and pestilence when they repent of their waywardness. In the nation of Fiji—where a single word, *vanua*, refers both to the people and to their land—a group of home-grown missionaries known as the Healing the

---

[73] See *Psalms 1–41: A Christian Union Bible Study*, Lesson 9, Day 2.

Land Team have been seeing God do just that. Since the early 2000s, these Fijians have been invited into many different villages that were rife with division and beset with various woes to lead the people through a process of repentance, reconciliation with God and each other, and a reconsecration of their lands and waters to the Lord. As of May 2019, when a group of Christian Union staff members went to learn from this ministry, all 120 villages that had invited the Healing the Land Team to lead them through this process had experienced miraculous transformation in the productivity of their croplands and fisheries, as well as restored social relationships.

In one village, a man joyfully showed us the enormous yams he had harvested, twice the size of what he used to get before his village repented—and from the same plot on which he had been growing them continuously, without rotation, for the last twenty years. We heard of trees bearing fruit year-round that had produced only seasonal crops before; of dead coral reefs suddenly coming back to life, with schools of fish coming right up to the children's nets by the shore; of the return of edible seaweeds and abundant crab harvests in the rivers; and also of an end to alcohol and tobacco addiction, quarrels between the members of different churches, and other societal ills. We saw (and ate of) this abundance, and we experienced the generous hospitality of communities that had recently been at each other's throats.

Most of us in the West live much less closely to the land than our sisters and brothers in Fiji. But let us not lose sight of the reality that God has made His people to be stewards of the territory we inhabit and that our prayers for His Kingdom to come and His Spirit to be poured out should anticipate a wholesale transformation of that territory, as well as the people and culture within it.

What might "healing the land" look like in your area? What particular woes seem prevalent there, and what lies at the root of them? How might your church be a part of reconsecrating the area to God?

Lesson Review

We began this lesson, in Psalm 63, with a view into David's heart as a true seeker after the Lord. While such a life was (and is) not without serious opposition, as evidenced in Psalm 64, God does intervene, vindicating those He has chosen and causing all to reap what they have sown. And as the last three psalms of this lesson have repeatedly attested, God's grace on our behalf is a sign to the world that we serve a true and living God, the knowledge of whose glory must ultimately extend over all the earth (see Hab 2:14).

6

LESSON SIX:

Psalms 68–72

This lesson brings us to the end of Book 2 of the Psalms, and to the end of David's collected prayers (though a few of David's prayers are scattered throughout the remaining books). In these final prayers of David, the psalmist looks forward to what God would ultimately accomplish through the Son of David, the Messiah who was to come (and is to come again). There are still troubles to be endured while we wait for Jesus' return, but let's allow these words from Psalm 68 to set our thoughts on course for the week: "God will arise, his enemies will be scattered," and "the righteous" will "rejoice" (68:1, 3).

DAY 1: PSALM 68

Psalm 68 anticipates God's final ascendancy over all His enemies, particularly the rulers and principalities over idolatrous nations. References to Mount Bashan (v. 15) and "the Rider on the Clouds" (v. 4) take aim specifically at Baal worship, asserting that Yahweh, not Baal, is Lord. Paul connects this psalm with Jesus' resurrection, ascension, and reign over the church (Eph 4:7-16; see also Col 2:15); meanwhile, we look forward to the psalm's ultimate fulfillment when Jesus returns. The psalm shows that not only is Yahweh strong in battle (see Ps 24), but He also cares and provides for those otherwise abandoned and helpless (vv. 5-6, 10).

FOR THE DIRECTOR. OF DAVID. A PSALM. A SONG.

1 *God will arise, his enemies will be scattered,*
   and his haters will flee before him.
2 *As smoke is blown away, you blow them away,*
      as wax melts before fire;
   the wicked perish from before God.
3 *But the righteous rejoice;*
   they exult before God,
   they exult with joy.
4 *Sing to God, make music to his name;*
   build up a highway for the Rider on the Clouds!
   Yah is his name; exult before him!

105

⁵ *Father of the fatherless and Judge for the widows,*
  God, in his holy dwelling.
⁶ *God, who settles those who are alone into a house,*
  brings out the captives into prosperity,
  though the stubborn inhabit scorched land.
⁷ *God, when you go out before your people,*
  when you stride through the wilderness, Selah
⁸ *earth shakes, even the heavens drop,*
  before God, the One of Sinai;
  before God, the God of Israel.
⁹ *You sprinkle very generous rain, God;*
  when your possession is weary, you establish it.
¹⁰ *Your community, they live in it;*
  you have provided in your goodness for the lowly, God.
¹¹ *My Lord gives a word;*
  the messengers are a great host:
¹² *Kings of hosts flee, they flee!*
  And she that is at home divides the spoil—
¹³ *though they stayed among the sheepfolds—*
  the wings of a dove covered with silver,
  its pinions with green gold.
¹⁴ *When the Almighty scatters kings on it,*
  it snows on Zalmon.
¹⁵ *Mountain of gods, Mount Bashan—*
  craggy mountain, Mount Bashan—
¹⁶ *why do you look with hostility, craggy mountains,*
  on the mountain God desires for his dwelling?
  Yes, Yahweh will abide there forever.
¹⁷ *The chariotry of God are myriads, thousands and thousands,*
  my Lord among them, Sinai in holiness.
¹⁸ *You went up to the height, you took captives,*
  you received gifts of mankind,
  even those who rebelled at Yah God's settling there.
¹⁹ *Blessed be my Lord.*
  Day by day, he carries our burdens,
  the true God, our Savior. Selah
²⁰ *The true God, to us a God of saving acts,*
  as to Yahweh, my Lord, belong escapes from death.
²¹ *Indeed, God smashes the head of his enemies,*
  the hairy crown of him who goes about in his trespasses.

²² *My Lord says,*
>   *"From Bashan I will bring back,*
>   *I will bring back from the depths of the sea,*

²³ *so that your foot may smash in blood,*
>   *your dogs' tongue have its portion from your enemies."*

²⁴ *They see your processions, God,*
>   *the processions of my God, my king, in holiness.*

²⁵ *Singers go in front, string players behind,*
>   *in the midst of virgins beating tambourines.*

²⁶ *In the assemblies bless God,*
>   *Yahweh, from the fountain of Israel.*

²⁷ *There Benjamin, the littlest, is ecstatic!*
>   *The chiefs of Judah, leading their shout!*
>   *The chiefs of Zebulun! The chiefs of Naphtali!*

²⁸ *Your God commands your strength.*
>   *Be strong, God, you who act for us.*

²⁹ *Because of your palace above Jerusalem,*
>   *kings shall bring you a gift.*

³⁰ *Rebuke the snake in the grass,*[74]
>   *the herd of bulls with peoples for calves.*
>   *Trampling those who love silver,*
>   *may you scatter the peoples who delight in war.*

³¹ *Gifts of bronze shall come from Egypt;*
>   *Cush shall bring them quickly with his hands to God.*

³² *Kingdoms of the earth, sing to God;*
>   *make music to my Lord, Selah*

³³ *to the One who rides in the ancient heaven of heavens—*
>   *behold, he gives his voice, his mighty voice.*

³⁴ *Give strength to God.*
>   *His majesty is over Israel, and his strength is in the skies.*

³⁵ *God is to be feared from your holy places—*
>   *the God of Israel,*
>   *He who gives strength and power to the people.*
>   *Blessed be God.*

---

[74] Literally, "living creature of the reed[s]."

WHO'S THE BOSS?

> *Sing to God, make music to his name;*
> *build up a highway for the Rider on the Clouds!*
> *Yah is his name; exult before him! (v. 4)*

It is good and right that people sing to God, but it is also terribly important that they know who God is and not give honor to some god other than the One who is worthy of worship. Israel's neighbors (and, as time wore on, the apostate within Israel) worshiped the great pretender Baal. One of Baal's epithets, attested in writings from Ugarit to the north of Israel, was "Rider on the Clouds." But Israel's neighbors were deceived. Baal is not the one who "mak[es] the clouds his chariot" (104:3) and comes to defend his people; that distinction belongs to Yahweh (also referred to in this psalm by the abbreviated form *Yah*).[75]

Moreover, one cannot rightly know God as Yahweh—the One Who Is—while remaining ignorant of His nature and character. So Psalm 68 goes on to elaborate that He is

> *Father of the fatherless and Judge for the widows,*
> *God, in his holy dwelling.*
> *God, who settles those who are alone into a house,*
> *brings out the captives into prosperity,*
> *though the stubborn inhabit scorched land. (vv. 5-6)*

Is He not worthy that we should sing His praises? Indeed, the worship of any other god is not just a sacrilege but also a tragedy, for no other god truly loves or helps those who worship. Christians often struggle to communicate this reality with people of other religions for the obvious reason that we do not want to offend and alienate the very people we wish to invite into a loving relationship with our heavenly Father. Telling people that their gods are worthless seems like a poor way of winning them over.

Of course, in such conversations a listening ear to the Spirit of God (and a lot of genuine love for people) is necessary. But with attention and discernment, you will find that many people really aren't happy with their gods. They may even feel enslaved to them (as indeed they are). In that case, you may be doing them the greatest kindness they have ever received by saying, "Look, this god you're serving isn't the true God. Let me tell you about my God and what He's done for me." (This suggestion would also apply to our conversations with nominal Christians—especially those who have been presented with a warped picture of God and have not yet come to know Him in truth.)

---

[75] Tate, *Psalms 51–100*, 163, 176. See also Deut 33:26; Ps 18:10; Isa 19:1. For *Yah* as an abbreviated form of *Yahweh*, see our "Note on the Divine Name (Yahweh)" in *Psalms 1–41: A Christian Union Bible Study*, Lesson 2.

Think of someone you care about who serves a different god (or many gods). What is he or she missing that can be found only in Jesus?

_____

_____

_____

_____

MAKING THEM JEALOUS

In verses 15-16, David asks Mount Bashan why its peaks are envious of Sinai, Yahweh's mountain. Bashan, to the north of Israel, was known as the gateway to the underworld, and it was a hub of demonic false religion.[76] David's taunt thus anticipates Isaiah's rebuke of Lucifer:[77]

> You said in your heart,
>> "I will ascend the heavens;
>>> above the stars of God I will raise my throne,
>>> and I will preside on the mount of assembly, in the heights of the north.
>> I will ascend above the cloudy heights;
>>> I will make myself like the Most High."
>> Ah! To Sheol you are brought down,
>>> to the depths of the pit. (Isa 14:13-15)

Whoever does not gladly serve God must be envious of Him. To Him belong the Kingdom, power, and glory forever—as well they should. And because His blessings abound to His people—He "carries our burdens" (v. 19) and performs "saving acts," which include breaking us free from death (v. 20)—so we who belong to God provoke the unsaved to jealousy (see Rom 11:11). Fortunately, they need not go away frustrated; if they acknowledge our God as Lord and forsake all others, they, too, will find a place at the table.

COME WILLINGLY . . . OR UNWILLINGLY

Verse 18 tells of the Lord taking captives, while verse 31 refers to kings seeking to appease Him with gifts. And in many other places, Scripture informs us that everyone must face God sooner or later. The question everyone ought to consider is, _Will He welcome me into His joy as a good and faithful servant_ (Matt 25:23) _or throw me out into the darkness_ (Matt 25:30)? So the final two verses of Psalm 68 wisely exhort us to "give [our] strength to God" in faithful submission and service, knowing that He is the One who actually gives us strength and power (vv. 34-35). "Blessed be God," the psalm closes (v. 35). Blessed be God indeed.

---

76 See Heiser, _Unseen Realm_, 201, 289-295.

77 The name Lucifer comes from the Latin rendering of the Hebrew _helel_, the "morning star" to whom these verses are directed (Isa 14:12).

Where is the Lord asking you to pour out your strength today? Are you filled with His strength for the task?

DAY 2: PSALM 69

Psalm 69 is the prayer of a God-fearing person suffering persecution. While it originally spoke of David's experience of vicious opposition to his reign, it also clearly anticipates the scorn and rejection Jesus would come to suffer. Consequently, it is the third most frequently cited psalm in the New Testament (after Psalms 110 and 22).[78] And as Jesus taught His disciples to expect the same treatment their Master received from sinful people, this psalm also speaks for all of us today who are hated on His account. The prayer begins as an urgent cry for help, but it ends with a beautiful vow of confidence that God will indeed save and establish His people forever.

FOR THE DIRECTOR. ACCORDING TO "LILIES." OF DAVID.

1 *Save me, God,*
for waters have come up to my neck.
2 *I have sunk deep in mire,*
and there is no foothold.
I have entered into deep waters,
and a flood washes over me.
3 *I have grown weary in calling,*
my throat is parched,
my eyes fail,
waiting for my God.
4 *More than the hairs of my head are those who hate me for nothing;*
many are those who would destroy me, my lying enemies;
what I did not steal, I must now return.
5 *God, you know about my folly,*
and my guilt is not hidden from you.
6 *Let not those who wait for you be ashamed because of me,*
my Lord Yahweh of Hosts;
let not those who seek you be dishonored because of me,
God of Israel.

---

78 Boice, *Psalms 42–106*, 569.

7 *For it is on your account that I bear reproach,*
   that dishonor covers my face.

8 *I have become a stranger to my brothers,*
   alien to my mother's sons.

9 *Because zeal for your house has consumed me,*
   and the reproaches of those who reproach you have
      fallen on me.

10 *Even when I weep and fast,*
   it brings reproaches on me.

11 *When I put on sackcloth for clothing,*
   I became a byword to them.

12 *Those who sit at the gate muse about me,*
   and the drunkards sing about me.

13 *As for me, my prayer is to you, Yahweh,*
   for a time of favor;
   God, in the greatness of your loyalty,
      answer me with your saving faithfulness.

14 *Rescue me from the mud and do not let me sink;*
   let me be delivered from my haters and from the watery depths.

15 *Let not a flood of waters wash over me,*
   nor the deep swallow me,
   nor the pit close its mouth over me.

16 *Answer me, Yahweh, because your loyalty is good;*
   according to the abundance of your mercies, turn to me.

17 *And do not hide your face from your servant,*
   for I am in distress; answer me quickly.

18 *Draw near to my soul—redeem it!*
   Because of my enemies ransom me.

19 *You know my reproach and my shame and my dishonor;*
   all my harassers are before you.

20 *Reproach—*
      it has broken my heart, and I am sick.
   I looked for condolence, but there was none,
      and for comforters, but I did not find any.

21 *But they gave me poison for food,*
   and for my thirst they gave me vinegar to drink.

22 *Let their table before them become a trap*
   and a snare for their allies.

23 *Let their eyes go dark so they cannot see,*
   and their loins shudder continually.

24   *Pour out on them your indignation,*
        and let the burning of your anger overtake them.
25   *Let their camp become desolate;*
        in their tents let no one dwell.
26   *Because you—whom you have struck, they pursue,*
        and to the pains of those you have pierced, they add.[79]
27   *Add guilt to their guilt,*
        and do not let them into your righteousness.
28   *Let them be blotted out of the book of life,*
        and do not let them be registered with the righteous.
29   *But I am lowly and in pain;*
        let your salvation, God, raise me to a secure height.
30   *I will praise God's name in song,*
        and I will magnify it with acknowledgment.
31   *This will be better for Yahweh than an ox,*
        a bull with horn and cloven hoof.
32   *The lowly see, they rejoice;*
        seekers of God, let your hearts be alive.
33   *For Yahweh is the one who listens to the needy,*
        and he does not despise his captives.
34   *Let the heavens and earth praise him,*
        the seas and everything that moves in them.
35   *For God will save Zion*
        and build the cities of Judah,
        and they will dwell there and possess it—
36   *the offspring of his servants will inherit it,*
        and those who love his name will abide there.

PRAYING INTO PERSPECTIVE

In the first two verses, the psalmist prays as a man on the verge of drowning. Verse 3 reveals that his situation is not just a sudden crisis; rather, he has been crying and searching so long and hard that his throat has gone hoarse and his vision has gone blurry. By verse 4, we start to get some clarity about what is actually causing his distress—a great many people are treating him with gratuitous hatred, cutting him down with lies and demanding restitution for wrongs he has not committed.

In an inspired move of humility, David leaves his defense to God, acknowledging that God knows better than he does anything he may have done to invite trouble: "God, you know about my folly . . ." (v. 5). Compare Paul's response to quarrelsome members of the church in

---

[79] MT has *yesapperu* ("they number/recount"); "add" follows LXX, which implies Hebrew *yosipu*.

Corinth, which the New Living Translation renders well: "It matters very little how I might be evaluated by you or by any human authority. I don't even trust my own judgment on this point. My conscience is clear, but that doesn't prove I'm right. It is the Lord himself who will examine me and decide" (1 Cor 4:3-4, NLT).

David's train of thought continues to move beyond himself, as in verse 6 he prays for others: "Let not those who wait for you be ashamed because of me." Notice, then, the progression of David's prayer: from natural self-concern amid overwhelming distress, to a recognition that God knows his situation, to a concern for how others are being affected by it. Thus, even before the external situation has been resolved, the ongoing shift in David's perspective demonstrates that the act of laying his burdens before the Lord is already having an effect.[80]

What concerns are most troubling you today? Write them down, offer them to God, and engage with Him in as vigorous a way as you need to until you can rest assured that He knows what is going on and is moving to take care of it.

THE REJECTED MESSIAH

Jesus told His disciples:

> If the world hates you, know that it hated me before you. . . . If I hadn't done such deeds among them as no one else did, they would not bear the guilt of sin; but now they have seen and hated both me and my Father. And the word written in their Scriptures must be fulfilled, that "they hated me for nothing." (John 15:18, 24-25)

The Scripture which Jesus declared as fulfilled is to be found in verse 4 of our psalm (or possibly 35:19). And in John's Gospel, consuming zeal for God's house (v. 9a) is what first set Jesus at odds with the religious leaders in Jerusalem (John 2:17). Truly, it can be said of Jesus more than anyone else that He bore the reproaches of those who were really taking issue with God (v. 9b; see Rom 15:3). Even today, people call out Jesus' name as a curse word when they are angry or frustrated.

But "in the days of his flesh, he offered up prayers and supplications to the one who was able to save him from death—with a loud cry and tears—and he was heard because of his reverence" (Heb 5:7). We see this kind of praying in verses 13-29, where the psalmist directs his prayer to Yahweh (v. 13), laments his deep distress (vv. 14-15, 17-21, 26, 29), and honors God by

---

[80] Kidner, *Psalms 1–72*, 264.

appealing to His loyalty, faithfulness, and abundant mercy (vv. 13, 16). And we see, by way of the confident testimony from verse 32 to the end of the psalm, that the prayer has been heard.

An important distinction to note here between David's prayer and Jesus' prayer in a time of persecution is that while David curses his persecutors (vv. 22-28), Jesus prayed for forgiveness for the very people who gave Him vinegar when He thirsted on the cross (Luke 23:34-36; see also Ps 69:21; Matt 27:48; John 19:28-29). Make no mistake—Jesus will have vengeance on those who remain His enemies in the end (see, e.g., Rev 6:15-17). But His desire is that those who hate Him presently would have every opportunity to repent, turn to Him, and receive mercy (Matt 23:37; 2 Pet 3:9).

Take a moment to thank Jesus for leading you to repentance. Having given thanks, think of people you know who hate God. Pray that God would use you to reconcile them to Himself through your representation of Jesus and His mercy (see 2 Cor 5:18-21), and write down any action steps He would have you take.

SCORNED ON HIS ACCOUNT

Jesus repeatedly made the point that just as the world hated Him for representing the Father, so it would hate us for representing Him (see, e.g., Matt 5:10-12; John 15:18-25). In turn, Peter tells us not to be surprised when persecution comes but to rejoice insofar as our suffering comes from fellowship with Christ (1 Pet 4:12-19). And Peter practiced what he preached (Acts 5:12-42).

We are not to act in ways that bring *justified* anger against ourselves, and we are also not to avoid the world's hatred by shirking the call to bold witness (Matt 5:13-16; 10:26-33). But what sort of animosity have you faced that has come not through any fault of your own (recall verse 5) but instead for representing Jesus? What sort of animosity are you prepared to face in the future?

DAY 3: PSALM 70

Psalm 70 is a prayer for God to intervene "quickly" (v. 1) and rescue the psalmist from trouble. Its text is nearly the same as the final verses of Psalm 40; here, it integrates closely with Psalms 69 and 71, sharing common language and expressing a common concern for rescue from adversaries.

FOR THE DIRECTOR. OF DAVID. FOR REMEMBRANCE.

> 1 *God, to rescue me,*
>   *Yahweh, to my help, come quickly!*
> 2 *Let them be ashamed and disgraced*
>   *who seek my life;*
>   *let them be turned back and humiliated*
>   *who delight in my distress.*
> 3 *Let them turn back because of their shame,*
>   *those who say, "Aha! Aha!"*
> 4 *Let them exult and rejoice in you,*
>   *all who seek you,*
>   *and may they say continually, "God be magnified!"*
>   *who love your salvation.*
> 5 *While I am lowly and in need,*
>   *God, come quickly to me!*
>   *You are my help and my deliverer;*
>   *Yahweh, do not delay!*

A CONCISE AND URGENT PLEA

Psalm 70 is simultaneously a concise plea for help, which the supplicant needs promptly, and a bridge between the much lengthier prayers which precede and follow it. In Psalm 69, the psalmist cried for rescue (69:14; see 70:1), had shame and disgrace heaped upon him (69:6, 19; see 70:2), was "lowly and in pain" but knew that Yahweh listens to the needy (69:29, 32-33; see 70:5), and prayed blessing over those who seek and love God (69:32, 36; see 70:4). Psalm 71 will continue in similar fashion, including a call for God to "come quickly to my help!" (71:12; see 70:1, 5).[81]

As short a prayer as Psalm 70 is, it nonetheless covers a number of important points that can be unpacked elsewhere at greater length. And it does so with elegantly simple poetic symmetry: from "me" and "my" urgent need for help, to the disgrace of enemies, to the blessing of fellow God-lovers, and back to "my" urgent need for help.

---

[81] See Futato, "Book of Psalms," 233-234.

While Psalms 62 and 65 extolled the goodness of resting calmly in God, Psalm 70 bids us to remember that there is "a time to be silent and a time to speak" (Eccl 3:7). Jesus, who invited us to come and find rest for our souls (Matt 11:28-30), also taught us to pray like the widow who so badgered a godless judge that he feared she would give him a black eye and granted her petition (Luke 18:1-8).[82] And while He was honoring John the Baptist as the greatest prophet to have lived under the old covenant, Jesus commended the large crowds who eagerly received John's message as "violent" people taking heaven by storm—that is not to say that a mob could besiege and capture the heavenly, but rather that these God-seekers were figuratively banging on the doors to get in (Matt 11:11-12). At one point some seekers, seeing that Jesus brought heaven's dominion with Him to the earth, literally tore the roof off a house to get to Him (Mark 2:1-12).

How many prayers have you prayed with the urgency and insistence of "God, come quickly to me! You are my help and my deliverer; Yahweh, do not delay!" (v. 5)? Is there anything you can't wait for God to do?

_____

_____

_____

_____

COVERING THE BASES

The heading of Psalm 70 marks it as being a prayer "for remembrance"—or more literally, "for causing to remember" or "for calling to mind." In other words, the psalmist wants God to direct His attention to him. While a longer plea follows, as we have said, in Psalm 71, Psalm 70 is more than a simple summons for God to get up and get on His horse. The psalm gives reasons why God should come and act, appealing both to God's own interest and to His love for the lowly. And it lays out a specific request for God to answer when He comes.

First, the psalmist gives the request: that God "turn back" in open shame those who have sought his demise (vv. 2-3). Second, he gives the supporting arguments: that God's action in saving the psalmist will cause "all who seek" God to worship Him (v. 4) and that the psalmist is "lowly and in need" (v. 5). The latter argument appeals to God's nature as the deliverer of the lowly and provider for the needy (see 35:10; 68:5-6). And the former argument, that God will win praise, is ultimately an appeal to justice. If you said to another person, "Help me out, and you will be widely praised as a hero," you would be appealing to that person's vanity. But God is not vain to desire praise; He properly deserves it, and we grow more alive and joyful as we learn to give it to Him. In granting the psalmist's request, God will simultaneously bring relief and justice.

---

[82] While translations typically render the end of Luke 18:5 along the lines of "lest . . . she weary me" (KJV), which accords with the figurative usage of the Greek verb _hypōpiazō_, the word literally means "to hit [someone] under the eye."

A MESSIANIC PRAYER

As Psalm 69 anticipated the time when Jesus would bear the reproach of those who spurned God, so Psalm 70 can be understood from the vantage point of the cross—particularly as the hecklers' cry of "Aha!" (v. 3) is echoed on Calvary (Mark 15:29). And where the psalm speaks of persecutors being ashamed and humiliated, we find a twofold fulfillment in Jesus. First, God put the "rulers and authorities"—the diabolical powers that sought Jesus' death—to shame by defeating death through the cross (Col 2:15). Second, many people soon became convicted of their sinfulness and repented as they were made to "look on [God] whom they have pierced and lament over him"[83]—and people continue to repent today wherever the gospel is preached.

Thank God that He does not keep us in shame but washes it away when we repent of our sins and entrust our lives to Jesus. Is there anything of which you still feel ashamed? Name it, and nail it to the cross.

DAY 4: PSALM 71

Psalm 71 is the prayer of a man with many years of history with God (vv. 9, 17-18). While the Hebrew manuscripts give the psalm no heading, it is closely connected with Psalm 70, and its place before Psalm 72—a prayer for the king's son at the end of the Davidic collection—suggests that it is a prayer of David as he was growing old.[84] The psalmist emphasizes his lifelong trust in Yahweh (vv. 5-6) as he waits for the Lord to rescue him once again (vv. 1-2, 14). In keeping with his view of God's faithfulness, which has been shown in the past, the psalmist concludes with a resounding vow of confidence (vv. 20-24).

> [1] *In you, Yahweh, do I seek refuge;*
> *let me not be put to shame forever.*[85]

---

[83] "They will look on me whom they have pierced and lament over him as one mourns an only son" (Zech 12:10; see John 19:37). We see a prompt fulfillment of this prophecy in the response to Peter's sermon at Pentecost, as three thousand were "pierced through the heart" and cried out for salvation at Peter's announcement that they had killed the Messiah (Acts 2:22-41).
[84] See Futato, "Book of Psalms," 236. The only other psalm in Book 2 without a heading in MT is Psalm 43, which, as we observed, is closely connected with Psalm 42. LXX of Psalm 71 includes a heading that reads "David's. Of the sons of Jonadab and the first of the exiles."
[85] Or "let me never be put to shame."

2   *In your righteousness rescue me and deliver me;*
      extend your ear to me and save me.

3   *Be for me a crag to dwell in,*
       to go into continually;
     you have commanded my salvation,
       for you are my rock and my stronghold.

4   *My God, deliver me from the hand of the wicked,*
      from the grip of the wrongdoer and the ruthless.

5   *For you are my hope, my Lord Yahweh,*
      my trust from my youth.

6   *On you have I leaned from the womb;*
      from my mother's belly you have borne me along.
      Of you is my praise continually.

7   *I have been a sign to many,*
      as you have been my strong refuge.

8   *My mouth is filled with your praise,*
      your glory all day long.

9   *Do not cast me off in the time of my old age;*
      as my strength is spent, do not abandon me.

10   *For my enemies talk about me,*
      and those watching my soul consult together,

11   *saying: "God has abandoned him;*
      pursue and capture him, for there is no one to rescue him!"

12   *God, do not be far from me;*
      my God, come quickly to my help!

13   *Let them be ashamed and perish*
       who are adversaries of my soul;
     let them be wrapped in reproach and dishonor
       who seek my harm.

14   *As for me, I will continue waiting,*
      and adding to all your praise.

15   *My mouth will recount your righteousness,*
      your salvation all day long,
      for they are more than I can count.

16   *I will come with the mighty deeds of my Lord Yahweh;*
      I will commemorate your righteousness, yours alone.

17   *God, you have taught me from my youth,*
      and up to the present I declare your wonders.

18   *So even to old age and gray hair,*
      God, do not leave me,

until I declare the strength of your arm to a generation,
your might to everyone who will come,
19 *and your righteousness, God, to high heaven,*
because you have done great things.
God, who is like you?
20 *Though you have made me see troubles,*
many and hard,
you will revive me again
and bring me up from the depths of the earth.
21 *You will increase my greatness*
and comfort me again.
22 *And I will acknowledge you with a lute,*
acknowledge your faithfulness, my God;
I will make music for you with the lyre,
Holy One of Israel.
23 *My lips will resound when I make music for you,*
with all my soul, which you have ransomed.
24 *And my tongue will muse on your righteousness all day,*
because they are shamed, they are abashed who sought my harm.

FAITHFUL TO THE END

Do not cast me off in the time of my old age;
as my strength is spent, do not abandon me. (v. 9)

What is a warrior such as David to do when he has grown too old and frail for combat? What are you to do as your body ages, or other circumstances change, and you are no longer able to do certain things that had once been a vital part of your identity? The more strongly you have linked your identity with a particular function in the world, the more of a crisis it can become to endure a change of circumstances. We may not know the immediate cause of David's cry for help in Psalm 71, but we do see him wrestling with the fear of abandonment as he grows incapable of contributing to society in the ways he previously had.

David would certainly not be the last person to wrestle with the thought of being useless. Nor is the thought unique to those of a particular age bracket or employment status. Healthy young people can be driven to workaholism by this same basic notion—that one's value is contingent on the output of one's labor. So we must return from time to time to the most fundamental of questions: *Why am I here?* and *Why does God love me?*

Our heavenly Father does desire, of course, that we be good stewards of the time and talents He has entrusted to us (Matt 25:14-30). But He also loved us and set His loyalty upon us before we did a single thing to earn it—before we were even born (see Rom 9:11-13;

Eph 1:3-6; 2:8-10). Even the apostles, whose title refers to the fact that they were "sent out" to do the Lord's work,[86] were chosen not for their capacity to execute the tasks Jesus would give them but because He desired to have them with Him; their assignment was secondary to their relationship (Mark 3:13-15).

If you are trying to earn God's love, what effort could possibly be enough? This is the trap: If you think God's love must be earned, you will work ever more frantically to prove your worth, knowing all the while that you haven't done enough, until you are finally forced to give it up. So remember: *God loved us first*, before we ever thought of reciprocating (1 John 4:19). Jesus gave His life, not for the perfect and the accomplished, but for the lost (Luke 19:10; Rom 5:8). As you yield to Him, God will work through you to do beautiful things; but He loves you right now, and will love you forever, just because you are His child.

In what area(s) of your life are you most tempted to measure your self-worth by your performance? What does the price Jesus paid for you on the cross say about your value in His eyes?

FRUITFUL IN EVERY SEASON

> *So even to old age and gray hair,*
> *God, do not leave me,*
> *until I declare the strength of your arm to a generation,*
> *your might to everyone who will come. (v. 18)*

While David may have grown too weak physically to lead a battle charge, he did find a purpose in what remained of his time on earth. Precisely because he had experienced God's mercy, power, and faithfulness in so many ways throughout his lifetime in the Lord's service, David was wonderfully qualified to teach the next generation about his righteous Savior (v. 15), who would also be theirs. David could still sing God's praises (vv. 22-24), and he could instill faith in those who would take his place. Indeed, an important part of our calling in the body of Christ is to raise up strong Christian leaders for the Lord's work in the next generation.

Even if you can't sing as well as you would like, you can bear witness to the God who made you who you are. In fact, you do so merely by *being* who you are, since you have been made in God's image (Gen 1:26). Yes, sinful behavior is not fitting for God's image bearers, and it clouds our witness; so yes, we do seek diligently to apply the means of grace God has made available

---

[86] The Greek word *apostolos* denotes one who is sent out on an assignment.

for our restoration as righteous sons and daughters. But we must learn that it is all grace, and we must receive that grace by faith as a gift from our ever-loving Father.

THE BEST IS YET TO COME

Though you have made me see troubles,
many and hard,
you will revive me again
and bring me up from the depths of the earth.
You will increase my greatness
and comfort me again. (vv. 20-21)

Even if you live to be 120 years old, your years in this life are but a brief preparation for the everlasting life that awaits, in which you are called to coreign with Christ in His eternal Kingdom. So as important as your work may be in the various roles you occupy here, make it your priority to know God, develop trust with Him, and grow in godly character. Then you will develop the kind of strength that never wears out.

What spiritual legacy do you hope to leave to the next generation? How is God leading you to prepare for that now?

DAY 5: PSALM 72

Psalm 72 marks a fitting end to Book 2 of the Psalter and the prayers of David (v. 20), as it is a prayer for David's son and successor. While Solomon is the prayer's immediate subject, its hopes for the king are so extravagant that Jewish and Christian readers have long read the psalm as a messianic prophecy.[87] The psalm envisions a king who judges justly, who loves and defends the poor and powerless, who reigns over all the earth, who brings the whole land into such flourishing that even the mountaintops yield abundant crops, and whose name will be honored forever.

---

[87] Kidner, *Psalms 1–72*, 273.

FOR SOLOMON.[88]

1 *God, give your judgments to the king,*
       and your righteousness to the king's son.

2 *May he judge your people rightly,*
       and your lowly ones with justice.

3 *May the mountains bring peace to the people,*
       and the hills righteousness.

4 *May he judge the lowly among the people,*
       save the children of the needy,
       and crush any oppressor.

5 *May they fear you[89] while the sun shines,*
       and before the moon, through all generations.[90]

6 *May he come down like rain on what is mown,*
       like showers that water the earth.

7 *Let the righteous blossom in his days,*
       and abundance of peace, until the moon is no more.

8 *And may he rule from sea to sea,*
       and from the river to the ends of the earth.

9 *Desert dwellers shall bow before him,*
       and his enemies lick the dust.

10 *Kings of Tarshish and distant shores shall render tribute,*
       kings of Sheba and Seba bring a gift.

11 *And all the kings shall bow down to him,*
       all the nations serve him.

12 *For he shall rescue the needy who cry for help,*
       the lowly, and those without a helper.

13 *He shall pity the weak and needy,*
       and the souls of the needy he shall save.

14 *From oppression and violence he shall redeem their souls,*
       and their blood shall be precious in his eyes.

15 *Let him live,*
           and let him be given gold from Sheba,
       and let there be continual prayer for him,
           all day blessing him.

16 *Let there be abundance of wheat in the land,*
       even on the top of the mountains;

---

[88] While the Hebrew phrasing is the same as for those psalms marked "of David" (see *Psalms 1–41: A Christian Union Bible Study*, Lesson 1, Day 2) and could thus indicate Solomonic authorship, LXX explicitly marks Psalm 72 as a prayer "for" (*eis*) Solomon, and the note at the end of the psalm marks this as the end of David's prayers. So we assume the psalm is one that David prayed on his son's behalf, though it would not substantially change our reading if Solomon were the psalm's author.

[89] LXX has "And may he remain," suggesting ויאריך ("And may he prolong/continue long") in place of ייראוך ("May they fear you").

[90] Literally, "generation of generations."

may his fruit wave like Lebanon,
and may they blossom from the city like the herbage of the land.
17 *Let his name endure forever;*
may his name spread as long as the sun shines;[91]
and may they bless themselves by him,
all the nations call him blessed.
18 *Blessed be Yahweh, God, God of Israel,*
who alone does wonders.
19 *And blessed be his glorious name forever,*
and may the whole earth be filled with his glory.
Amen and Amen!
20 *The prayers of David son of Jesse are ended.*

GREAT DAVID'S GREATER SON

David certainly had greater hopes for the king to come after him than he ever realized in his own lifetime. Not only would David's son rule "from sea to sea, and from the river to the ends of the earth" (v. 8)—which is to say, over all the world[92]—but people around the world would forever regard him as a source of blessing (v. 17), as his reign would bring justice (v. 2) and well-being (vv. 3, 7).

Solomon came closer than any king of Israel (or Judah) to realizing these hopes. He ruled "over all the kingdoms from the river [i.e., the Euphrates] to the land of the Philistines, and to the border of Egypt. And they brought tribute and served Solomon all the days of his life" (1 Kgs 4:21). The populations of Judah and Israel were abundant and well fed (1 Kgs 4:20). Solomon became famous for requesting and receiving uncommon wisdom to judge his people (1 Kgs 3), and he received abundant wealth from distant monarchs—most notably the queen of Sheba, who also blessed his kingdom and his God upon seeing how well Solomon governed (1 Kgs 10).

But Solomon also famously failed. He loved and married many women from idolatrous nations. The Lord had specifically instructed His people not to intermarry, knowing that these foreigners would persuade the Israelites to join them in worshiping other gods. In his later years, Solomon did worship his wives' gods, and Israel's faithful but jealous God punished this apostasy by dividing the kingdom (1 Kgs 11:1-13; see also Exod 23:31-33; 34:12-16; Deut 7:1-4).

So Solomon's reign offered Israel both a foretaste of what was to come and a bitter reminder that it was only a foretaste and not the true fulfillment of God's promise. As successive kings wavered between faithfulness and further idolatry, the situation in Israel and Judah grew worse and worse, until finally the Davidic king was carried off into exile, and a puppet leader was installed in his place to oversee Jerusalem as a vassal of Babylon (2 Kgs 25). Nonetheless, in

---

91 Literally, "before/in the presence of the sun."
92 As VanGemeren writes, "It is unnecessary to restrict the meaning to a particular sea . . . or river . . . , for v. 8 speaks of the Lord's universal rule, encompassing seas, rivers, and lands" (VanGemeren, *Psalms*, 551).

advance of this calamity, Isaiah received a word from the Lord giving assurance that God would yet fulfill the promise:

> A shoot will emerge from the stump of Jesse;
>   a sprout from his root will bear fruit.
> And upon him will rest the Spirit of Yahweh—
>   the Spirit of wisdom and understanding,
>   the Spirit of counsel and might,
>   the Spirit of knowledge and the fear of Yahweh.
> And he will savor the fear of Yahweh;
>   not by what his eyes see will he judge,
>   nor by what his ears hear will he make decisions,
> but he will judge in righteousness for the poor
>   and decide in uprightness for the lowly in the land;
>   he will strike the earth with the rod of his mouth,
>   and with the breath of his lips he will kill the wicked.
> Righteousness will be the belt around his waist;
>   truth shall gird his loins. (Isa 11:1-5)

Compare Isaiah's prophecy with Psalm 72, and note as many similarities as you can. What attributes of the messianic King most capture your attention today?

ALREADY, AND STILL TO COME

We know that Jesus is the "shoot" (Isa 11:1) that emerged from the house of David to reign as King forever. We know not only that the sevenfold Spirit of God (Isa 11:2; see Rev 1:4; 3:1; 4:5; 5:6) rested upon Him during His ministry on earth in the flesh but also that He still reigns through the Spirit while abiding at the Father's right hand. And we know to Whom Psalm 72 looks forward.

But while Jesus inaugurated a new era with His appearance two thousand years ago, and we still see signs of His reign wherever the gospel of the Kingdom is proclaimed and His word is carried out in faith, we continue to await His return in glory, when He will finally crush oppressors, exalt the lowly, fill the earth with His peace, and receive the honor which is ever due to His Name. "Until that day," Mark Futato writes, "we pray that God would give us his justice and righteousness, and that we might do the will of God in bringing blessing to those who are in need and cannot do for themselves what God can do for them through us."[93]

---
[93] Futato, "Book of Psalms," 240.

Sometimes our desire to help the poor can become overly abstract as we try to tackle problems on a grand scale. Whom do you know (by name) that is presently in need of help? How could you assist that person in some very practical way? Make a plan to connect with that person today (or as soon as possible) and to keep yourself accountable to following up over the long term.

Lesson Review

At the beginning of this lesson, Psalm 68 announced a coming day when "God will arise," His enemies will be blown away like smoke, and the righteous will rejoice (68:1-3). In Psalms 69–71, we saw the struggle that must precede God's final day of rest—a struggle most poignantly endured on the cross, where Jesus secured eternal victory through the shedding of His own blood. Finally, Psalm 72 bids us to look forward to the consummation of our hope in the King of kings:

> Blessed be Yahweh, God, God of Israel,
>   who alone does wonders.
> And blessed be his glorious name forever,
>   and may the whole earth be filled with his glory.
> Amen and Amen! (72:18-19)

7

LESSON SEVEN:

Psalms 73–77

We now enter Book 3 of the Psalms. With the exception of Psalm 86 ("a prayer of David"), all of the psalms in Book 3 are attributed to the music leaders David had appointed to minister in the Tabernacle (and subsequently in the Temple). Psalms 73–83 are all attributed to Asaph (whom we first encountered in Psalm 50). While these psalms provide no direct historical reference point, Psalm 74 seems self-evidently to be a lament over the destruction of the Temple, which occurred when Nebuchadnezzar conquered Jerusalem in 586 BC. So "Asaph" may indicate the sons of Asaph who continued to serve as music leaders in those days (see 2 Chr 35:15).

The psalms in this lesson repeatedly draw our attention to God's power and decisiveness in judgment and war. Amid moments of lament, the psalmist recalls God's mighty deeds of old and looks forward to His coming again to judge the wicked and vindicate the just.

DAY 1: PSALM 73

Psalm 73 begins with an affirmation of God's fidelity, which the psalmist immediately follows with a confession of his doubts (vv. 2-16). If God promises to bless the just and sweep away the wicked (see Ps 1), then why does the exact opposite seem to be happening? But then the psalmist gains divine insight (v. 17), which enables him to conclude with a beautiful declaration of trust and devotion to God, his "rock" and his everlasting inheritance (v. 26). The psalm thus encourages us to be honest about our doubts while looking to the Lord for the understanding we need to overcome them.

A PSALM OF ASAPH.

1 *Surely God is good to Israel,*
    to the pure in heart!
2 *But I—my feet nearly turned aside,*
    my step nearly slipped,
3 *because I envied the boastful,*
    the well-being of the wicked that I saw,

⁴ *because there are no fetters for their death,*
  and their bellies are fat.

⁵ *In the toil of mankind they have no part;*
  they do not bear Adam's affliction.

⁶ *Consequently, pride is their necklace;*
  they clothe themselves with violence.

⁷ *From their padded interior comes forth iniquity;*[94]
  the imaginings of their heart overflow.

⁸ *They mock and speak of evil;*
  from their elevated position they speak of extortion.

⁹ *They set their mouth in the heavens,*
  and their tongue ranges over the earth.

¹⁰ *So his people turn to them,*
  and they drain the waters of abundance.[95]

¹¹ *And they say, "How would God know?"*
  and "Does the Most High have knowledge?"

¹² *Behold, these are the wicked;*
  and ever at ease, their wealth increases.

¹³ *Surely for naught have I kept my heart pure*
  and washed my hands in innocence.

¹⁴ *I have been struck all day,*
  and my reprimand comes every morning.

¹⁵ *If I said, "I will recount thus"—*
  behold, I would have betrayed the generation of your children.

¹⁶ *When I purposed to comprehend this,*
  it was trouble in my eyes,

¹⁷ *until I entered God's holy places,*
  that I might perceive their end.

¹⁸ *Surely you set them on slippery places;*
  you make them fall into deceptions.

¹⁹ *How they are ruined in a moment!*
  They come to a complete end through terrors.

²⁰ *Like a dream after one wakes,*
  my Lord, when you rouse yourself you will disdain their image.

²¹ *When my heart was soured*
  and my insides pierced,

²² *I was brutish and ignorant;*
  I became a beast before you.

---

[94] "Iniquity" follows LXX, implying עון in place of MT's עין ("eye"). "From their padded interior" is literally "from fat."

[95] Literally, "waters of full will be drained for them." LXX has "length of days will be found for them." (In Hebrew, "days" and "waters" differ only by one *yod*, the smallest letter.)

23 *But I am still with you;*
    you hold my right hand!
24 *With your counsel you lead me,*
    and afterward, you will receive me in glory.
25 *Who is for me in the heavens?*
    And beside you there is nothing I desire on earth.
26 *Though my flesh and my heart fail,*
    God is the rock of my heart and my portion forever.
27 *For behold, those who are far from you perish;*
    you annihilate all who play the harlot from before you.
28 *As for me—God's drawing near is good for me;*
    I have made my Lord Yahweh my refuge,
    so as to recount all your works.

WHY DO THE BAD PEOPLE HAVE IT SO EASY?

The question here is essentially the same question David addressed at length in Psalm 37. If *shalom* ("well-being" or "peace") is supposed to come through justice and righteousness, as indicated in Psalm 72, then why do the wicked seem to have more of it than everybody else?[96] They are quite literally, as the old expression puts it, fat and happy (see v. 4). And in this context, *fat* is by no means an insult, as modern people might take it to be—just the opposite, it is a point of envy (v. 3), because it signifies being well fed and free from the hard labor to which God sentenced Adam and his descendants (v. 5; see Gen 3:17-19).

But these people, so carefree and seemingly blessed, are *wicked* (v. 3)! They are arrogant, violent, mocking and oppressive of others, and disrespectful of God (vv. 6-11). And yet God's people want to join their club (v. 10), and they just keep getting richer (v. 12). Little wonder, then, that the psalmist questions why he has worked so hard and faithfully for far less; seeing these faithless people at ease every morning is like a slap in the face (vv. 13-14). It's just not fair.

But that is not the right way to look at this situation (v. 15). The crux of the lesson in Psalm 73 comes in verses 16-17:

When I purposed to comprehend this,
    it was trouble in my eyes,
until I entered God's holy places,
    that I might perceive their end.

As verse 16 expresses, the injustice that the psalmist perceived was simply too much for him to think about. Why get all worked up about a problem you're never going to be able to solve? But then the psalmist did the "one thing" David often sought to do: He went to the sanctuary,

---

96 See Futato, "Book of Psalms," 243.

where he might see God's beauty and inquire of Him (v. 17; see also 27:4). And his whole perspective changed.

In Psalm 37, David counseled us not to be upset by the prosperity of the wicked, because their day would end soon enough—"Like grass they quickly wither"; "They shall end in smoke" (37:2, 20). We might imagine Asaph hearing these very words on that day he entered the sanctuary, as he is struck with a revelation: "How they are ruined in a moment!" (v. 19). In any case, his vexation ends with the same insight that Psalm 37 put forward: When God arises in judgment, the wicked will be like a dream shaken off in the morning (v. 20), while the faithful will remain with Him in everlasting glory (vv. 23-26).

This goes to show that the big, perennially nagging questions—such as *What are we here for?* and *Why is there so much evil in the world?*—might not prove so troublesome if we look to what the Bible has already said about them. If the writer of Psalm 73 came to the same conclusion as David in Psalm 37, maybe we don't have to reinvent the wheel. Then again, sometimes hearing the right answer from someone else isn't enough; we need God to pierce through the crust that has formed around our hearts and let His light shine in. When it comes to biblical insight, it is His Spirit who makes the truth go from words on a page to living reality in our understanding and in our being.

Is there a particular moral or philosophical question that has been bothering you for some time? If so, write it down. Take it to the Lord in prayer, and search the Scriptures to see what they say about it.

CONFESSING DOUBT HONESTLY

When Christians experience doubts about God, they often respond in one of two ways: Either they feel bad about having such doubts and try to pretend they believe what they're really not sure of, or they come to embrace the notion that doubting is healthy and make peace with their uncertainty. Neither of these alternatives is what the Bible teaches.

The problem with the first option should be obvious: Faith is only faith when we actually believe, and we must not be double-minded (Heb 11:1; Jas 1:6-8). Saying "I believe" when you don't believe is false. Option two is honest, insofar as one acknowledges one's doubts. But to make peace with unbelief is to make peace with sin. Like any other sin, doubting that God will stand by His word—by implication impugning His character—is to be confessed *and repented of*, and we are to seek God's grace to become free from it.

In Psalm 73, Asaph provides a model for dealing with doubt. After beginning with the statement in verse 1 that God is surely good to the pure in heart, he readily acknowledges that he is having a very hard time believing it. He even had a difficult time finding the energy to think about it. Asaph is refreshingly transparent. But he does make the effort to search out an answer, and he does so specifically by drawing near to God's presence in a place of worship. He recognizes that the way he had been thinking was off base; in fact, teaching young people to think that same way would have been a betrayal of their budding relationship with the God who is faithful and true (v. 15). By God's grace, he comes to a place where he no longer speaks doubtfully of God's justice; instead, he recounts God's works (v. 28).

Which of God's works serve most to ground your faith in His character? What concrete action can you take today to ensure that you remind yourself often of these things?

DAY 2: PSALM 74

Psalm 74 is a lament over God's ostensible abandonment of Israel as evidenced by the total ruin and desecration of His sanctuary in Jerusalem. Unlike Psalm 44, which also addressed Israel's defeat, there is no appeal here to the people's innocence; prayer is made solely on the basis of God's honor.[97] And while the present circumstances are horrific, hope rises on the basis of what God has done in the past: He has shown Himself exceedingly strong in delivering His people from captivity (vv. 12-15). Indeed, He is the Creator and Ruler of heaven and earth (vv. 16-17). So we look for Him to come again and vindicate His great Name.

A MASKIL OF ASAPH.

> *1　Why, God, do you reject us utterly?*
> 　　*Why does your anger smoke against the flock of your pasture?*
> *2　Remember your congregation, which you acquired long ago,*
> 　　*which you redeemed as the tribe of your inheritance,*
> 　　*Mount Zion, where you have dwelt.*
> *3　Pick your steps over the utter ruins,*
> 　　*all the damage the enemy has done in the sanctuary.*
> *4　Your foes roared in the midst of your meeting place;*
> 　　*they set up their signs as signs.*

---

97 Goldingay, *Psalms 42–89*, 423.

⁵ *It looked like the raising of axes*
     over a thicket of trees.
⁶ *And then all of its carvings*
     they struck down with axes and pikes.
⁷ *They set fire to your sanctuary, burning it to the ground;*
     they defiled the dwelling place of your name.
⁸ *They said in their heart, "Let us put them down altogether!"*
     They burned all the meeting places of God in the land.
⁹ *Our signs we do not see;*
     there is no longer any prophet,
          nor one among us who knows for how long.
¹⁰ *How long, God, shall the foe taunt,*
     the enemy utterly disrespect your name?
¹¹ *Why do you withdraw your hand, your right hand?*
     Take it out of the fold of your garment and put an end to them!
¹² *And God, my king from long ago,*
     worker of salvation in the midst of the earth,
¹³ *you parted the sea with your strength,*
     you smashed the heads of the dragons upon the waters;
¹⁴ *you crushed the heads of Leviathan;*
     you gave him as food to the desert dwellers;
¹⁵ *you broke open both spring and stream;*
     you dried up ever-flowing rivers.
¹⁶ *Yours is the day, and yours also is the night;*
     you set in place the lamp and the sun.
¹⁷ *You set up all the earth's boundaries;*
     summer and harvesttime, you formed them.
¹⁸ *Remember this: The enemy has taunted, Yahweh;*
     a foolish people have disrespected your name.
¹⁹ *Do not give the life of your dove to a wild animal;*
     the life of your lowly ones, do not utterly neglect.
²⁰ *Look on the covenant,*
        for they fill the dark places of the land,
           abodes of violence.
²¹ *Let not the crushed turn back humiliated;*
     let the lowly and needy praise your name.
²² *Arise, God, defend your case;*
     remember your taunting from a foolish people all day long.
²³ *Do not forget the clamor of your foes,*
     the roar of those who rise against you, going up continually.

WHY, GOD? AND HOW LONG?

Psalm 74 is not the first psalm to lament apparent abandonment by God. Psalms 13 and 22 famously open with individual cries of abandonment, and Psalm 44 is a corporate lament in the face of military defeat. But Psalm 74 is striking, as it is situated right on the ruins of the Temple in Jerusalem, where Yahweh's Name was supposed to dwell forever (2 Chr 7:16). What's more, while Yahweh had made it His rule not to act without first revealing His purposes to the prophets (Amos 3:7), "there is no longer any prophet, nor one among [the people] who knows for how long" this desolation will last (v. 9).[98]

The bewildered mourners are neglecting some crucial information as they say this. God plainly foretold through Moses, before the people had even entered the Promised Land, that idolatry would lead to their destruction and removal from the land but that from exile they would seek the living God and find Him when they sought Him wholeheartedly. And He would not forget His covenant with their ancestors (Deut 4:25-31). As to "how long" Jerusalem would remain forsaken, God had said through Jeremiah that the people would serve Babylon for seventy years (Jer 25:11)—a fact recognized by the exiled Daniel as he applied his faith in prayer and fasting (Dan 9).

Perhaps the sternest (and most pertinent) rebuke to the Judeans came through Ezekiel, a great prophet who was in exile himself:

> The land is full of bloody judgment, and the city is full of violence. So I will bring in the most evil of nations, and they will possess their houses; and I will put an end to the arrogance of the strong, and their holy places will be defiled. When anguish comes, they will seek peace, but there shall be none. Disaster upon disaster comes, and report after report. And they seek a vision from a prophet, while law[99] is lost to the priest and counsel is lost from the elders. (Ezek 7:23-26)

Herein lies a timeless and important point: If you want to hear from God, see to it that you are walking in accordance with what He has already said. He hates lawlessness but blesses those who hear His words and act on them (Matt 7:21-27). So if you want God to speak to you about what you should do next, the best way to position yourself for such revelation is by faithfully doing what He has already asked of all of us in the Scriptures, as well as anything the Holy Spirit has specifically prompted you to do. As a general rule, obedience precedes further understanding.

---

98 Derek Kidner (*Psalms 73–150: An Introduction and Commentary*, TOTC 16 [London: Inter-Varsity Press, 1975], 296) notes, "Historically, this cry could well be that of the derelict community left in the homeland after the deportations to Babylon and the emigration to Egypt (Jer. 43:5-7) which had removed first Ezekiel and then Jeremiah."

99 While in the Psalms the word *torah* is mostly used as a general term for "instruction," here it likely refers more specifically to God's commandments and instructions given to the people and preserved in writing (cf. 2 Kgs 22:8-20).

Are you longing to hear God's voice? Is there anything you know He's asked of you that you've been neglecting? If so, don't fall into the trap of self-condemnation, but do acknowledge specifically how you have failed and ask God to set you back on track in His grace.

BEGINNING TO SEE CLEARLY

Having asked God why He has withdrawn His power and allowed heathens to desecrate holy ground (v. 11)—a question which, as we have seen, Moses had already answered—the psalmist moves in the right direction by looking back to the Exodus story (vv. 12-15). Moreover, he sets his appeal for restoration on a strong, three-legged stool: the honor of God's Name (vv. 18, 22-23), the covenant God made with Israel (v. 20), and God's loving concern for the lowly and needy (vv. 19, 21).

In the generations prior to Jerusalem's destruction, the city's apostasy and corruption had reached catastrophic levels—just consider the scene where the high priest himself stumbles across a Torah scroll in the Temple of Yahweh. He had never read it before—and neither had the king (2 Kgs 22:8-20)! Whatever happened to the expectation that Israel's leaders would keep a copy of the Torah continually before them and ruminate on it morning and evening (Deut 17:18-20; Josh 1:8), or that the priests would read it aloud to the whole gathered nation every seven years (Deut 31:9-13)? Such a thorough departure from God's word, and the corruption that comes with that departure, requires the most drastic corrective measures—not only must the defiled land lie fallow for seventy years (after which virtually all of the psalmist's generation will have died), but the throne of David must remain unoccupied until the Son of God Himself comes to claim it at the cost of His own life.

Throughout the Exile, God was still faithful as ever to those who were faithful to Him (see the books of Daniel and Esther). But for a nation as a whole to avoid judgment, the collective faithfulness of God's people must be great enough to stay the wickedness of the ungodly. As God said through Ezekiel, even if Noah, Daniel, and Job (three figures singled out as being righteous amid corrupt generations) were found together in a land under God's just judgment, they could not change His verdict, though their own lives would be saved (Ezek 14:12-23).

Many nations today face a similar situation; that is, God continues to shepherd His faithful remnant, but the clamor of iniquity in the land rises more loudly than the prayers of God's people. If we, as God's people, wish to see our nations healed and our neighbors receive the same grace we pray that God would grant us, we must collectively lift our hands and our voices to the Lord. He has said, "If my people—those who are called by my name—will humble themselves, and pray, and seek my face, and turn from their wicked ways, then I will hear from the heavens and forgive their sin and heal their land" (2 Chr 7:14). This is why Christian Union routinely calls believers across the United States to join together in times of repentance with prayer and fasting[100] and why we encourage you, in whatever nation you live, to gather with others in seeking the Lord on your nation's behalf.

Are you aware of networks of people in your area who pray together for God's good purposes to prevail against the current of rebellion and unbelief? How might you get involved or call others to become part of such a group?

DAY 3: PSALM 75

In a dramatic contrast to Psalm 74, Psalm 75 speaks of God's wrath in eager anticipation of the justice it will finally bring about—the execution of which the speaker himself hopes to participate in (v. 10). As other psalms have testified, God's righteous judgment is perceived very differently depending on which side of it one is on. Also noteworthy is that God Himself is the speaker for a considerable portion of this psalm (at least verses 2-3 but probably through verse 5 and quite possibly through verse 8, since God sometimes speaks of Himself in the third person).[101]

FOR THE DIRECTOR. "DO NOT DESTROY." A PSALM OF ASAPH. A SONG.

> *1   We have acknowledged you, God;*
> *we have acknowledged that your name was near;*
> *your wonders declared it.[102]*
> *2   When I appoint a time,*
> *I will judge with equity.*
> *3   When the earth totters, and all its inhabitants,*
> *I am the one who steadies its pillars.* Selah
> *4   I say to the boastful, "Do not boast,"*
> *and to the wicked, "Do not lift up a horn.*

---

[100] See https://www.dayandnight.org.
[101] See Goldingay, *Psalms 42–89*, 439. As the biblical writers do not use quotation marks, we cannot say with certainty where the speaker changes, except that verse 9 is obviously a worshiper's vow to praise God.
[102] Or "they recounted your wonders." Many versions render this entire verse in the present tense, while LXX has it as a vow for the future: "We will acknowledge you, God; we will acknowledge and call upon your name" (see further comment in the lesson text).

⁵ *Do not lift up your horn on high*
　　　or speak with an insolent neck."
⁶ *Indeed not, from the east or from the west,*
　　　nor from the wilderness to the mountains.
⁷ *For God is the judge;*
　　　he puts this one down and raises this one up.
⁸ *Indeed, there is a cup in Yahweh's hand,*
　　　and the wine foams, fully mixed;
　　when he pours it out,
　　　　they must surely drain it out to the dregs;
　　　all the wicked of the earth shall drink.
⁹ *As for me, I will proclaim forever;*
　　　I will make music for the God of Jacob,
¹⁰ *and all the horns of the wicked I will lop off;*
　　　the horns of the righteous will be lifted up.

GOD WILL SET THINGS RIGHT

Psalm 74 lamented that God had abandoned His "meeting place" and left the sanctuary to ruin, with none of the survivors knowing when He might return (74:4, 7, 9). One way of reading Psalm 75 is as a response to that lament. In verse 2, when God speaks of an appointed "time," the Hebrew word is actually the same word translated as "meeting place" in Psalm 74 (see 74:4, 8), and God's utterance here specifically addresses both His ability to hold things together through calamity ("When the earth totters . . ." [v. 3]) and His commitment to subdue the insolent and exalt the righteous. Compare the cry of the heathen pillagers in Psalm 74:8—"Let us put them down altogether!"—with the imperatives here in Psalm 75 that the wicked not "lift up a horn" (vv. 4-5; cf. v. 10) and the reminder that God is the one who "puts down" and "raises up" (v. 7).

The worshiping congregation's status at the beginning of Psalm 75 is uncertain. While most translations render verse 1 in the present tense, John Goldingay observes that the Hebrew verbs in this verse are of a different form than those in the remaining verses and that it makes sense (thematically as well as grammatically) to render verse 1 in the perfect tense. That is, we can understand the congregation here as petitioning God to act, testifying that they have faithfully acknowledged God's presence and have seen His wonders in the past.[103]

In any case, God responds by affirming that He is indeed going to act, though His judgment will come at a time of His own choosing (v. 2). Meanwhile, God's people experiencing turmoil on the earth are reminded that He is the One who laid the earth's foundations and that He will keep it from falling apart, no matter how chaotic things may appear (v. 3). Recall the faithful testimony of Psalm 46: "We shall not fear, though the earth shifts, though the mountains stagger into the heart of the seas . . ." (46:2).

---

[103] Goldingay, *Psalms 42–89*, 441.

Recall also that God the Son authorized the destruction of His own body, declaring, "Destroy this temple, and in three days I will raise it up" (John 2:19). He Himself, in faithful obedience to the Father, is put down and raised up (see v. 7), and in Him, through whom and for whom all things were created, all things hold together (Col 1:15-20).

When you think of God's appointed Day of Judgment, do you envision it as something in the remote future, or do you eagerly hope to see it come soon?

_____

_____

_____

_____

THE CUP OF WRATH

> Mine eyes have seen the glory of the coming of the Lord:
> He is trampling out the vintage where the grapes of wrath are stored . . .[104]

> *Indeed, there is a cup in Yahweh's hand,*
> *   and the wine foams, fully mixed;*
> *   when he pours it out,*
> *   they must surely drain it out to the dregs;*
> *   all the wicked of the earth shall drink. (v. 8)*

There is wine that "gladdens the heart" (104:15); there is the "new wine" of the Holy Spirit (see Matt 9:17; Acts 2:13-18; Eph 5:18); and then there is the wine that causes people to stagger, the cup of God's wrath (Ps 60:3; Isa 51:17). The image here is certainly foreboding, as people "must surely drain . . . to the dregs" the spiced concoction that is going to make them reel and collapse. What's more alarming is how John's vision takes up this image and actually intensifies the violence of it (Rev 14:17-20; 16:17-21).

We cannot forget that Jesus, truly "gentle and lowly in heart" (Matt 11:29), so zealously cares for His little ones that He warns it would be better to die by drowning than to suffer His vengeance for causing a child to stumble (Matt 18:6). At the same time, we remember— mercy of mercies!—that Jesus Himself freely stood in our place and, so fully aware of what was coming that His sweat became as drops of blood in anguished anticipation, drank the cup of wrath we had brought upon ourselves by our rebelliousness (Luke 22:39-44). It is by His sacrifice, and His sacrifice alone, that the just Judge grants us a verdict of "not guilty" (Rom 3:23-26).

---

[104] Julia Ward Howe, "Battle Hymn of the Republic" (1862).

Imagine yourself, to the extent that you are able, in Jesus' place as He was being dragged before the Sanhedrin, before Pilate and Herod, being flogged, mocked, crucified, and abandoned. Give thanks and praise to your gracious Lord, who in love suffered more than you can fathom. Use this space to write down any particular reflections that stir your heart.

DAY 4: PSALM 76

In Psalm 74, we saw a longing for God to come and restore what was broken. In Psalm 75, that longing became a confident expectation. In Psalm 76, the Lion of Judah has already come, and we meet Him returning from a successful hunt. Justice has been served.

FOR THE DIRECTOR. WITH STRINGS. A PSALM OF ASAPH. A SONG.

   1   *God is known in Judah;*
          in Israel his name is great.
   2   *In Salem is his lair,*
          his den in Zion.
   3   *There he broke the fiery arrows,*
          shield and sword and war. Selah
   4   *You are enveloped in light,*
          majestic returning from the mountains of prey.
   5   *The stouthearted have been plundered;*
          they slumbered their sleep,
          and all the men of valor could not find their hands.
   6   *At your rebuke, God of Jacob,*
          both chariot and horse fell unconscious.
   7   *You—you are fearsome!*
          Who will stand before you after the time of your anger?
   8   *From the heavens you made your judgment heard;*
          the earth feared and was quiet
   9   *when God rose for judgment*
          to save all the lowly in the earth. Selah

10   *For the rage of man is crushed;*
        the remnant of rage you bind.[105]
11   *Make vows and fulfill them to Yahweh your God;*
        let all around him bring a gift to the Fearsome One.
12   *He cuts off the breath of leaders,*
        he is fearsome to the kings of earth.

THE LION OF JUDAH

   "I'd thought he was just a man. Is he—quite safe? I shall feel rather nervous about meeting a lion."

   [. . .]

   "Safe? . . . Who said anything about safe? 'Course he isn't safe. But he's good. He's the King, I tell you."[106]

While Psalm 76 never uses the word *lion* directly, the image of God as the Lion of Judah (see Gen 49:9; Rev 5:5) runs throughout. In verse 2, the psalmist refers to Jerusalem as His "lair" and "den." In verse 4, he returns from "the mountains of prey," and just as a pouncing lion goes for the jugular, "he cuts off the breath of leaders" who rebel against Him (v. 12).

And His ferocity is absolutely stunning. While verse 5 may suggest a group of warriors caught sleeping in their tents and unable to lift a hand in self-defense, it certainly alludes to the sleep of death into which they fell after the Lion's visit. In verse 6, we find that His "rebuke" is enough to lay out cold both horses and chariots. (Compare this depiction with images of the Messiah striking the earth "with the rod of his mouth" [Isa 11:4] or with a "sharp sword" coming out of His mouth [Rev 19:15].) Even the psalmist seems to stammer as he tries to describe the Lord in this moment:

You—you are fearsome![107]
Who will stand before you after the time of your anger? (v. 7)

Our Lord is wonderfully "compassionate and gracious, slow to anger and abounding in loyalty and faithfulness" (Exod 34:6). He allows us to wrestle with Him as we struggle to learn and grow, allowing an astonishing amount of give-and-take (see Gen 32:22-32). And He patiently bears with the rebellious, giving them a long time to come around to a change of heart (2 Pet 3:9). But when He does finally say that enough is enough, there's no more argument. It's

---

105 Since antiquity, translators and commentators have differed widely in their understanding of this verse. Our reading follows that of J. A. Emerton ("A Neglected Solution of a Problem in Psalm Lxxvi 11," *Vetus Testamentum* 24 [1974]: 136-146), which best upholds the integrity of MT.

106 C. S. Lewis, *The Lion, the Witch and the Wardrobe* (London: Geoffrey Bles, 1950), ch. 8, "What Happened after Dinner."

107 In many contexts, this word is translated as "awesome." That is quite correct, at least historically, but the meaning of that term in English has drifted over time, and today we easily forget that the word *awe* means *fear*. The Hebrew word in verse 7, *nora'* (from *yare'*), denotes an object of fear.

over. If you still stand against the Lion of Judah, He will kill you. If you are submitted to Him, He will welcome you in love forever.

> From the heavens you made your judgment heard;
>   the earth feared and was quiet
> when God rose for judgment
>   Oto save all the lowly in the earth. (vv. 8-9)

As we have seen so often in the Psalms, God stands and judges on behalf of the lowly. The Scriptures repeatedly exhort us to humble ourselves (e.g., Matt 23:12; 1 Pet 5:6; see also Exod 10:3), and well we should. If you do not humble yourself, then God will humble you. And you do not want that. Do not pray "Lord, humble me"—it is not a biblical prayer. Humble yourself. Get on your knees and acknowledge your dependence on God's grace. Lift your hands and your voice in praise of His greatness. Honor Jesus, both in your private prayers and out in the open.

Fasting, which Christians in the modern West have often neglected, is one tool for promoting humility. One reason fasting helps in this regard is that when we are hungry, things tend to come out that we would normally do a better job of keeping under wraps. (Consider the recently popularized word *hangry*, born of the recognition that people often become irritable when their blood sugar runs low.) As unregenerate parts of our personalities are thus exposed, we are both reminded of our ongoing need for grace and given an opportunity to acknowledge specific sins before the Lord and seek His healing for our souls. Sunlight is the best disinfectant.

When you get hungry or tired, are there specific traits that tend to emerge?

FEAR OF GOD AMONG THE RIGHTEOUS

> Make vows and fulfill them to Yahweh your God;
>   let all around him bring a gift to the Fearsome One. (v. 11)

One of the most amazing realities of the gospel is that the Lord raises His servants to the status of friends (John 15:15). But we pervert the meaning of this statement if we fall into a lackadaisical, "Jesus is my homeboy" attitude, thinking that we're squared away with Him no matter what we do. Read what Jesus said immediately before conferring the status of "friend" on His disciples: "You are my friends if you do what I command you" (John 15:14). And John, whose joy it was to call himself "the disciple Jesus loved" (see, e.g., John 19:26), still fell flat on his face when he saw Jesus in glory (Rev 1:12-18).

So Psalm 76 tells those of us who have found favor with God and not fallen under judgment that we should still be diligent to fulfill our vows to God and that we should not come before Him empty-handed.

What gift can you bring to the Giver of every good and perfect gift (Jas 1:17)? Review Psalms 50 and 51, along with Psalm 100:4 and Micah 6:6-8. What offering will you bring to the Lord today?

DAY 5: PSALM 77

While Psalms 75 and 76 moved us forward in expectation of the fulfillment of God's day of reckoning, we now return to the place of Psalm 74—if not to the literal ruins of the sanctuary, at least to a place of feeling abandoned by God. The psalmist looks back to God's great miracles in the exodus from Egypt and wonders why He isn't doing now as He did before. The psalm does not give an answer but simply ends in remembrance of the past. Thus, it teaches us to hold fast to the testimony of God's Word while we wait for the Lord to deliver us from present distress.

FOR THE DIRECTOR. ACCORDING TO JEDUTHUN. OF ASAPH. A PSALM.

1   With my voice, to God I cry out;
my voice to God, that he might listen to me.
2   In the day of my distress I have sought my Lord;
my hand by night has been stretched out without falling numb,
and my soul has refused to relent.
3   I remember God and groan;
I muse, and my spirit feels faint. Selah
4   You lay hold of my eyelids;[108]
I am troubled but cannot speak.
5   I consider former days,
the years of old.

---

[108] Literally, "the guards of my eyes." Most translations take this line to mean "You hold my eyelids *open*," i.e., "You keep me awake," but Goldingay (*Psalms 42–89*, 464) argues that "God's action (or inaction) has been keeping the supplicant's eyes *shut* in the sense of giving these eyes nothing to see, no act of deliverance. . . . The parallel reference to not speaking supports this understanding" (emphasis added).

6   *I will remember my song in the night;*
      with my heart I will muse, and my spirit searches.

7   *Will it be forever that my Lord spurns,*
      and will he never again be favorable?

8   *Will his loyalty cease completely,*
      his word come to an end for generation after generation?

9   *Has God forgotten to be gracious,*
      or shut up his compassion in anger? Selah

10 *So I say, "What weakens me is this:*
      the changing of the Most High's right hand!"

11 *I remember the deeds of Yah;*
      indeed, I remember your wonders of old,

12 *and I ruminate on all your works, and on your deeds I muse.*

13 *God, in holiness is your way;*
      what god is great like God?

14 *You are the wonder-working God;*
      you have made known your might among the peoples.

15 *You redeemed your people with your arm,*
      the sons of Jacob and Joseph. Selah

16 *Waters saw you, God;*
      waters saw you and writhed;
      even the depths trembled.

17 *Clouds poured out water,*
      the skies gave sound,
      and your arrows flew about.

18 *The sound of your thunder was in the whirling;*
      lightning flashes lit up the world;
      the earth trembled and shook.

19 *Through the sea was your way,*
      and your paths were through great waters,
      though your footsteps were not observable.

20 *You led your people like a flock*
      by the hand of Moses and Aaron.

PERSEVERANCE

Psalm 77 speaks from a place of confusion and abandonment. The psalmist feels spurned by God, seeing ample evidence of God's anger but not His mercy or compassion (vv. 7-9). We know from our discussions of previous psalms what the psalmist must do: He must seek the Lord with all his might and not lose heart, like the persistent widow of Jesus' parable

(Luke 18:1-8). And from the beginning of his testimony, the psalmist declares that this is exactly what he has been doing so far:

> *In the day of my distress I have sought my Lord;*
>   *my hand by night has been stretched out without falling numb,*
>   *and my soul has refused to relent. (v. 2)*

And so he continues. Though he may be past the point of being able to articulate himself clearly ("I am troubled but cannot speak" [v. 4]), he still resolves to *consider, remember, muse,* and *search* (vv. 5-6). We hear his musing in verses 7-9:

> *Will it be forever that my Lord spurns,*
>   *and will he never again be favorable?*
> *Will his loyalty cease completely,*
>   *his word come to an end for generation after generation?*
> *Has God forgotten to be gracious,*
>   *or shut up his compassion in anger?*

Given the thoughts that have been stirring in the psalmist's mind, it is little wonder that he should have a hard time speaking. These questions express raw, heartbreaking pain—the kind that cannot be assuaged simply by stating that the answer to all his questions is clearly *no*. The worst part, as the psalmist himself says, is that his present experience does not square at all with what he knows of God from the past; the Most High, he declares, has changed (vv. 10-11). More specifically, His "right hand"—which represents His power—has changed.

The Scriptures make plain elsewhere that God's character does not change (e.g., Num 23:19; Mal 3:6; Heb 13:8), nor has His arm shrunk so that He cannot save (Num 11:23; Isa 59:1). What the psalmist expresses in verse 10 is not factually correct. But it is what he honestly feels.

The point here is not to excuse bad theology when we get upset. Rather, when we get frustrated or angry at God, He'll let us unload those feelings on Him as long as we come as children to our Father seeking relationship. The psalmist is not an enemy trying to cast off God's authority; he is crying out to God for help.

And he persists. Though he cannot see God at work in the present, he turns his attention to what God has done in the past, laying it before the Lord (and before his own soul) as a testimony and a precedent, setting the expectation that God should act similarly again.

It often happens that when we feel an acute hunger for God to come and do something, we pray very fervently about it that day; but we do not often persevere in prayer and anticipation if the answer does not immediately appear. While a delayed answer could be the result of spiritual battles above and beyond us (Dan 10:2-14), it may also serve to test our resolve and our level of trust in God's word. Do we really want what we're asking for enough to keep on badgering God about it? Are we so assured of His integrity that we expect Him to do as He has promised, even though time has passed without evidence of change or an explanation as to why we must wait?

John Wimber, a pastor and author, used to lead conferences in which he taught people to pray for healing of the sick. Inevitably, he would get responses from people who had tried praying for somebody but saw no visible result. Because the person didn't get healed, they concluded that this type of prayer didn't work. Wimber would give his standard response: "Why don't you pray for a thousand somebodies, and then let's talk."[109]

Have you ever prayed urgently for something and not received it? How long did you keep praying, and what led you to stop?

HOLD ON TO THE TESTIMONY

Psalm 119:2 declares blessing on "the keepers of [God's] testimonies." On one level, this refers to obeying the commandments God gave Israel in their covenant. But on a more basic level, it refers to remembering what God has said and done. Everything recorded in the Scriptures and everything God has done in your life is a testimony of who He is and what He does—the One who is the same yesterday, today, and forever (Heb 13:8).

So here in Psalm 77, while the psalmist waits for God to reveal Himself again, he recalls the foundational story of Israel's exodus from Egypt—just as we observed in Psalm 74. These events formed the basis of Israel's covenant with God, as He Himself indicated while laying out the terms of that agreement: "I am Yahweh, your God, who brought you out from the land of Egypt, from the house of servitude. You shall not have other gods . . ." (Exod 20:2-3). By recounting the Exodus as he does here, the psalmist implicitly appeals to the covenant, in which God promised that although He would punish apostasy in increasing measure as the people fell into idolatry, He would indeed regather and restore them when they turned back to Him (see Deut 28:15-68; 30:1-10). So while we do not always see God's response as quickly as we might like, we press on in faith that it will be forthcoming.

Is there anything you feel a burden to pray for now, especially anything for which you have struggled to persevere? What word or testimony can you hold on to in order to help you keep going?

---

[109] Videos of Wimber teaching on his five-step prayer model can be readily found online. Interested readers may also wish to consult his writings on healing (see especially John Wimber and Kevin Springer, *Power Healing* [San Francisco: HarperSanFrancisco, 1987; repr., San Francisco: HarperOne, 2009]).

Lesson Review

The Asaphite psalms take us through high highs and low lows. The common thread running through them is that we are utterly dependent on God, whose action (or inaction) makes all the difference. It has been said that the Western church today can carry on with most of its business without relying on the Holy Spirit—we can preach sermons, sing songs, run soup kitchens, and so on, by mere human effort. We should do all those things, of course, but woe to us if we stop depending on God to do far more in our midst than we can manufacture by ourselves. There is a huge difference between a learned person's reflections and a sermon birthed by the Holy Spirit through prayer; between singing the right notes and entering into God's throne room; between doling out a meal and manifesting the spiritual gift of hospitality; between praying thoughtful prayers for the sick and seeing them healed. Let us follow Asaph's example of honestly assessing where we are and refusing to rest until we see God move.

8

LESSON EIGHT:

Psalms 78–80

The psalms for this lesson all deal with the sins of God's people and their consequences. Psalm 78 calls God's people to remember their history so as not to repeat it, while Psalms 79 and 80 are prayers offered upon the fall of Judah and Israel, respectively. These psalms are sobering in their communication of God's judgment on rebellious nations, but they also look forward to the hope of mercy and restoration through the Messiah.

DAY 1: PSALM 78 (PART 1)

Psalm 78 is significantly longer than any of the psalms we have studied thus far—at seventy-two verses, it is the second-longest psalm in the Psalter, surpassed only by Psalm 119. Today we will consider its opening remarks, which serve as an introduction, and give an overview of the testimony that follows, which we will examine more closely over the next two days. Psalm 78 is, in essence, a retelling of Israel's history with the aim that future generations would not repeat the sins of the past.

A MASKIL OF ASAPH.

1 Give ear, my people, to my instruction;
  extend your ear to the words of my mouth.
2 I will open my mouth with a proverb,
  pour out riddles from of old,
3 things which we have heard and known,
  which our fathers recounted to us.
4 We will not hide them from their children,
    recounting them to the next generation:
  the praises of Yahweh and his might,
    and the wonders he has done.
5 He set up a testimony in Jacob,
    teaching he put in Israel,

which he commanded our fathers
to make known to their sons,
⁶ *so that the next generation would know,*
the sons to be born
would arise and recount them to their sons,
⁷ *and they would put their confidence in God*
and not forget God's deeds
but keep his commandments,
⁸ *and not be like their fathers,*
a stubborn and rebellious generation,
a generation that did not keep its heart steadfast,
and whose spirit was not faithful to God.

. . .

INTRODUCTION

Give ear, my people, to my instruction;
extend your ear to the words of my mouth.
I will open my mouth with a proverb,
pour out riddles from of old. (vv. 1-2)

The opening verses of Psalm 78 clearly indicate that the psalm is intended for instruction in wisdom (using similar language to Psalm 49). The psalmist presents a "proverb," apparently not in the usual sense of offering a brief saying but rather by condensing much of Israel's history into a readily digestible nugget so that children might easily learn a lesson their forebears learned the hard way (v. 6). The aim of the lesson is given in verses 7-8; namely, that

they would put their confidence in God
and not forget God's deeds
but keep his commandments,
and not be like their fathers,
a stubborn and rebellious generation,
a generation that did not keep its heart steadfast,
and whose spirit was not faithful to God.

This is much the same wisdom that Ecclesiastes seeks to convey: "The end of the matter, when all has been heard: Fear God, and keep his commandments" (Eccl 12:13). Here in the psalm, emphasis is placed on the importance of remembering the past, as the experience of previous generations provides copious examples both of how things can go off the rails when we fail to keep God's ways and also of God's mercies, which ought to incline our hearts toward Him.

Before we get into the specifics of the historical narrative that follows, let us take heed of the value of learning history in general. Some of us may have been put off by history during our school years, when we may have struggled to memorize names and dates for our exams and missed the point of many of the stories. If so, that is most unfortunate, for there really is truth in the old adage that those who do not know their history are doomed to repeat it. Names and dates are, of course, ancillary to the real lessons of history, whereby we can trace how various ideas and choices have played out in the world. Many ideas that have proven empirically bad in history have come back around because they still sound plausible and good to those who haven't looked squarely at the historical data. Whether the examples under consideration come from ancient Israel, medieval Europe, or twentieth-century China, the wise person will find valuable lessons to be gleaned about God's world as it exists and operates, not in theory, but in reality.

Are there any particular lessons of history that you want to pass on to the next generation? What are they, and how might you be intentional in conveying them?

_____

_____

_____

_____

A SUMMARY OF THE HISTORICAL TESTIMONY IN PSALM 78

The remainder of Psalm 78 recalls Israel's exodus from Egypt and conquest of Canaan. As others have helpfully observed, the testimony follows a pattern that is laid down in verses 9-39 and repeated from verse 40 to the end. We can outline the psalm as follows:[110]

Prologue (vv. 1-8)
The first recital (vv. 9-39)
    God's people forgot and rebelled (vv. 9-11)
    God's wonders in Egypt/Zoan[111] (vv. 12-16)
    God's people rebelled against the "Most High" (vv. 17-20)
    God "heard and became furious" (vv. 21-33)
    God moved with compassion to forgive (vv. 34-39)
The second recital (vv. 40-72)
    God's people forgot and rebelled (vv. 40-42)
    God's wonders in Egypt/Zoan (vv. 43-55)

---

[110] The following outline is taken (with only slight adaptation) from Futato ("Book of Psalms," 259-260), who cites J. Clinton McCann Jr. ("Psalms," in 1 and 2 Maccabees, Job, Psalms, vol. 4 of The New Interpreter's Bible [Nashville: Abingdon, 1996], 990) and Richard J. Clifford ("In Zion and David a New Beginning: An Interpretation of Psalm 78," in Traditions in Transformation: Turning Points in Biblical Faith, ed. Baruch Halpern and Jon D. Levenson [Winona Lake, IN: Eisenbrauns, 1981], 121-141).

[111] As Tate writes, "Zoan (LXX, Tanis) was a city in northeastern Egypt, known also as Avaris, and possibly the same as Raamses/Rameses in Exod 1:11, though this identification is now questioned" (Psalms 51–100, 281).

GGGGG

God's people rebelled against the "Most High" (vv. 56-58)
God "heard and became furious" (vv. 59-64)
God chose Zion and David (vv. 65-72)

We will cover these two recitals in the course of the next two days. For now, consider what the overall pattern of the narrative seeks to highlight: Rebellion against God is outrageous, and He is rightly angered by it. We do not want to repeat the sins of those who went before us. Meanwhile, we give thanks to God for His persistence in shepherding a stubborn people and doing what had to be done to redeem them, not out of any obligation, but as a result of His own choosing.

How often have you forgotten God's goodness and strayed from His directives? How faithful has He been to keep working on you?

DAY 2: PSALM 78 (PART 2)

Today we examine the first wave of the narrative arc we outlined yesterday. God's people "forgot his deeds" and rebelled (vv. 9-11). The psalmist reminds us of God's wonderful deeds, which they should have remembered (vv. 12-16). Failing to do so, they continued in unbelief (vv. 17-20) and angered God (vv. 21-33), who yet had compassion and restrained Himself from destroying them entirely (vv. 34-39).

. . .

9 The sons of Ephraim, equipped as bowmen,
    turned back on the day of battle.
10 They did not keep God's covenant
    but refused to follow his instruction.
11 They forgot his deeds
    and his wonders that he had shown them.
12 Before their fathers he did a wonder,
    in the land of Egypt, the territory of Zoan.[112]
13 He split the sea and brought them through it;
    he made the waters stand up like a heap.

---

[112] A place in Egypt (see note in Lesson 8, Day 1).

¹⁴ *And he led them in a cloud by day,*
    and all night in firelight.
¹⁵ *He split crags in the wilderness*
    and gave them to drink, as much as the deeps.
¹⁶ *He brought forth streams from the cliff,*
    made waters run down like rivers.
¹⁷ *But they continued to sin against him,*
    to defy the Most High in the desert,
¹⁸ *and they tested God in their heart,*
    asking food according to their will,[113]
¹⁹ *and they spoke against God, saying,*
    "Can God prepare a table in the wilderness?
²⁰ *See, he struck a crag and waters flowed,*
        torrents overflowed—
    can he also give bread
        or arrange meat for his people?"
²¹ *Thus Yahweh heard and became furious,*
    and a fire was kindled against Jacob;
    yes, wrath arose against Israel,
²² *because they did not have faith in God*
    and did not trust in his salvation.
²³ *And he commanded the skies from above,*
    the doors of the heavens he opened,
²⁴ *and he rained down on them manna to eat;*
    the grain of the heavens he gave to them!
²⁵ *Each ate the bread of the valiant;*[114]
    provision he sent them aplenty.
²⁶ *He set the east wind blowing in the heavens,*
    and by his strength he drove the south wind,
²⁷ *and he rained down on them meat like dust,*
    winged birds like the sand of the seas;
²⁸ *he made them fall in the midst of his camp,*
    round about his dwelling place.[115]
²⁹ *So they ate and were exceedingly full,*
    as he brought them their desire.

---

[113] Literally, "for their *nefesh* [soul]." This Hebrew word can refer to one's self as a whole or, as in this case, to the mind, will, and emotions. Recall from the Exodus narrative that God had miraculously given them food, but they complained that it wasn't to their liking.
[114] LXX has "angels." In this context, the "valiant" clearly refers to the heavenly host.
[115] Or "tabernacle."

30 *They had not turned from their desire—*
   their food was still in their mouth,
31 *and God's wrath rose against them,*
   and he killed some of their stoutest;
   and the young men of Israel he brought to their knees.
32 *With all this, they still sinned,*
   and they did not believe despite his wonders.
33 *So he ended their days in a breath,*
   their years in sudden terror.
34 *When he killed them they would seek him;*
   they would turn and seek God.
35 *And they remembered that God was their rock,*
   God Most High their redeemer.
36 *But they enticed him with their mouth,*
   and with their tongue they lied to him.
37 *Their heart was not steadfast with him,*
   and they were not faithful to his covenant.
38 *But he is compassionate;*
   he covered their iniquity and did not destroy them,
   but frequently turned back his anger
   and did not stir up all his rage.
39 *He remembered that they were flesh,*
   a wind that passes and does not return.

   . . .

FORGETTING AND DISOBEYING

The sons of Ephraim, equipped as bowmen,
   turned back on the day of battle.
They did not keep God's covenant
   but refused to follow his instruction.
They forgot his deeds
   and his wonders that he had shown them. (vv. 9-11)

The psalmist does not tell us specifically what incident he has in mind here; however, the closing portion of the psalm contrasts rejected Ephraim with chosen Judah (vv. 67-68), and Ephraim is often a biblical shorthand for the northern tribes of Israel collectively. Thus, the relevant narrative here is likely that of Judges 1, which contrasts Judah's diligence in conquering southern Canaan with the northern tribes' laxity (see especially Judg 1:27-36). The northern tribes did not drive out the various peoples that God had explicitly commanded them to destroy lest they lead Israel into idolatry (Deut 7:1-5).

People often object to God's command that the Israelites annihilate and dispossess these peoples, and it is little wonder why. We all know too many cases where people have slaughtered one another and thought wrongly that they were doing the Lord's work. But the Lord, who alone gives life and has the right to take it, was manifestly present and unambiguous in His directives to Moses and Joshua. The reason Israel had to wait four hundred years in Egypt was that God would not bring such a sentence on the inhabitants of Canaan until their iniquity had grown to such proportions as warranted their destruction (see Gen 15:16). But when God did give the command—and there was no question that God had indeed spoken[116]—it didn't matter how the people felt about it; their task was to obey. As Jeremiah would later pronounce, "Cursed is the one who does Yahweh's work with slackness; cursed is the one who holds back his sword from bloodshed" (Jer 48:10).

The effects of Israel's incomplete conquest bear this out. They did conform to their neighbors' wickedness, sometimes even sacrificing their children to false gods, failing to honor the true God to such an extent that He scattered them into exile.

While there are times and places where the use of military force remains necessary, clearly the Christian call to arms is more broadly a call to defeat sin and the spiritual forces of wickedness. And in the spiritual battle, it is no less true that God would have us give the enemy no quarter. We may not deal violently with others, but we should aggressively root out sin in ourselves, as Jesus said: "If your right hand causes you to stumble, cut it off and throw it away; for it is better for you that one of your members should perish than that your whole body go into hell" (Matt 5:30).

Are there sins in your life that you have been lax about putting to death? If so, name them, and plead with God for mercy through the blood of Jesus and for strength to overcome through the Holy Spirit.

REMEMBERING AND PASSING ON

Having called out the northern tribes' forgetfulness, the psalmist points out what they should have kept in mind ("Before their fathers [God] did a wonder" [v. 12]). The ensuing narrative recalls how the previous generation had experienced God's deliverance from Egypt through the

---

[116] This caveat is a response countering those today who think they have heard a word from God telling them to execute vengeance on some person or group. Any prophecy must be tested, with the whole counsel of Scripture as the touchstone. The Israelites under Moses and Joshua knew exactly what God had said, and His words were confirmed by His manifest presence in the cloud and clear signs of His participation in early battles (e.g., lengthening the daylight during one battle [Josh 10:12-14]).

miraculously parted sea, and it remembers how He miraculously provided water and food along their way through the desert (see Exod 14–17). The people of that generation had themselves been doubters and complainers against God despite witnessing His extraordinary miracles, and thus they provoked His anger (verses 18-31 recall Numbers 11).

> *With all this, they still sinned,*
> *   and they did not believe despite his wonders. (v. 32)*

Shortly after the debacle of Numbers 11 came the great manifestation of unbelief when the people received the scouts' report of the Promised Land and its inhabitants (Num 13–14). The Israelites thought Yahweh was incapable of dealing with the people who stood in their way, so they resolved to choose a new leader to replace Moses and go back to Egypt (Num 14:1-4). It was for this unbelief that God made them wander for forty years until that generation died out, bringing only their children (plus faithful Joshua and Caleb) into the land of Canaan.

This generation of children that grew up in the wilderness eating manna and watched their rebellious parents die in the wilderness is the very same generation (along with their own children) that failed to prosecute the conquest of Canaan with due diligence. Such hardheadedness defies comprehension.

And yet in our own day, disobedience persists despite plain knowledge of God's power and goodness. Every one of us has to fight the temptation in our own hearts to do as the Israelites did, doubting God when we really must know better. Thankfully, God is compassionate (v. 38). "He remembered that they were flesh" (v. 39), and He knows what we are made of as well.

God has given us His Spirit so that we might not walk according to the flesh (see Rom 8:1-11). "His divine power has given us everything necessary for life and godliness, through the knowledge of the one who called us to his own glory and excellence" (2 Pet 1:3). We have resources that Ephraim could only dream of. Let us not neglect to draw on those resources.

What is something God has enabled you to do that you know for certain you could not have done without the Holy Spirit?

DAY 3: PSALM 78 (PART 3)

Today we look at the psalmist's second recital of the people's rebellion in the wilderness (vv. 40-42) after being saved from Egypt (vv. 43-54) and of a subsequent generation who, having been brought into the Promised Land (v. 55), also wickedly rebelled against God and provoked Him to anger (vv. 56-64). Again, God's final word is mercy, but the outpouring of that mercy is qualified: He chooses and establishes the faithful while rejecting the rebellious (vv. 67-72).

. . .

40   *How they rebelled in the wilderness*
    and grieved him in the desert!
41   *Repeatedly they tested God;*
    the Holy One of Israel they provoked.
42   *They did not remember his hand,*
    the day he redeemed them from the adversary,
43   *how he set his signs in Egypt*
    and his wonders in the territory of Zoan;
44   *how he turned their rivers to blood,*
    and their streams they could not drink.
45   *He sent against them a swarm, and it devoured them,*
    and frogs, which ruined them.
46   *And he gave their produce to the consuming insect,*
    their labor to the locust.
47   *He killed their vine with hail*
    and their sycamore figs with ice.[117]
48   *He gave over their cattle to the hail,*
    their livestock to the firebolts.
49   *He sent against them his burning anger,*
    fury and indignation and distress,
       a detachment of angels of calamities.
50   *He cleared a path for his anger.*
    He did not spare their souls from death,
       but he handed their lives over to the plague.
51   *And he struck every firstborn in Egypt,*
    the firstfruits of their virility in the tents of Ham.
52   *And he led out his people like a flock;*
    he drove them like a herd in the wilderness.

---

[117] The exact meaning of this Hebrew word (*khanamal*) is uncertain, as it occurs only here, but it is obviously being used in parallel with "hail" (Exodus 9:25 indicates that the same plague ruined both trees and smaller plants). LXX has *pachnē* ("frost").

⁵³ *And he guided them in safety, and they were not in dread;*
    but their enemies, the sea covered.

⁵⁴ *And he brought them within the border of his holiness,*
    to the mountain his right hand had acquired.

⁵⁵ *And he drove out nations from before them*
    and allotted to them with lines an inheritance,
    so settling in their tents the tribes of Israel.

⁵⁶ *But they tested and rebelled against God Most High*
    and did not keep his testimonies.

⁵⁷ *They drew back and acted faithlessly like their fathers;*
    they turned like a loose bow.

⁵⁸ *And they angered him with their high places,*
    and with their idols they aroused his jealousy.

⁵⁹ *God heard and became furious,*
    and he thoroughly rejected Israel.

⁶⁰ *He abandoned the tabernacle at Shiloh,*
    the tent where he dwelt with mankind,

⁶¹ *and he let his might go into captivity,*
    his splendor into the hand of the adversary,

⁶² *and he handed his people over to the sword,*
    while he was furious with his possession.

⁶³ *Fire consumed his*[118] *young men,*
    and his virgins were not praised.[119]

⁶⁴ *His priests fell by the sword,*
    and his widows did not weep.

⁶⁵ *But my Lord awoke like one asleep,*
    like a strong man shouting because of wine,

⁶⁶ *and he struck his adversaries in the backside;*
    he gave them everlasting reproach.

⁶⁷ *And he rejected the tent of Joseph;*
    the tribe of Ephraim he did not choose,

⁶⁸ *but he chose the tribe of Judah,*
    Mount Zion, which he loved,

⁶⁹ *and he built his sanctuary like the heights,*
    like the earth which he founded for eternity.

⁷⁰ *And he chose David his servant,*
    and he took him from the sheepfolds;

---

[118] Or "its" (referring to Israel, God's "possession" [v. 62]), so throughout this verse and the next.

[119] This means, presumably, that the young women never saw their wedding days, whereupon they would have been praised by those in attendance. Alternatively, LXX treats the verb (Hebrew *hullalu*) as a form not of *halal* ("to praise") but of *yalal* ("to lament").

> *71* *from tending ewes he brought him*
> *to shepherd Jacob his people,*
> *Israel his possession.*
> *72* *And he shepherded them according to the integrity of his heart,*
> *and with the skill of his hands he led them.*

CIRCLING BACK

In the first wave of this psalm's historical narrative, the psalmist began with the northern tribes' disobedience during the conquest, then reflected back on what their parents and grandparents had done during the journey out of Egypt and in the wilderness. In today's reading, while the narrative follows the same basic outline, it begins with the wilderness generation (v. 40) and moves up to the psalmist's day.

While the reference in verse 43 to God's "signs in Egypt and his wonders in the territory of Zoan" clearly echoes verse 12, the emphasis in what follows is different. While verses 13-16 were all about God leading Israel and providing for them, verses 44-51 are about His wrath on the Egyptians. Both the positive and the negative—the provision and the plagues—are "wonders" that testify to God's distinct power.

The plagues on Egypt (see Exod 7–12) are also "signs" (v. 43), meaning they point to something beyond themselves. So what do they signify? First, the succession of plague after plague indicates the stubbornness of Pharaoh—if he had let the Israelites go earlier, he and his people would not have had to endure all that devastation. We can learn the same lesson from Pharaoh that we learn from Israel: Rebellion against Yahweh is foolish and leads to tragic consequences. Second, Yahweh used the plagues (combined with Pharaoh's stubbornness) as an occasion for showing off His utter supremacy over the gods of Egypt, who were powerless to fend off His attacks. Finally, the last plague, the death of the firstborn (vv. 50-51), from which the faithful were spared by marking their houses with the blood of a lamb (Exod 12), pointed to the Lamb who was to come, the "firstborn of all creation" (Col 1:15) who died that we might be saved (cf. vv. 52-55). This event (Passover) was particularly to be remembered and celebrated.

God used the series of plagues to break Pharaoh's stubborn will to resist. Some (though by no means all) of the afflictions people suffer today are God-ordained means of spurring them to change their ways.[120] Have you ever experienced a form of suffering that you equated with the rod of God's discipline? If so, how did you respond, and what happened afterward?

---

120 See *Psalms 1–41: A Christian Union Bible Study*, Lesson 10, Day 1, as well as Lesson 5, Day 4 in the present volume.

DEFEAT BY THE PHILISTINES

> *He abandoned the tabernacle at Shiloh,*
> *the tent where he dwelt with mankind,*
> *and he let his might go into captivity,*
> *his splendor into the hand of the adversary. (vv. 60-61)*

The likening of the people to a "loose bow" in verse 57 brings us back to where we started this saga in verse 9 with the failure of Israel's "bowmen" to be God's instrument of judgment against the Canaanites. And again we are reminded that Israel fell into idolatry (v. 58). The episode then described in verses 60-66 corresponds to the narrative of 1 Samuel 4–5, when the Israelites, desperate after a defeat by the Philistines, brought the Ark of the Covenant—the throne of God's "might" and "splendor" (v. 61)—from the Tabernacle in Shiloh to the battle-field. God, who had allowed Israel's defeat as a consequence of their corruption, was not about to be manipulated by such measures into changing His verdict, so He allowed the Philistines to capture the Ark. Not only that, but thirty thousand Israelite fighters died, as did the corrupt priests (1 Sam 4:10-11; see Ps 78:62-64).

> *But my Lord awoke like one asleep,*
> *like a strong man shouting because of wine,*
> *and he struck his adversaries in the backside;*
> *he gave them everlasting reproach. (vv. 65-66)*

While the Lord refused to be manipulated by His wayward people, He also had no intention of letting the Philistines believe they had defeated Yahweh. Not only did He cause the statue of their god to fall prostrate before the Ark, and then lose its head and hands entirely (1 Sam 5:1-5), but He also struck the inhabitants of the Philistine town holding the Ark with what was likely either hemorrhoids or some sort of abscess (1 Sam 5:6-12). Hence, when the psalmist says in verse 66 that God "struck his adversaries in the backside" and "gave them ever-lasting reproach," he is telling us, in so many words, that God humbled the haughty Philistines by making them the butt of a joke.

God laughs at people who think they are superior to Him (see 2:4). And it turns out not to be a pleasant experience for them. We are to remain humble before the One who is truly in control.

GOD WINS

The psalm ends not with God abandoning the Tabernacle at Shiloh but with God establish-ing Jerusalem as the new place of worship and appointing "David his servant" as the shepherd of God's people. As much as this psalm has dwelt on the foolishness and outrageousness of rebellion against the wonder-working, nation-saving God, the final word has to be that God is faithful and good. He uses both the carrot and the stick to draw His people to Himself. And if we are smart, we will avoid the stick and run after the carrot: His presence, love, protection, and provision, which He gladly and generously gives to those who trust Him.

How would you summarize the lessons of Psalm 78 in your own words? How might you teach it to your children (or to others)?

_____

_____

_____

_____

DAY 4: PSALM 79

Psalm 79, like Psalm 74, evidently comes from those who witnessed the destruction of Jerusalem by Nebuchadnezzar's army in 586 BC. As in Psalm 74, there is no appeal here to the people's innocence, but mercy is sought (v. 8) and petition is made on the basis of God's honor (vv. 9-13). "While there is pathos in the psalm," one commentator observes, "its prevailing tone is one of indignation."[121] Whatever iniquities the Israelites may have committed to bring judgment upon themselves, the Babylonians have acted atrociously, and God is called upon to rebuke them and vindicate His good name.

A PSALM OF ASAPH.

1   *God, the nations have entered your possession;*
        they have defiled your holy palace;
        they have laid Jerusalem to ruins.
2   *They have given the corpses of your servants*
            as food for the birds of the heavens,
        the flesh of your loyal ones to the animals of the earth.
3   *They have poured out their blood like the waters,*
        all around Jerusalem,
        with no one to bury them.
4   *We have become a reproach to our neighbors,*
        an object of mocking and derision to those around us.
5   *How long, Yahweh, will you be angry? Forever?*
        How long will your jealousy burn like fire?

---

121 Kidner, *Psalms 73–150*, 316.

6   *Pour out your wrath on the nations who do not know you,*
      on the kingdoms that do not call upon your name.
7   *For he has consumed Jacob,*
      and they have made his abode desolate.
8   *Do not call to mind against us former iniquities;*
      let your mercies hasten to meet us,
        for we are brought very low.
9   *Help us, God of our salvation,*
      for the sake of the glory of your name;
      deliver us and atone for our sins
        for your name's sake.
10   *Why should the nations say,*
      "Where is their God?"
      Let it be known among the nations before our eyes—
        vengeance for the blood of your servants poured out.
11   *Let the groan of the prisoner come before you;*
      in accordance with the greatness of your arm,
        spare the sons of death,[122]
12   *and pay back to our neighbors sevenfold, to their bosom,*
      their reproach with which they reproached you, my Lord.
13   *And we, your people, the flock you shepherd,*
      will acknowledge you forever;
        generation after generation we will recount your praise.

THE LORD'S JUDGMENT

Before the Babylonian siege was laid upon Jerusalem, Yahweh pronounced the following judgment:

Of deadly diseases they shall die. They shall not be lamented, nor shall they be buried. They shall serve as manure on the ground. By the sword and by hunger they shall perish, and their corpses shall be food for the bird of the heavens and for the beast of the earth. (Jer 16:4)

Here in Psalm 79, we see its fulfillment:

They have given the corpses of your servants
  as food for the birds of the heavens,
    the flesh of your loyal ones to the animals of the earth.

---

122 I.e., those doomed to die.

They have poured out their blood like the waters,
  all around Jerusalem,
  with no one to bury them. (vv. 2-3)

Jeremiah's prophecy is hardly the sort of word one takes pleasure in recalling so as to say "I told you so." The Lord made a point of announcing His judgments in advance of carrying them out so that people might take heed and repent and He would stay His hand. This is precisely the story of Nineveh in the book of Jonah (see Jon 3), and it is the general principle Yahweh teaches in Jeremiah 18 (see especially Jer 18:7-8). In other words, the fact that God has pronounced judgment does not mean that it must come to pass. It means: Repent now *or* it will come to pass.

God's word to Jeremiah was clear about what Judah and Jerusalem had done:

When you report all these words to this people, and they say to you, "Why has Yahweh spoken against us all this great evil?" and "What is our iniquity?" and "What is our sin, which we have sinned against Yahweh our God?" then you shall say to them: "Because your fathers abandoned me, declares Yahweh, and went after other gods and served them and bowed down to them; but me they abandoned, and my law they did not keep. And you have done more evil than your fathers. Behold, you go on, every man after the stubbornness of his evil heart, without listening to me." (Jer 16:10-12)

How accurately might that same indictment apply to the people and nation where you live? Remember that the Scriptures have recorded these words for our instruction and correction (2 Tim 3:16). We do not want our nation to face anything like the judgment the psalmist witnessed, which came as a result of Judah's failure to heed God's rebuke. How mindful of God's word are the people of your nation?

MOVING IN THE RIGHT DIRECTION

Do not call to mind against us former iniquities;
  let your mercies hasten to meet us,
  for we are brought very low. (v. 8)

The image of mercies hastening to meet God's sinful children calls to mind the parable from Luke 15 wherein the loving father hikes up his robes and runs to embrace the prodigal son who has ventured back home.[123] Like the people of Israel collectively, the son in the parable had abandoned his father, brought sin and shame upon himself, and was without excuse. He, too, was "brought very low," having spent time in the muck of pigsties, envious of the hogs' fodder. But when he swallowed his pride and returned to the father he had dishonored, he was received with open arms and great joy.

Like the parable, the psalm teaches us not to make excuses but simply to admit that we need mercy. The psalmist goes on to identify Yahweh, whose jealous anger was recognized as the source of the present calamity (v. 5), as "God of our salvation" (v. 9). He will forgive and restore His people because He is merciful.

But the psalmist also recognizes that forgiving Israel is only a part of setting things right. God Himself has borne the reproach of Israel's neighbors because of their iniquity, and the remainder of the psalm is concerned with the restoration of His good name. Israel brought dishonor upon Him, and if they had the ability to rectify that, it would be their responsibility to do so. But they cannot vindicate God. He will have to come and act on His own behalf.

None of us can adequately repay God for the damage our stubborn, prideful behavior has done to His good name. What we can do is humbly receive the forgiveness of our debt, paid in full by our King. We can join His people in the psalm's final vow (v. 13), acknowledging Him forever and recounting His praise from generation to generation.

What word of praise stirs in your heart now? How might you pass it on to the next generation?

_____

_____

_____

_____

DAY 5: PSALM 80

Here in Psalm 80, desolation and exile are again in view, but this psalm far predates the fall of Jerusalem. It speaks instead of the conquest of the northern tribes (vv. 1-2) by the Assyrians nearly a century and a half earlier. Though the Asaphite singers lived in Jerusalem and the northern and southern kingdoms had long been divided by this point, they still pray with and for their northern brothers as one family, asking God to "restore us" (vv. 3, 7, 19). The final lines show a distinctly messianic hope (v. 17) that God's judgment will finally give way to revival (v. 18).

---

[123] See Kidner, _Psalms 73–150_, 318.

FOR THE DIRECTOR. ACCORDING TO "LILIES." A TESTIMONY. OF ASAPH. A PSALM.

1   *Shepherd of Israel, give ear;*
        you who guide Joseph like a flock,
        who sit enthroned upon the cherubim, shine forth!

2   *Before Ephraim and Benjamin and Manasseh,*
        rouse your strength
            and come for our salvation.

3   *God, restore us,*
        and make your face shine that we may be saved.

4   *Yahweh, God of Hosts,*
        how long will you fume at your people's prayer?

5   *You have fed them tears for bread*
        and given them tears to drink by the quart.[124]

6   *You have made us a source of contention to our neighbors,*
        and our enemies mock us among themselves.

7   *God of Hosts, restore us;*
        make your face shine that we may be saved.

8   *A vine you uprooted from Egypt;*
        you drove out nations and planted it.

9   *You cleared before it*
        and planted its roots,
        and it filled the land.

10   *Mountains were covered with its shade,*
        and with its branches the cedars of God.

11   *It extended its boughs to the sea,*
        and to the river its shoots.

12   *Why have you broken through its walls,*
        so that all who pass by pluck it?

13   *A boar from the forest tears it up,*
        and wild animals graze on it.

14   *God of Hosts, please turn,*
        look down from the heavens and see,
        and attend to this vine,

15   *the stock that your right hand planted,*
        and to the son you made strong for yourself.

16   *It is burned with fire, cut down;*
        from the rebuke of your face they perish.

---

[124] Literally, "by the third" (of some unspecified measure; see also Isa 40:12).

¹⁷ *Let your hand be upon the man of your right hand,*
  upon the son of Adam you made strong for yourself.
¹⁸ *And we will not draw back from you;*
  revive us, and we will call upon your name.
¹⁹ *Yahweh, God of Hosts, restore us;*
  make your face shine that we may be saved.

DO FOR JOSEPH AS YOU DID FOR DAVID!

Shepherd of Israel, give ear;
  you who guide Joseph like a flock,
  who sit enthroned upon the cherubim, shine forth!
Before Ephraim and Benjamin and Manasseh,
  rouse your strength
    and come for our salvation. (vv. 1-2)

In Psalm 18, David testified that he had called on Yahweh in his distress, and that when he did so, his cry came to Yahweh's ears (18:6). Yahweh "rode upon a cherub and flew" (18:10), and there was "brightness before him" (18:12) as He rained hail, fire, and all manner of destruction on the enemy. Now, in Psalm 80, the praying community asks Yahweh, the "Shepherd of Israel" (cf. 23:1), to come and do likewise for the descendants of Rachel, Jacob's favorite wife.[125]

Even as God is asked to "shine forth" with blinding ferocity against the adversary, He is also asked to "shine" on His people with the blessing of salvation. "God, restore us, and make your face shine that we may be saved" (v. 3) becomes the psalm's refrain, with God's name amplified at each occurrence (vv. 7, 19). This refrain recalls the blessing God instructed the high priest to speak over all Israel (Num 6:22-27), and it speaks to the unity of the one people Yahweh redeemed for Himself out of Egypt—the Asaphites don't pray "Restore *them*" but rather "Restore *us*," and they ask God to cease rejecting "your people's prayer" (v. 4).

The psalm therefore reminds us of our calling to identify with, and intercede on behalf of, our brothers and sisters in the body of Christ: "If one member suffers, all the members suffer with it; if one member is honored, all the members rejoice with it" (1 Cor 12:26). This is obviously easier to do when our fellow members of the body behave as they ought, and harder to do when they are caught in some sin or have set themselves at odds with us in some way. It is no wonder that Jesus specifically instructs us to love and pray for those who are antagonistic toward us (Matt 5:38-48).

As we discussed in our study of Psalm 78, Ephraim and the other northern tribes were hardly models of good behavior. After Jeroboam's generation rejected the authority of the king in Jerusalem and established distinct worship practices, successive generations in the north

---

[125] Ephraim and Manasseh were Joseph's sons, born in Egypt, whom Jacob claimed as his own (Gen 48:5). They became the most prominent of the northern tribes. Therefore, as previously observed, "Ephraim" is often used to signify all the northern kingdom.

fell deeper and deeper into idolatry and wickedness. They earned the judgment God was now bringing against them by the hand of Assyria. But the Temple singers in Jerusalem still prayed for them—they prayed as though standing in their shoes.

Let's face it: Lots of other Christians have done, and continue to do, things with which we strongly disagree. But the Lord does not want His house divided (see John 17:20-23), and He commands us to love each other as He has loved us (John 13:34-35). (Which one of us earned the love Jesus has given?) Christ abides in us, and His love is perfected in us as we choose to love each other (1 John 4:12). Disunity in the body makes onlookers scorn us (see v. 6). Christian unity—not plastering over disagreement or neglecting to give and receive necessary correction but exhibiting genuine love and common purpose in allegiance to Christ Jesus, our Head—tells the world who our King is.

Is there a specific Christian group (perhaps a denomination, a particular church, or a ministry organization) that you have a hard time honoring as fellow members of Christ? Take time now to pray on their behalf, and write down any specific petitions you might continue to offer in pursuit of God's best for them.

TENDING THE VINE

God of Hosts, please turn,
  look down from the heavens and see,
  and attend to this vine,
the stock that your right hand planted,
  and to the son you made strong for yourself. (vv. 14-15)

Jesus tells us that He is the True Vine and that God the Father is the One who planted and tends the Vine. We are branches on the Vine, so our lives are bound up with Jesus' life (John 15:1-11). So here in Psalm 80, while the "vine" and the "son [God] made strong for [him]self" clearly refer to Israel as a people, they also anticipate the true King of Israel and Son of God who was to be revealed in due course. The vine being burned and cut down (v. 16) speaks of Israel being conquered and carried off to Assyria, but it also speaks of the One who "was pierced because of our rebellions, broken to pieces for our iniquities" (Isa 53:5).

The Father did indeed attend to the Vine. The people prayed, "Let your hand be upon the man of your right hand, upon the son of Adam you made strong for yourself" (v. 17). God raised Jesus from the dead and exalted Him to His right hand, whence the Son of Man will come again in glory to judge the living and the dead, and His Kingdom will have no end.

As you ponder what it means to be a branch of that Vine, remember that God not only cuts off the unfruitful branches but also prunes the good branches so they bear more fruit. And He prunes us by His word (John 15:3). Is there any habit the Lord has been prodding you to dispense with?

Lesson Review

Psalm 78 warned us not to forget. If we forget how prior generations went wrong, we will likely go the same way. If we forget the miracles God has done to get us here, we will not trust Him as we ought to lead us onward. And if we forget that He judges rebellion with vengeance, we will fail to honor Him as King and will find ourselves, before we know it, as slaves of other gods. Psalms 79 and 80 both drive home the point that He will not be disobeyed without real consequences. Yet everything He does, even His stamping out rebellion, He does with a view to this end: that He might conform us to the likeness of Jesus and thus make us fit to reign with Him forever as true sons and daughters of our holy Father.

9

LESSON NINE:

Psalms 81–85

These five psalms speak from different vantage points and address different occasions, but they all speak of coming before the Lord. Psalm 81 is a proclamation to pilgrims who have gathered in Jerusalem for a festival, and it carries admonishment directly from God concerning the people's refusal to follow His instructions. Psalms 82 and 83 finish out the set of Asaphite psalms begun in Psalm 73, and they likewise treat rebellion against God, but in different quarters—Psalm 82 addresses rebellion in the heavens, while Psalm 83 concerns the nations conspiring to destroy Israel. Psalm 85 addresses God's judgment on disobedience and is a prayer for forgiveness and the restoration of His favor upon His covenant people. Meanwhile, Psalm 84 stands out as the rapturous prayer of a weary traveler who has finally arrived at God's house and is beholding the blessings of His sanctuary; it also speaks of the transformative impact pilgrims can have upon the lands they pass through on their journeys.

DAY 1: PSALM 81

While this festival psalm begins with a call to praise God, what follows is a testimony from Yahweh's own lips exhorting Israel to honor no other god. As in previous Asaphite psalms, the judgment of exile is in view as a consequence of unfaithfulness. Meanwhile, we hear the cry of the Lord's heart that His people would choose the way of life, which is the way of obedience to His instructions (vv. 12-13; see also Ps 1). He is ready to help His people, if only they will listen.

FOR THE DIRECTOR. UPON THE GITTITE.[126] OF ASAPH.

1 *Give a ringing cry to God, our strength;*
    raise a shout to the God of Jacob.
2 *Lift up a song and sound a timbrel,*
    the melodious lyre with the harp.
3 *Blow a ram's horn at the new moon,*
    at the full moon for the day of our festival.

---

126 Probably a type of lyre. Or the term may mean "at the winepress" (implying that it was sung at the Feast of Booths).

4   For it is an ordinance for Israel,
         a rule of Jacob's God,
5   a testimony in Joseph that he set
              in his going forth over the land of Egypt.
         A voice[127] I did not know, I heard:
6   "I have relieved his shoulder of its burden;
         his hands shall move on from the basket.
7   In distress you called, and I delivered you;
              I answered you in the concealment of thunder;
         I tried you at the waters of Meribah. Selah
8   Hear, my people, and I will bear witness against you,
         Israel, if you will listen to me.
9   There must not be among you a strange god,
         and you must not bow down to a foreign god.
10   I am Yahweh, your God,
              who brought you up from the land of Egypt.
         Open wide your mouth, and I will fill it.
11   But my people did not listen to my voice;
         Israel was unwilling toward me.
12   So I sent them away in the stubbornness of their heart;
         they walked in their own counsel.
13   Oh that my people would listen to me,
         that Israel would walk in my ways!
14   I would easily humble their enemies
         and turn my hand against their oppressors.
15   Haters of Yahweh would wither before him,
         and it would be their doom forever.
16   And he would feed him[128] from the fattest wheat;
         with honey from the crag I would satisfy you."

A FESTIVAL FOR REMEMBRANCE

Blow a ram's horn at the new moon,
    at the full moon for the day of our festival. (v. 3)

The setting for Psalm 81 is almost certainly the Feast of Booths (Sukkoth).[129] The seventh
month of Israel's calendar was to begin with a horn blast and a holy convocation, followed by

---

[127] Literally, "A lip," representative as an organ of speech. In some contexts, this word is translated as "language" (e.g., Gen 11:1),
    but what follows implies hearing Yahweh's voice for the first time.
[128] "Him" is a reference, presumably, to Israel.
[129] See Kidner, Psalms 73–150, 323-324.

the Day of Atonement (Yom Kippur) on the tenth day of the month. Sukkoth commenced at the midpoint of the month (Lev 23:24, 27, 34). Hence, both the new moon and the full moon correspond to festival days. It was at Sukkoth that God's Law was to be read aloud to the people every seven years (Deut 31:10-13).

Psalm 81 is clearly an exhortation to observe God's Law. Whereas one might expect the opening call—to shout and make music to God—to lead into a catalog of His wonderful actions and attributes, what we find here instead is an appeal to covenant obligation: The people are to gather and offer loud praise because "it is an ordinance for Israel, a rule of Jacob's God" (v. 4). We then do hear of God's goodness, but not by way of the congregation's address to Him—Yahweh Himself shares His heart with the assembly through a word the psalmist has heard from His lips (vv. 5-16).

As with the giving of the Ten Commandments (Exod 20:1-17), Yahweh's prefatory remarks speak of His having brought Israel up out of Egypt (vv. 6-7; see also v. 10). What follows is an indictment that Israel has failed to obey the first and greatest commandment. Moses had issued the summons that was to be passed down through the generations: "Hear, Israel: Yahweh our God, Yahweh is one. And you shall love Yahweh your God with all your heart and with all your soul and with all your strength" (Deut 6:4-5). Now, in Psalm 81, God admonishes the wayward:

> *Hear, my people, and I will bear witness against you,*
> *Israel, if you will listen to me.*
> *There must not be among you a strange god,*
> *and you must not bow down to a foreign god. (vv. 8-9)*

We hear God's lament that His people "did not listen" (v. 11). They were sent away (v. 12), having done exactly what Psalm 1 tells us is doomed to fail—"they walked in their own counsel" and not according to Yahweh's instruction (vv. 12-13). We also hear the heart of the Father, who loves to give His children good gifts (Matt 7:11), as He laments Israel's squandering of opportunities to turn to Him and find help readily available (vv. 13-16; see also 46:1). Our God loves us and desires to be our refuge and strength, but we cannot serve two masters (Matt 6:24). Idolaters, along with others who disregard God's ordinances, will not inherit the Kingdom (Matt 7:21-23; 1 Cor 6:9-10).

As you continue to seek the Lord, are there any areas of your life where you find Him calling you anew to lean on Him and forsake old sources of comfort or support?

GATHERING TODAY

As we have said, the occasion for this psalm's proclamation was the Feast of Booths (Sukkoth). During this celebration, the people of Israel would assemble in Jerusalem for a week, staying in makeshift huts to remind themselves of their ancestors' journey through the wilderness after leaving Egypt. Here they would worship the God of their deliverance and recall the covenant He had made with them. Six months later, they would return for Passover and the Feast of Unleavened Bread, with much the same purpose—to spend a week in corporate worship and remembrance.

We would do well to recognize God's wisdom in ordaining these weeklong, semiannual gatherings for the good of His people. As countless saints can testify, life-changing encounters with the voice and Spirit of God often come when believers set aside multiple days in a row to seek God together. And historically, great revivals of biblical faith have begun with such gatherings.

A scriptural example of such revival can be seen in Hezekiah's restoration of the Passover celebration (2 Chr 30), whereupon the people were so filled with joy that they extended the feast for a second week. Likewise, when the returning exiles observed Sukkoth (Neh 8:13-17), they were profoundly moved by the teaching of God's word and came to rejoice greatly.

Another remarkable example comes from the United States, shortly after independence from England. While we know how the early Puritan pilgrims sought to build a Christian society in America, few today are aware of just how unchurched the new nation was in the early days of the republic—particularly in the frontier territories, where historical records show that not one person in a hundred practiced biblical religion. "Rampant alcoholism and avaricious land-grabbing were matched by the increasing popularity of both universalism (the doctrine that all will be saved) and deism (the belief that God is uninvolved in the world)."[130] But when people came from miles around to a camp meeting at Cane Ridge, Kentucky, thousands were converted and baptized in the Holy Spirit. This revival and others like it sparked a movement that we now call the Second Great Awakening—a movement which influenced many of the other great reform movements of the nineteenth century, including the abolition of slavery, as the church swelled both in numbers and in zeal.

The modern convention of time off from work for vacation actually derives from the nineteenth-century practice of traveling to Christian camp meetings like the one at Cane Ridge. We at Christian Union strongly encourage you to consider how you (and your family or friends) might benefit from following the biblical pattern of coming together regularly for multiday gatherings for worship, fellowship, and teaching twice a year. You can expect to draw close to God, to find joy and strength in a fresh filling of the Holy Spirit, to understand Him more deeply, and to connect with other Christians whose testimonies will encourage your faith.

---

[130] Mark Galli, "Revival at Cane Ridge," *Christian History* 45 (1995), accessed online at https://christianhistoryinstitute.org/magazine/article/revival-at-cane-ridge/.

What do you expect God might do if you set aside a week to meet with Him? How can you make that happen?

_____

_____

_____

_____

DAY 2: PSALM 82

Psalm 82 gives us a window into the biblical worldview concerning the unseen authorities God created (see Col 1:16). As in the opening lines of Psalm 58, we find God rebuking the spiritual authorities that have turned rebellious and are now working contrary to the laws of God's Kingdom. Having heard God's statement of judgment to the divine assembly (v. 1), the psalmist prays in the final verse that God would promptly bring this judgment into effect.

A PSALM OF ASAPH.

> 1 *God stands in the divine assembly;*
> *in the midst of the gods he judges:*
> 2 *"How long will you judge for the unjust*
> *and lift up the face of the wicked?* Selah
> 3 *Judge for the weak and the orphan;*
> *justify the lowly and the poor.*
> 4 *Rescue the weak and needy;*
> *deliver from the hand of the wicked.*
> 5 *They neither know nor understand;*
> *in darkness they go about;*
> *all the earth's foundations are shaken.*
> 6 *I said, 'You are gods*
> *and sons of the Most High, all of you.'*
> 7 *But surely like Adam shall you die,*
> *like one of the rulers shall you fall."*
> 8 *Arise, God! Judge the earth,*
> *for you hold patrimony over all the nations.*

LORD OF HEAVEN AND EARTH

Psalm 82 offers a somewhat expanded view into the realities we discussed in studying Psalm 58—namely, that God has created beings "visible and invisible" (Col 1:16) and delegated authority to them in the administration of His Kingdom, and that human beings are not the only ones who have rebelled. To get a better grasp of this biblical worldview, let us turn for a moment to the Bible's account of Creation.

Having organized and populated the heavens with sun, moon, and stars, and the earth with all sorts of plant and animal life, God said: "Let *us* make man [Adam] in our image, according to our likeness; and let them rule over the fish of the sea and over the birds of the heavens and over the beasts and over all the earth, over every moving thing that moves on the earth" (Gen 1:26). To whom was God speaking when He said this? Christian readers might suppose that this was merely an intra-Trinitarian conversation, but the Scriptures suggest a wider audience. When Yahweh appears in a whirlwind to respond to Job, He highlights the mortal man's ignorance of creation, asking, "On what were [the earth's] pillars set, and who laid its cornerstone, while the morning stars resounded and all the sons of God shouted?" (Job 38:6-7). Both "morning stars" and "sons of God" are terms for members of the heavenly host. This affirms that God was surrounded by divine attendants when He created humankind.[131]

As God had created various orders of spiritual authorities in what is (to us) the invisible realm, so His intention for human beings was that we would likewise ("according to our likeness") exercise authority as God's representatives ("in our image") on the earth. We know, of course, that Adam and Eve fell into disobedience and brought humanity under the dominion of sin until Christ Jesus came as the second Adam to restore us to our created purpose (see Gen 3; Rom 5). From the story of Adam and Eve's failure, we know that at least one figure, the serpent—which was clearly no ordinary reptile—had already set himself against God's designs. Then in Genesis 6:1-5, we read of an untold number of divine beings (called "sons of God") who further corrupted humanity in the days before the Flood.

In an allusion to the story of the tower of Babel (Gen 11)—in which God disrupts rebellious humanity's attempt to storm the heavenly castle, as it were, and scatters the people to form diverse nations over the earth—Moses states that God "established the boundaries of the peoples according to the number of the sons of God" (or, as the New Living Translation helpfully translates, "according to the number in his heavenly court"). Yahweh assigned divine overseers to each nation while retaining the governance of Israel for Himself alone (Deut 32:8-9).[132]

Verses 2-5 of Psalm 82 attest to what is all too evident around the world: These principalities over the nations have encouraged all sorts of injustice, while the people go about in darkness. Hence, we find God judging the principalities.

[131] For a more extensive treatment of what the Bible teaches about supernatural beings and the divine council, see Heiser, *Unseen Realm*.
[132] MT of Deuteronomy 32:8 has "sons of Israel" (*bene Yisra'el*), but this is clearly an act of censorship by later scribes. Ancient Hebrew manuscript fragments found among the Dead Sea Scrolls have "sons of God," as MT retains in Job 38:7. LXX's *angelōn theou* ("angels of God") corresponds to this wording.

Both because of differences among cultures and because of the influence of the different principalities that have shaped those cultures, different nations tend to manifest different characteristic sins. For example, one nation may incline toward unbelief and another toward witchcraft; one may be marked by endemic arrogance, while yet another may suffer under a spirit of rejection. What particular spiritual ills do you find most prevalent in your nation?

ON EARTH AS IN HEAVEN

I said, "You are gods
and sons of the Most High, all of you."
But surely like Adam shall you die,
like one of the rulers shall you fall. (vv. 6-7)

Adam was made (together with his wife) to rule the earth under God's authority and as His representative. He died, of course, for his disobedience in eating the forbidden fruit. Likewise here, God pronounces the same sentence over His disobedient subjects in the spiritual realm. (Recall from Lesson 4, Day 1 that *'elohim* ["gods"] can refer generally to various orders of spiritual beings created by Yahweh, whom we call "God" with a capital *G*, to serve Him in His divine council.)

But just as Adam and Eve's sentence of mortality did not result in immediate death—they lived many more years and had children—so we find that God's decree regarding the death of the spiritual hosts of wickedness has not yet come to full effect. This will come in the end on the great Day of Judgment when they shall be thrown into the lake of fire (Rev 20:7-15). Meanwhile, we wait for and hasten that day, living lives of holiness (2 Pet 3:11-12) and proclaiming the gospel in all the earth (Matt 24:14). And we pray, as the psalmist does:

Arise, God! Judge the earth,
for you hold patrimony over all the nations. (v. 8)

When God consigned wayward nations to the jurisdiction of spiritual principalities, He did not surrender ownership. The whole earth along with everything and everyone in it are rightfully His (24:1). Jesus warned human religious leaders that they were but tenants given the care of God's vineyard (Matt 21:33-46; Mark 12:1-12; Luke 20:9-19). So must the "gods" of the nations relinquish their holdings when the Lord makes His claim.

And that is precisely what Jesus came to do, as seen in His announcement: "The time is fulfilled, and the kingdom of God is at hand; repent, and believe the good news!" (Mark 1:15).

He came to set the captives free and give sight to those who have been stumbling in darkness (Luke 4:18; see Ps 82:5). And He commissions us to go in His authority, proclaiming the arrival of His Kingdom and making disciples, baptizing and teaching as many as will receive Him as their Lord (Matt 28:18-20).

When sharing the gospel with non-Christians, people often invite their hearers to acknowledge that they are sinners and ask Jesus to forgive them. This is quite right, but we must not forget that Jesus also says we must teach them "to keep all that I have commanded you" (Matt 28:20). How forthright have you been in proclaiming obedience to Jesus' lordship as an integral part of the good news of salvation?

_____

_____

_____

_____

DAY 3: PSALM 83

Having heard in Psalm 82 Yahweh's assessment of the spiritual powers over the nations, we find in Psalm 83 a prayer for protection against the nations' schemes to eliminate Israel. While the psalmist uses vivid imagery to describe the defeat he wishes the aggressor nations to suffer, his ultimate hope is that their defeat would lead these enemies to forsake their gods and seek Yahweh, the God of gods (vv. 16, 18). This is the last of the Asaphite psalms.

A SONG. A PSALM OF ASAPH.

> 1 *God, let it not be quiet for you;*
>   *do not be deaf, and do not be still, God.*
> 2 *For behold, your enemies roar,*
>   *and your haters lift up their head.*
> 3 *Against your people they devise schemes;*
>   *they conspire against your treasured ones.*
> 4 *They say, "Come, let us wipe them out as a nation,*
>   *and let the name of Israel be remembered no more."*
> 5 *For they have conspired with one heart;*
>   *against you they are making a covenant.*
> 6 *Tents of Edom and Ishmaelites,*
>   *Moab and Hagrites,*
> 7 *Gebal and Ammon and Amalek,*
>   *Philistia with the inhabitants of Tyre.*

8 *Assyria also is joined with them;*
they have become an arm for the sons of Lot. Selah

9 *Do to them as with Midian;*
as with Sisera and Jabin at the Wadi Kishon—

10 *they were destroyed at En-dor;*
they became manure for the ground.

11 *Make them, their nobles, like Oreb and Zeeb,*
and like Zebah and Zalmunna all their princes,

12 *who said, "Let us possess for ourselves*
the pastures of God."

13 *My God, make them like a whirl,*
like stubble before the wind.

14 *Like a fire that burns a forest,*
and like a flame that sets mountains ablaze,

15 *so may you pursue them with your tempest*
and dismay them with your storm wind.

16 *Fill their faces with dishonor,*
and let them seek your name, Yahweh.

17 *Let them be ashamed and dismayed forever,*
and let them be abashed and perish.

18 *And let them know that you—*
whose name is Yahweh, you alone—
are the Most High over all the earth.

TIME FOR A SHOWDOWN

God, let it not be quiet for you;
do not be deaf, and do not be still, God.
For behold, your enemies roar,
and your haters lift up their head. (vv. 1-2)

The psalmist's opening appeal that God be neither "deaf" nor "still" might be understood as a variant of the typical plea that He "hear my prayer" and "answer me when I call," which we have found in so many psalms. Taken with the next verse, however, the appeal is rather that God respond to the "roar" of Israel's enemies and make some noise of His own. The psalmist puts the case before God that His people are being conspired against and that the enemies' objective is nothing less than total annihilation (vv. 3-4). God must therefore not confine Himself to the peace and quiet of His heavenly sanctuary (v. 1) but rouse Himself to action.

This is plainly an appeal to Israel's covenant relationship with God, whereby Yahweh is responsible for scattering Israel's enemies so long as the people uphold their end of the agreement

(Deut 28:7). (Notice that Israel's enemies are also "making a covenant" [v. 5], but theirs is to unite with each other *against* God.)

The idea that the psalm constitutes a legal appeal for God to act in keeping with His covenant may help explain why the psalm contains no first-person references to the psalmist or to Israel (with the exception of "*my* God" in verse 13).[133] There is no cry to "rescue me" or "deliver us," but instead it reads something like a prosecuting attorney's argument in the case of *Israel v. Edom et al.* We hear a charge laid against conspirators (vv. 2-5), along with their identification (vv. 6-8), followed by an appeal to precedent in requesting sentencing (vv. 9-12). (The full story behind verses 9-12 can be found in Judges 4–8.)

The list of conspirators includes more nations than we know to have allied against Israel at any one moment, so the prayer may reflect not so much a particular confrontation as the general reality of being surrounded by hostile neighbors. If we were to connect the psalm with a single recorded conspiracy, the likeliest candidate would be the events of 2 Chronicles 20, when an international army came from Edom and was led by Moabites and Ammonites (and it was an Asaphite who prophesied that Yahweh would destroy the enemy without requiring Israel to take up arms; see 2 Chr 20:14-17).[134]

In any case, Psalm 83 reminds us that in addition to asking God for provision as Father and Friend (Matt 7:11; Luke 11:5-13), we can also appeal to God the Judge for relief from oppression (Luke 18:1-8; see also Heb 12:22-24). And as the episode in 2 Chronicles 20 readily attests, He is quite capable of fighting our battles for us when He finds cause to do so.

Are there any spiritual battles in which you've been fighting but are struggling to hold or gain ground? How might you ask the Judge for an injunction against your opposition?

BEYOND VICTORY AND DEFEAT

> Fill their faces with dishonor,
>   and let them seek your name, Yahweh. (v. 16)

The second half of verse 16 comes as a rather unexpected add-on to what has preceded it. But it is perfectly in keeping with God's character to use punitive discipline as a means of correction. Unlike the enemies' desire that Israel cease to exist (v. 4), the psalmist's call for Israel's enemies

133 See Goldingay, *Psalms 42–89*, 573.
134 Kidner, *Psalms 73–150*, 330-331; cf. Futato, "Book of Psalms," 273.

to "perish" (v. 17) does not speak about extermination. Rather, the plea is that these enemies would get a thorough (and well-deserved) thrashing and that *through* defeat they would resolve to forsake the false gods that failed to protect them and seek the one God who can actually deliver. Verses 17-18 expand on the twofold plea of verse 16; while these enemies should be ashamed and humiliated for all their wicked scheming, the psalmist's ultimate concern is for them to know that Yahweh, and Yahweh alone, is "the Most High over all the earth" (v. 18).

Because much of the church today neglects to teach on God's continuing use of punitive discipline to accomplish His purposes, we remind readers of what the New Testament says on this point. Not only does Hebrews 12:3-11 clearly testify that God disciplines the children He loves (and in ways that "seem painful rather than pleasant"), but Peter also declares that judgment must begin with those of us who are in the household of God (1 Pet 4:17). To receive God's chastening discipline and accept correction is a mercy, moving us into alignment with His ways and allowing His Holy Spirit to flow freely in and through us.

We can also readily apply the psalm's insight into the corrective nature of God's discipline to our own prayers wherever we see injustice. We can pray both for the relief of the victims and their restoration to wholeness and also for the perpetrators—that they might repent of the evil they have done, escape from their servitude to the prince of darkness, and come to seek the God who is both just and merciful to those who humble themselves before Him.

Is there anyone in particular whose actions have enraged you? What would you ask God to do with that person?

DAY 4: PSALM 84

We now move from the psalms of Asaph to those of another group of David's appointed song leaders, the sons of Korah (whom we first encountered in Lesson 1). Like Psalm 81, Psalm 84 speaks of a pilgrimage to Jerusalem and to the house of Yahweh. Having come to God's house, the psalmist delights in it and expresses his desire to remain there (v. 10) while also praying God's blessing on the king (v. 9) and on all who trust God, wherever they may be (vv. 5-6, 11-12).

FOR THE DIRECTOR. UPON THE GITTITE.[135] OF THE SONS OF KORAH. A PSALM.

1 *How lovely are your dwelling places,*
  Yahweh of Hosts!
2 *My soul longed, and even came to an end,*
  for the courts of Yahweh;
 my heart and my flesh cry out
  to the living God.
3 *Even the bird finds a house,*
  and the swallow a nest for herself,
 in which she can put her young,
  near your altars, Yahweh of Hosts,
  my king and my God.
4 *Blessed inhabitants of your house,*
  who continually praise you! Selah
5 *Blessed mankind*[136] *whose strength is in you,*
  with a highway in their heart!
6 *Those passing through the valley of the balsam tree*
  make it a spring,
 and the early rain wraps it with blessings.
7 *They go from strength to strength;*
  the God of gods appears in Zion.[137]
8 *Yahweh, God of Hosts, hear my prayer!*
  Give ear, God of Jacob! Selah
9 *Look at our shield, God,*
  and regard the face of your anointed.
10 *For better is a day in your courts than a thousand elsewhere;*
  I would rather stand at the threshold in the house of my God
  than dwell in the tents of wickedness.
11 *For sun and shield is Yahweh God;*
  grace and glory Yahweh gives;
 he does not withhold good from those who walk in integrity.
12 *Yahweh of Hosts,*
  blessed mankind who trusts in you!

---

135 See note on the heading of Psalm 81.
136 The Hebrew here uses the singular *'adam* ("Adam/man"), with the plural at the end of the verse suggesting a collective sense. Note the same language in verse 12.
137 Or "he appears to God in Zion," meaning (presumably) that each pilgrim appears before God as required in Exodus 23:17.

COME TO THE SANCTUARY

Psalm 84 begins with a sigh of relief and delight at having arrived at God's house after a long journey. The psalmist recalls, "My soul longed, and even came to an end, for the courts of Yahweh" (v. 2); but now that he is there, he exclaims, "How lovely!"[138] From the very threshold of God's house (v. 10) he can look within and survey a blessed company—even the birds find sanctuary and give God praise with their cheerful songs (vv. 3-4).

At the same time, the psalm recognizes that God's bountiful presence is not limited to any one structure or location. He is with His people, such that those who have a mind to come before Him—"a highway in their heart" (v. 5)—will find His blessings poured out all along the way, even through otherwise dry or sorrowful places (v. 6).

The reference to the "valley of the balsam tree" in verse 6 is laden with allusive meaning. On the one hand, the Hebrew name for the tree (*baka'*) sounds like the verb that means "to weep" (*bakah*), such that translations going all the way back to the Septuagint have taken it as simply a variant spelling of *bakah* and given us the familiar "vale of tears." If we retain *baka'* with the meaning of "balsam tree," as in 2 Samuel 5:23-24 and 1 Chronicles 14:14-15, we get both the immediate sense of a desert environment (as balsams are prominent in arid places) and a potential reference to the balsam's association with the Rephaim (see 2 Sam 5:22; 1 Chr 14:9), the ancient giants whom God sentenced to death.[139] Any way you parse it—and the psalmist likely intended to evoke all of these associations[140]—the valley of *baka'* is antithetical to the life-giving loveliness of God's house.

But God doesn't just sustain His people through the weary valley; by His grace, they "make it a spring, and the early rain wraps it with blessings" (v. 6). This grace similarly rests on us as we walk in our calling as Christ's ambassadors, proclaiming and representing the reality of His Kingdom wherever we go. For though we may suffer in the world, God will use us to reconcile the world to Himself (2 Cor 5:17-21). So Jesus sent His first representatives out "to the lost sheep" of Israel with the assignment to proclaim that the Kingdom of the heavens has come near and to heal the sick, raise the dead, cleanse lepers, and expel demons (Matt 10:6-8). As a Spirit-filled disciple of Jesus, you are to transform the dry and weary valley into a source of abundance as rivers of living water flow out of you (John 7:38).

The Christian life, then, is about more than simply securing your personal salvation. Your assignment, together with other believers, is to transform the society and territory you inhabit, by the power of the Holy Spirit, into a place where God's will is done on earth, as it is in heaven. This is why the Spirit bestows His various gifts for the work of ministry, and why it is imperative that you develop and utilize your gifts in the context of a community that seeks God's Kingdom and righteousness wholeheartedly.

---

[138] Many translations render all of verse 2 in the present tense. But as John Goldingay astutely observes (*Psalms 42–89*, 588), the Hebrew verbs in verse 2a-b are of a form that suggests past tense (in contrast to the similar sentiments expressed in the present tense in Psalm 42), and past tense fits the context here. The time of yearning and fainting is over, as the psalmist stands at the threshold of God's house (v. 10) and marvels at what he sees (vv. 1, 3-4).

[139] See Deut 2:11, 20-21; Josh 11:21-22; 12:4; 14:12; Isa 14:9; see also Heiser, *Unseen Realm*, 221-231.

[140] See Goldingay, *Psalms 42–89*, 593.

Are you currently receiving consistent input from mature believers to help you develop your spiritual gifts and leadership ability? What sort of mentorship are you able to provide for newer believers?

_____

_____

_____

_____

EYES ON THE PRIZE

> *For better is a day in your courts than a thousand elsewhere;*
> *I would rather stand at the threshold in the house of my God*
> *than dwell in the tents of wickedness. (v. 10)*

It is with good reason that many believers have committed verse 10 to memory. The psalmist's testimony helps to remind us where we draw our life, joy, and strength from, lest we allow "the cares of the age and the lure of wealth" to entangle us (Matt 13:22). God's presence really is better than anything the world has to offer, as indeed every good thing in the world points back to Him as its Source.

A parable has been told of a Christian who, before he died, was informed that he could bring one suitcase of earthly possessions with him to heaven. Wanting to maximize the value of what he could carry, and with hopes of a beneficial exchange upon arrival, he converted his assets into solid gold ingots and packed them into a suitcase. When he died and the angels escorted him to the gates of heaven, St. Peter asked the man what he had chosen to bring. The man then opened his suitcase to show Peter the shining bricks. Upon seeing them, the apostle scratched his head in perplexity and asked, "So you brought . . . pavement?"

Obviously this story takes a few liberties, but it illustrates our point nonetheless. All the worldly riches one might amass won't amount to a pile of paving stones in heaven, and many people's most ardent pursuits will yield nothing of eternal value whatsoever. Indeed, those who "dwell in the tents of wickedness" will not enter God's Kingdom at all; they will be sent away to where there is wailing and gnashing of teeth. As Psalm 1 informs us, "The way of the wicked will fail" (1:6). However, there is rejoicing in the assurance that Yahweh gives "grace and glory" and "does not withhold good from those who walk in integrity" (v. 11).

So let us heed this psalm's testimony of the surpassing goodness of God's house, and let us continually focus our attention on what will prove enduringly valuable, as the apostle Paul also exhorts us:

> If then you have been raised up with the Messiah, seek the things above, where the Messiah is seated in the glory of God. Think about what is above, not what is on the earth; for you have died, and your life is hidden with the Messiah in God. (Col 3:1-3)

Look at your calendar and consider how you are investing your time and energy. What will you look back on from eternity's perspective as time wasted? What changes might you make now to redeem the time that remains ahead of you?

DAY 5: PSALM 85

Psalm 85 is another Korahite psalm. A prominently recurring word in this psalm is *shub*, meaning "to turn/return/restore." This is a prayer that Yahweh's blessing would return upon the land, that He would turn away His anger, and that His people would be reconciled to Him and not return to the foolish ways that brought them under judgment. The form of judgment in view seems to be drought and food shortage (v. 12), but the psalm is not otherwise tied to any distinct historical setting.

FOR THE DIRECTOR. OF THE SONS OF KORAH. A PSALM.

1 *You have favored, Yahweh, your land;*
   you have wrought the restoration[141] of Jacob.
2 *You have lifted the iniquity of your people;*
   you have covered all their sin. Selah
3 *You have withdrawn all your fury;*
   you have turned back from your burning anger.
4 *Restore us, God of our salvation,*
   and annul your vexation with us.
5 *Is it forever that you will be angry at us?*
   Will you draw out your anger to generation after generation?
6 *Is it not you who will turn and revive us,*
   that your people may rejoice in you?
7 *Show us, Yahweh, your loyalty,*
   and give us your salvation.

---

[141] This verse uses a good deal of wordplay in the Hebrew. In the first line, the verb for "favor" (*ratsah*) resembles the noun for "land" (*'erets*), and in the second line, the verb and object come from the same root—a literal rendering would be something like "You have turned the turning of Jacob," which clearly doesn't come across well in translation. This same root (*shub*) recurs in verse 4 ("restore") and verse 6 ("turn").

> ^{8} *Let me hear what God, Yahweh, will say,*
> *for he will speak peace*
> *to his people, to his loyal ones,*
> *and they shall not return to folly.*
> ^{9} *Indeed, his salvation is near to those who fear him,*
> *so that glory may dwell in our land.*
> ^{10} *Loyalty and faithfulness have met;*
> *righteousness and peace have kissed.*
> ^{11} *Faithfulness shall spring up from the earth,*
> *as righteousness from the heavens has looked down.*
> ^{12} *Yes, Yahweh will give what is good,*
> *and our land will give its produce.*
> ^{13} *Righteousness will go before him*
> *as he sets his feet on the path.*

THE PEOPLE AND THE LAND

In our study of Psalm 67 in Lesson 5, we related how a group of Christians in Fiji, for whom the notions of "people" and "land" are encapsulated in the same word, have been experiencing the miraculous restoration of both social harmony and natural resources wherever people have repented of their sins and reconsecrated their land to God. This is precisely the sort of dynamic Psalm 85 has in view, beginning with the recollection that Yahweh had previously forgiven His people's sins and favored their land (vv. 1-3).

At present, the people are suffering under what they discern to be God's anger (vv. 4-5), which they have brought upon themselves by way of "folly" (v. 8). Whatever errant ways may have led to the current crisis, it should come as no surprise that God would punish sin with a poor harvest (see v. 12), as He explicitly named the fruitfulness or unfruitfulness of the land among the blessings and curses contingent on Israel's covenant obedience (Deut 28:2-5, 15-18, 38-40).

In Ezekiel 22, God responds to Israel's sin by telling the prophet to proclaim His judgment over the land: "Son of Adam, say to her, 'You are a land that is not cleansed or rained on in the day of indignation'" (Ezek 22:24). God then catalogs the sins committed in the land, beginning with the leaders—prophets, priests, and princes who have profaned what is holy and shed blood for selfish gain (Ezek 22:25-28)—and expanding to the people at large who have extorted, robbed, and otherwise oppressed the lowly, the needy, and the sojourner (Ezek 22:29). Then, in an often excerpted and quoted pronouncement, God declares, "I sought a man among them to build up the wall and stand in the gap before me on behalf of the land, to avert its destruction, but I found none" (Ezek 22:30).

What do we learn from this? We see that as it goes with leadership, so it goes with the people; and as it goes with the people, so it goes with the land. If we want God's blessing to be upon our land, it is imperative that we be proactive in raising up leaders who will walk in integrity and the fear of the Lord. Just as the praying community in Psalm 85 asks God, "Is it not you who will turn and revive us?" (v. 6), so they declare the answer: "Indeed, his salvation is near to those who fear him, so that glory may dwell in our land" (v. 9).

In recognition of the profound impact of leadership for the better or worse of society, Christian Union seeks to develop and connect transformative Christian leaders at America's most influential universities and in key cities.[142] **What are you doing within your sphere of influence (e.g., your family, friend group, church, school, or business) to develop a culture around what God values and requires?**

RECONCILIATION IN CHRIST

Loyalty and faithfulness have met;
righteousness and peace have kissed.
Faithfulness shall spring up from the earth,
as righteousness from the heavens has looked down. (vv. 10-11)

Healing and wholeness come to the land when God finds that His loyalty is met with our faithfulness. When we walk in righteousness, He embraces us with His *shalom* (translated "peace" here, but the term also refers more generally to well-being). The sweet imagery of these verses encourages us to pursue righteousness and be as faithful as we possibly can be, but the psalm also recognizes that we need God's grace to overcome our weakness. "Yes, Yahweh will give what is good," verse 12 declares, not because we pulled ourselves together by our own unaided willpower, but because He, in His loyalty, has turned us, revived us, and given us His salvation (vv. 6-7).

The ultimate meeting place of God's loyalty and human faithfulness (or of righteousness and peace) is in the person of Jesus Christ. Thus, in verse 11, the psalmist looks forward to His coming and continues in that same anticipation through the final pronouncement that "righteousness will go before him as he sets his feet on the path" (v. 13).

Jesus "set his feet on the path" as the "blessed man" who walked in the way God prescribed (Ps 1)[143] and who blazed the trail for us to follow (Heb 12:2). Not only has He shown us the way, He *is* the Way by which we come to the Father (John 14:6). When we let our old selves die and take up a new identity *in* Christ Jesus, His righteousness becomes our righteousness, His

---

[142] If you would like to partner with us in that work, please visit our website at ChristianUnion.org.
[143] See *Psalms 1–41: A Christian Union Bible Study*, Lesson 2, Day 1.

faithful Spirit infuses His character into us, and we find ourselves reconciled to God in Him, receiving peace through the blood of His cross (Col 1:20).

As you reflect on Jesus' loyalty, faithfulness, righteousness, and peace, and as you apply yourself to "furnish your faith with virtue" (2 Pet 1:5), what virtue(s) are you most keenly endeavoring to develop at present? What measures have you taken to cultivate the virtue(s) you seek?

_____

_____

_____

_____

Lesson Review

As the Psalms have consistently maintained, righteousness and faithful obedience are absolute requirements for those who would dwell in God's house. Psalms 81–83 testify to God's judgment on those who refuse to listen to and obey His directives, even as Psalm 81 makes plain that God would much rather see His people repent than suffer the consequences of sin. Psalm 84 is a beacon of hope, declaring not only that the pilgrim finds joy and rest in God's house but also that those who set their hearts to seek the Lord will transform the weary land through which they journey, bringing God's blessings upon it. Psalm 85 reminds us that we need to be transformed, "turned" by the grace of God and made new in Christ Jesus, so that we may be clothed in righteousness and learn to walk in the obedience of faith. In sum, we are reminded that God's blessings flow from His presence as we walk in step with Him, faithfully doing as He, in His righteousness and wisdom, instructs us. We are also reminded of His instruction, highlighted in two psalms of pilgrimage (Pss 81, 84), that we are to gather regularly with other believers for dedicated times of fellowship, admonishment, and encouragement.

10

LESSON TEN:
Psalms 86–89

We now come to the end of Book 3 of the Psalms (Pss 73–89), where we find resolute hope amid a very dark hour. Psalm 86 recalls the Davidic laments of Books 1 and 2 as the king cries to God for rescue from an assembly of enemies. Psalm 87 speaks prophetically of the glorious day when the Gentiles would be counted among God's people. Meanwhile, Psalm 88 expresses the pain of abandonment experienced by Yahweh's suffering Servant. Finally, Psalm 89 combines the celebration of Yahweh's faithfulness with bewilderment at His having allowed Jerusalem and the Davidic monarchy to fall. In sum, these psalms cry out for God to prove His righteousness, which He would do in sending Jesus to fulfill His promises, reign as King forever, and open the way of salvation for people from every nation (see Rom 3:21-26).

DAY 1: PSALM 86

Psalm 86 is the only prayer in Book 3 attributed to David (recall that the collection of David's prayers "ended" with Psalm 72, the last psalm of Book 2). This lament reminds us of the precarious position of David's line and the promise made to him of an unending dynasty (which Psalm 89 will address explicitly). In the present context, this particular prayer is appropriate, as it is a prayer for help in a time of distress. Meanwhile, David himself represents the messianic hope to which the remaining psalms in this section must look forward.

A PRAYER OF DAVID.

> ¹ *Extend, Yahweh, your ear; answer me,*
> *for I am lowly and in need.*
> ² *Watch over my soul, for I am loyal;*
> *save your servant—you are my God—*
> *who trusts in you.*
> ³ *Be gracious to me, my Lord,*
> *for to you I call all day long.*
> ⁴ *Gladden the soul of your servant,*
> *for to you, my Lord, I lift up my soul.*

⁵ *For you, my Lord, are good and forgiving,*
  and abounding in loyalty to all who call to you.

⁶ *Listen, Yahweh, to my prayer,*
  and attend to the sound of my supplication.

⁷ *On the day of my distress, I call to you,*
  for you answer me.

⁸ *There is none like you among the gods, my Lord,*
  and nothing like your deeds.

⁹ *All nations, which you have made,*
  shall come in and bow down before you, my Lord,
  and glorify your name.

¹⁰ *For great you are, and worker of wonders;*
  you alone are God.

¹¹ *Teach me, Yahweh, your way;*
  I will walk in your faithfulness;
  unite my heart to fear your name.

¹² *I will acknowledge you, my Lord, my God, with all my heart,*
  and may I glorify your name forever.

¹³ *For your loyalty is great over me,*
  and you have delivered my soul from deepest Sheol.

¹⁴ *God, presumptuous ones have risen against me,*
  and a terrifying assembly seek my life;
  they do not set you before themselves.

¹⁵ *But you, my Lord, are a compassionate and gracious God,*
  slow to anger and abounding in loyalty and faithfulness.

¹⁶ *Turn to me and be gracious to me;*
  give your strength to your servant, and save the son of your handmaiden.

¹⁷ *Do with me a sign for good,*
  that my haters may see it and be ashamed,
  because you, Yahweh, have helped me and comforted me.

PETITION AND PRAISE

Like many of David's psalms we studied in earlier lessons, Psalm 86 is composed in the form of a chiasm,[144] with concentric motion from an outer frame or context toward a central point of focus. In this case, the context is an immediate need for help (lines A and A' below), while the heart of the prayer (line E) is that the psalmist might learn God's ways and honor His Name forever. We may outline the psalm as follows:

---

[144] See Lesson 3, Days 4 and 5. For several more examples, see *Psalms 1–41: A Christian Union Bible Study*.

A. Save "your servant" (vv. 1-4)

  B. You are "abounding in loyalty" (vv. 5-6)

    C. The present crisis ("the day of my distress") (v. 7)

      D. All nations shall "glorify your name" (vv. 8-10)

        E. Teach me to honor your name (v. 11)

      D'. Let me "glorify your name" (vv. 12-13)

    C'. The present crisis (enemies "seek my life") (v. 14)

  B'. You are "abounding in loyalty" (v. 15)

A'. Save "your servant" (vv. 16-17)[145]

The flow of this composition follows the understanding that we live for God's purposes, which extend far beyond ourselves. As Yahweh brought renown to His Name by delivering a whole nation out of bondage in Egypt (Exod 7:5; 9:16), so His every saving act at an individual level is an opportunity to give Him glory. Here David stands in need of help *so that* he can faithfully execute his duties as God's servant, ever learning his Lord's ways and giving honor to His Name.

When was the last time God got you out of a tight spot? How did you use that opportunity to give Him recognition—to honor His Name, as David prays here?

FAITHFULNESS IS GOD'S GIFT

Like the psalm as a whole, the central verse (v. 11) forms a mini-chiasm, a sandwich of imperative-vow-imperative:

Teach me, Yahweh, your way;
   I will walk in your faithfulness;
unite my heart to fear your name.

David's intention is to walk in God's faithfulness (or truth; Hebrew *'emeth*). This must be our aim as well. When Paul wrote his epistle to the Romans, he stated that the purpose of his

---

145 Adapted from Tate, *Psalms 51–100*, 378.

apostleship was to bring about, among all nations, faithful obedience to God for the sake of His Name (Rom 1:5; see also Rom 16:26).[146] And like Paul, David understands that to walk faithfully will require the help of God's grace—hence the twin imperatives: "Teach me . . . your way" and "Unite my heart."

This latter phrase may sound unusual. But we know that it is not good to have a divided heart or to be double-minded (Ps 12:2; Jas 1:8); rather, we are to love, serve, and (in this case) fear God with singleness of heart, which is to say, wholeheartedly. We can do that, David recognizes, only if God works the requisite transformation in us.

So also, verse 12 underscores the need for God's help to do what honors Him. While the first verb in verse 12 is indicative ("I will acknowledge you"), the second is cohortative[147] ("May I glorify your name"). In other words, it is within our power to verbalize gratitude for what God has done, but in order to give His Name the glory it deserves, we will need the Holy Spirit to sanctify and empower us.

David's hopes for an affirmative answer to his prayer rest, as usual, on the nature of God Himself: He is "good," "forgiving," "compassionate," "gracious," "slow to anger," and "abounding in loyalty" to all who seek Him (vv. 5, 15).

As for those who don't seek Yahweh—as evidenced by their hatred for His servant—David hopes that they will be ashamed of having opposed God when He demonstrates His love for the one they have scorned. Recall the mocking voices at the cross—"Let [God] deliver him, if he delights in him" (22:8; see Matt 27:43)—and recall the intense contrition that was expressed when Peter testified that God had indeed raised from the dead the One they so abused (Acts 2:22-41). Praise God, three thousand people repented and were saved that day. May your life be marked by such faithfulness that God's signs of approval would serve to correct those who mistreat you.

God loves you and has always loved you, even before the world was made (Eph 1:4). But your actions can please or displease Him (Rom 8:8; Gal 1:10; 1 Thes 2:14-16; 4:1). When do you most experience signs of God's pleasure? Is there any doubtful habit in your life that He would rather you put away?

---

[146] The Greek phrase *eis hypakoēn pisteōs* ("unto obedience of faith") indicates the kind of obedience that proceeds from faith, hence "faithful obedience," though translations of this phrase vary.

[147] Hebrew grammarians use this term for first-person exhortations, typically translated "may I/we" or "let me/us"; here, it is used to express the desired outcome of the psalmist's acknowledgment.

DAY 2: PSALM 87

This Korahite psalm has been described as "terse, abrupt, enigmatic, like a prophetic oracle"[148]—because it *is* a prophetic oracle.[149] Building on the transnational outlook of Psalm 86:8-9, and in anticipation of the Messiah's completed mission, Psalm 87 "depicts Zion as the metropolis of the universal kingdom of God, into which all nations are adopted as citizens. The franchise of Zion is conferred upon them as though it were theirs by right of birth."[150]

OF THE SONS OF KORAH. A PSALM. A SONG.

1   *His foundation is on holy mountains.*
2   *Yahweh loves the gates of Zion*
        more than all the dwellings of Jacob.
3   *Glorious things are spoken of you,*
        City of God! Selah
4   *I will mention Rahab and Babylon to those who know me;*
        behold, Philistia and Tyre, and also Cush:
        "This one was born[151] *there."*
5   *And to Zion it shall be said,*
        "Each was born in her,
        and the Most High himself will establish her."
6   *Yahweh will record in the register of the peoples:*
        "This one was born there." Selah
7   *And they sing as they play the pipe:*
        "All my springs are in you."

BORN IN ZION

Do not be astonished that I said to you, "It is necessary that you be born again."[152]
(John 3:7)

Like these words to Nicodemus, which the Pharisee was unable to comprehend, Psalm 87 speaks of the mystery that was revealed in Christ Jesus: that as many as are "baptized into his death" find new life and a new identity in Him, having been predestined for adoption in Him before the foundation of the world (Rom 6:3-5; 2 Cor 5:17; Eph 1:4-5).

---

[148] A. F. Kirkpatrick, *The Book of Psalms: With Introduction and Notes* (Cambridge: Cambridge University Press, 1902), 518.
[149] Goldingay, *Psalms 42–89*, 632.
[150] Kirkpatrick, *Psalms*, 519.
[151] Or "fathered" (so throughout the psalm). The Hebrew verb *yalad*, when used in the active voice, can refer to either parent's role in bringing a child into the world (see, e.g., Gen 3:16; 4:18).
[152] Like the Hebrew verb for "born/fathered" in the psalm (noted above), the Greek verb *gennaō* does not distinguish between the father's and mother's roles in procreation (see, e.g., Matt 1:2; Luke 1:13).

Two ambiguities enshroud the mystery. First, Zion, the object of the psalmist's celebration, denotes both God's heavenly city and Jerusalem, the locus of God's reign on earth. Second, being "born" or "fathered"—in both the psalm and in Jesus' words to Nicodemus—is not restricted to natural procreation (see also 2:7). Hence the Bible speaks of God's chosen ones as His "sons" (Exod 4:22; Matt 5:9), and of the unregenerate as "sons of wickedness" (89:22) or "sons of the devil" (John 8:44; Acts 13:10). As John summarizes in the prologue of his Gospel, "To all who received [Jesus], he gave the right to become children of God—to those trusting in his name, who were born not by blood nor by the will of the flesh nor by the will of man but of God" (John 1:12-13).

No matter the circumstances of your natural birth, if you surrender your life to Jesus, you will be registered in heaven as a child of Zion and as a child of God. And you will gain all the authority and inheritances appropriate to that birthright.

To know what authority and privileges you have as a child of Zion and to prevent the enemy from denying you your birthright, you need to know the Scriptures and commit God's promises to memory. Is there a particular area of life in which you are now eager to step into your authority as a believer?

MANY WHO ARE LAST SHALL BE FIRST

> *I will mention Rahab and Babylon to those who know me;*
> *behold, Philistia and Tyre, and also Cush:*
> *"This one was born there." (v. 4)*

Rahab denotes a great sea dragon, and the title is used here as an epithet for Egypt.[153] The first nations listed are Israel's original enslaver (Egypt) and their latter-day conqueror (Babylon), followed by Canaanite neighbors who led them into idolatry (Philistia and Tyre). Meanwhile, Cush (Ethiopia) is emblematic of faraway places.[154] No nation is written out of God's redemption story.

This is not to say, by any means, that everyone from these nations will be saved. But in the end there will be "sons of Zion" from every nation, just as there are "sons of hell" from Jerusalem proper (Matt 23:15). All people have sinned, and all are offered the same means of grace (see Rom 11:32): There is "one Lord, one faith, one baptism, one God and Father of all" (Eph 4:5-6).

---

[153] See also Ps 89:10; Isa 30:7; 51:9-10.
[154] See Kidner, *Psalms 73–150,* 347.

What sorts of interactions have you had with Christians from other nations? Have you ever tried to distinguish the norms and values instilled in you by your own nation's culture from the Bible's norms and values?

DAY 3: PSALM 88

Psalm 88 is the bleakest of all the psalms. It speaks of death and dying, of descent to the underworld, and of a sense of total abandonment by God. The closest it gets to anything like hope is a series of questions to God (the expected answer to all of which is, sadly, *no*—but more on that in a moment) and the psalmist's refusal to give up praying (v. 13). Psalm 88 has long been understood as speaking for Jesus as He bore God's wrath (see v. 16) and died in our stead. It has also been a lifeline for many others, giving words to express raw pain to God in moments of grief so deep that hope feels lost.

A SONG. A PSALM OF THE SONS OF KORAH. FOR THE DIRECTOR. ON *MAKHALATH-LE'ANNOTH.*[155] A MASKIL OF HEMAN THE EZRAHITE.[156]

> *¹ Yahweh, God of my salvation,*
> *   on the night I cry out before you,*
> *² let my prayer come before you;*
> *   extend your ear to my cry.*
> *³ For my soul is sated with miseries,*
> *   and my life has come to Sheol.*
> *⁴ I am reckoned with those descending the pit;*
> *   I have become like a strong man without strength.*
> *⁵ Among the dead I am released, like the slain,*
> *   who lie in the grave,*
> *   whom you remember no more,*
> *   as they have been cut off by your hand.*
> *⁶ You have set me in the lowest pit,*
> *   in the dark places in the depths.*

---

155 The meaning of these words is uncertain. *Makhalath* appears only here and in the heading of Psalm 53. *Le'annoth* could mean "to be answered" (as in LXX), "for singing" (*The Hebrew and Aramaic Lexicon of the Old Testament* [*HALOT*], s.v. "ענה"), or "for affliction/humbling" (as in the NLT).

156 Heman was one of David's appointed music leaders from among the descendants of Korah (1 Chr 6:31-37).

[7] *Upon me has lain your wrath,*
    and with all your waves you have put me down. Selah
[8] *You have put my friends far from me;*
    you have made me an abomination to them,
    shut up so I cannot get out;
[9] *My eye grows faint from my affliction;*
    I have called you, Yahweh, every day;
    I have spread out my hands to you.
[10] *Will you do a wonder for the dead?*
    Will the Rephaim rise and acknowledge you? Selah
[11] *Will your loyalty be declared in the grave?*
    Your faithfulness in Abaddon?
[12] *Will your wonder be made known in the darkness,*
    or your righteousness in the land of forgetfulness?
[13] *But I—to you, Yahweh, I have cried out,*
    and in the morning my prayer will come before you.
[14] *Why, Yahweh, do you reject my soul,*
    hide your face from me?
[15] *I have been lowly and expiring from boyhood;*
    I have borne your terrors; I am numb.
[16] *Your burnings of anger have swept over me;*
    your terrors have annihilated me.
[17] *They have surrounded me like waters all day long;*
    they have encompassed me altogether.
[18] *You have put lover and friend far away from me;*
    those who know me . . . darkness.

IS THIS THE END?

In Psalm 22, we saw the movement from the moment of agony on the cross—"My God, my God, why have you abandoned me?" (22:1)—to the joyous praise of resurrection: "You have answered me!" (22:21). Psalm 88 brings us to a similar place of intense suffering, when all seems lost—"My soul is sated with miseries, and my life has come to Sheol" (v. 3). But this time, the prayer ends with the psalmist still in darkness.

Thomas H. Troeger, professor emeritus at Yale Divinity School as well as a pastor and a prolific hymn writer, tells of a time he went to the hospital to visit a woman from his church. She was heartbroken and angry, suffering in the face of disease and feeling abandoned by God. The kindly pastor asked if he might sit with her for a while and read a psalm. Without any signs of expecting this to do much good, the woman nonetheless said that he could. So he began to read Psalm 88. As he did so, he could see the woman paying very close attention. And when he finished, she eagerly took the book from his hands, reading and rereading the psalm for herself. Stunned that such words of raw pain and despair addressed to God could be found *in the Bible*, she clung to this prayer as her own all that day. It was the only prayer she felt she could honestly pray. In time, as she wrestled with God through Psalm 88, she found her faith and hope returning, and she was able to move on to other prayers.[157]

People sometimes feel that God has left them for dead but don't know they have permission to tell Him that. It may seem impious to say to God, "I am . . . like the slain . . . whom you remember no more. . . . You have set me in the lowest pit . . ." (vv. 5-6). But that is what the psalmist says, and these words are preserved in the Bible for our edification.

Have you ever gone through a season when you were blinded by pain and unable to see hope? If so, how did God meet you with grace?

_____

_____

_____

_____

LOOKING INTO THE ABYSS

> *Will you do a wonder for the dead?*
> *Will the Rephaim rise and acknowledge you?*
> *Will your loyalty be declared in the grave?*
> *Your faithfulness in Abaddon?*
> *Will your wonder be made known in the darkness,*
> *or your righteousness in the land of forgetfulness? (vv. 10-12)*

The irony of these rhetorical questions is that while the assumed answer to each of them is *no*, in Christ Jesus each question finds its *yes*. This is most obviously the case with the first question, as Jesus was miraculously raised from the dead. The remaining questions connect with what Peter tells us Jesus did after being put to death in the flesh—namely, He went and made an announcement to "the spirits in prison . . . who disobeyed in time past . . . in the days of Noah" (1 Pet 3:18-20). These are the Rephaim (also known as the Nephilim),[158] the spawn of rebellious angels who fueled human depravity (Gen 6:1-5). The book of Enoch, which was well known to the New Testament writers (and which the Ethiopian Orthodox Church includes in its canon of Scripture), identifies the spirits of dead Rephaim with what the New Testament writers call "unclean spirits" and "demons."[159]

---

157 Thomas H. Troeger, spoken remarks in a lecture at Yale Divinity School, spring 2013.
158 Deut 2:10-11, 20-21; Num 13:32-33; see also Heiser, *Unseen Realm*, 195, 335-339.
159 Heiser, *Unseen Realm*, 325.

In short, Jesus did declare God's loyalty in the grave and did make known His wonders in the darkness. And while the unclean spirits may not have wished to, they could not help but "confess that Jesus Christ is Lord, to the glory of God the Father" (Phil 2:11; see also Mark 1:24; 5:7).

The psalmist goes on to ask why he had to endure God's anger (vv. 14-18). Insofar as the psalm anticipates the suffering and death of Jesus, how would you answer that question (see Isa 52:13–53:12)?

CONCLUDING REFLECTION

The resurrection of Jesus fundamentally changes the way we understand suffering, grief, and death. We are called to have confident assurance in God's promise to bring us through every trial, and we should never be in total despair. But God may test us right up to the breaking point as He seeks to establish us in faith. Psalm 88 can be tremendously helpful as a prayer for someone right on the edge of that breaking point. It is the prayer of someone who doesn't know what else to say besides "Please listen" (see v. 2) and "I am numb" (v. 15) but who persists in calling out to God rather than giving up.

May the Lord save you from the time of trial, and may your hope in the Resurrection never fade.

DAY 4: PSALM 89 (PART 1)

Psalm 89 is the prayer of a man whose experience does not accord with his expectations: Though he proclaims Yahweh's eternal loyalty and faithfulness, recalls His history of helping Israel, and quotes God's own words of promise to David, the psalmist turns suddenly to call out the apparent failure of God's promised faithfulness: "You have spurned and rejected . . . your anointed. You have renounced the covenant of your servant" (vv. 38-39). What do we do when our experience seems to contradict God's word? Psalm 89 offers essential understanding for navigating a crisis of faith.

A MASKIL OF ETHAN THE EZRAHITE.[160]

1 *Of Yahweh's loyalties I shall sing forever;*
    to generation after generation I will make known your faithfulness with my mouth.

2 *For I have said, "Loyalty has built the heavens forever;*
    your faithfulness is established in them."

3 *"I have made a covenant with my chosen one;*
    I have sworn to David my servant:

4 *'I will establish your offspring forever*
    and build your throne for generation after generation.'" Selah

5 *So the heavens proclaim your wonder, Yahweh,*
    and your faithfulness in the assembly of holy ones.

6 *For who in the clouds can be set alongside Yahweh?*
    Who is like Yahweh among the sons of God—

7 *God, inspiring great terror in the council of the holy ones,*
    and feared above all who are around him?

8 *Yahweh, God of Hosts, who is like you, mighty Yah,*
    with your faithfulness all around you?

9 *You rule over the rising of the sea;*
    when it lifts its waves, you still them.

10 *You have crushed Rahab as one slain;*
    with your mighty arm you have scattered your enemies.

11 *Yours are the heavens, yours also the earth;*
    the world and what fills it: You established them.

12 *North and south:[161] You created them;*
    Tabor and Hermon: In your name they resound.

13 *Yours is an arm with strength;*
    your hand is powerful;
    your right hand reaches high.

14 *Righteousness and justice are the foundation of your throne;*
    loyalty and faithfulness are before your face.

15 *Blessed are the people who know the shout;[162]*
    Yahweh, in the light of your face they will walk.

16 *In your name they shall rejoice all day long,*
    and in your righteousness they shall be exalted.

---

160 If this Ethan is the contemporary of David mentioned in 1 Chronicles 15:17 (note the mention of Heman in that same verse and in the heading of Psalm 88), he may have written verses 1-37, while the remainder of the psalm may be a reflection on his words by another author after the Exile.

161 Or "Zaphon and the sea," Zaphon being the mountain of God in the north (see Ps 48:2; Isa 14:13), and following LXX in reading "sea" (Hebrew *yam/yammim*) in place of MT's "south" (*yamin*).

162 The Hebrew word *teru'ah* can indicate a "shout or blast of war, alarm, or joy" (BDB, s.v. "תְּרוּעָה"). Hence, this phrase may indicate "those who hear the joyful call to worship" (NLT) or those who recognize the call to battle and join Yahweh's forces. Of course, these may be one and the same. Observe that the preceding verses address Yahweh as powerful Ruler and Commander, while the following verse speaks of the joy of the saints.

¹⁷ For you are their glorious strength,
   and by your favor you raise our horn.

¹⁸ For Yahweh's is our shield,
   and to the Holy One of Israel belongs our king.

¹⁹ You spoke once in a vision to your loyal ones, and you said:
   "I have put help on a mighty one;
   I have raised up a chosen one from the people.

²⁰ I found David, my servant;
   with my holy oil I anointed him,

²¹ whom my hand will support.
   Indeed, my arm will strengthen him.

²² No enemy shall exploit him,
   nor shall a son of wickedness humble him,

²³ but I will pound his foes before him,
   and those who hate him, I will strike.

²⁴ My faithfulness and my loyalty will be with him,
   and in my name his horn will be uplifted.

²⁵ And I will set his hand upon the sea,
   his right hand upon the rivers.

²⁶ He will call me: 'You are my Father,
   my God and the rock of my salvation.'

²⁷ And I will make him the firstborn,
   the highest of the kings of the earth.

²⁸ Forever I will maintain my loyalty to him,
   and my covenant will prove reliable for him.

²⁹ I will appoint his offspring forever,
   and his throne as the days of the heavens.

³⁰ If his sons forsake my instruction
   and do not walk by my judgments,

³¹ if they profane my ordinances
   and do not keep my commandments,

³² then I will attend to their rebellion with the rod,
   to their iniquities with plagues.

³³ But my loyalty I will not break off of him,
   and I will not betray my faithfulness.

³⁴ I will not profane my covenant,
   and what has come forth from my lips I will not change.

³⁵ Once have I sworn by my holiness:
   If I should lie to David . . .

³⁶ His offspring shall be forever,
   and his throne like the sun before me.

> ^{37} *Like the moon he shall be established forever,*
> *with a witness in the clouds proving true.* "Selah
> . . .

GOD IS FAITHFUL

> *Of Yahweh's loyalties I shall sing forever;*
> *to generation after generation I will make known your faithfulness with my mouth. (v. 1)*

As we have seen throughout the Psalms, loyalty and faithfulness are defining attributes of God's character. On Day 1 of this lesson, in Psalm 86:15, we heard David affirming God's self-description to Moses:

> Yahweh, Yahweh, God compassionate and gracious,
> slow to anger and abounding in loyalty and faithfulness,
> who maintains loyalty to the thousandth generation,
> who takes away iniquity and rebellion and sin;
> though in acquitting he does not leave unpunished,
> visiting the iniquity of the fathers upon children and upon children's children,
> to the third and to the fourth generation. (Exod 34:6-7)

In Psalm 89, the words *loyalty* and *faithfulness* each occur eight times. Verses 30-32 affirm God's justice in disciplining those who go astray, but verses 33-34 immediately assert that the imposition of judgment does not mean an end of God's covenant faithfulness to David. God is no despot. His will is not to destroy but to raise up a people who walk by faith in His holiness and righteousness. Thus, while His unique power as the Creator would seem sufficient to establish His rulership over creation (vv. 6-13), the psalm declares that "righteousness and justice are the foundation of [his] throne" and that "loyalty and faithfulness are before [his] face" (v. 14). If we wish to stand before God, we must acquire these virtues, which His Word and Spirit work to impart to us.

In what area(s) of faithfulness do you find God's Spirit most stretching and strengthening you these days?

GOD'S PROMISE TO DAVID

> *I will establish your offspring forever*
>   *and build your throne for generation after generation. (v. 4)*

The context in which God made this promise to David is recorded in 2 Samuel 7. David wished to build a house for Yahweh (i.e., a temple), but Yahweh flipped the script: Playing on the various meanings of the word *house*, He declared: "Yahweh will make you a house [household/ family/lineage]. . . . I will raise up your offspring after you . . . and I will establish the throne of his kingdom forever" (2 Sam 7:11-13).

The obvious way to understand this promise during the days of the ancient monarchy would have been in terms of an unending dynastic succession. Solomon's reign marked the initial fulfillment of the promise, and a series of direct descendants did hold the throne of Judah (though no longer of all Israel) until the Babylonian captivity. On this reading, the fall of the monarchy is unthinkable; hence, the psalmist accuses God of renouncing His covenant with David (v. 39).

But there is another way to understand the "offspring" (or "seed") that God vowed to establish forever. The Hebrew noun is grammatically singular, and from this side of the Cross we can see that it is the one Son of David, not an ongoing series of descendants, who will reign forever. This is precisely how Paul reads God's promise of blessing through the *offspring* of Abraham (Gal 3:16).

Paul tells us that *all* of God's promises are fulfilled in Jesus (2 Cor 1:20). Besides the promises to David and Abraham we have just mentioned, what are some other old-covenant promises that come to mind? How do they point to Jesus?

DAY 5: PSALM 89 (PART 2)

Today we continue with Psalm 89, beginning with the turning point at which God's loyalty to David appears to have failed.

> . . .
>
> 38   *But you have spurned and rejected;*
>   *you have become furious with your anointed.*

39   *You have renounced the covenant of your servant;*
      you have laid his crown in the dirt.
40   *You have breached all his walls,*
      laid his fortifications to ruin.
41   *All passersby have plundered him;*
      he has become a reproach to his neighbors.
42   *You have raised the right hand of his adversaries,*
      gladdened all his enemies.
43   *Yes, you turn back the edge of his sword;*[163]
      you have not upheld him in battle.
44   *You have put an end to his splendor,*
      and his throne you have thrown down to the ground.
45   *You have shortened the days of his youthful vigor;*
      you have clothed him with shame. Selah
46   *How long, Yahweh? Will you hide forever?*
      How long will your anger burn like fire?
47   *Remember me, of what duration I am,*
      for what nothingness you have created all the sons of Adam.
48   *Who is the man who can live and not see death,*
      who can deliver his soul from the hand of Sheol? Selah
49   *Where are your former loyalties, my Lord?*
      You swore to David by your faithfulness.
50   *Call to mind, my Lord, the reproach of your servants;*
      I carry in my bosom all the many peoples,
51   *because your enemies have reproached, Yahweh,*
      because they have reproached the steps of your anointed.
52   *Blessed be Yahweh forever.*
      Amen and Amen!

UNSEEING AND CONFUSED

The psalmist could not see ahead to the day when Jesus would come through David's line and take up His everlasting place as the King of kings. Therefore, seeing the monarchy overthrown, the psalmist could only surmise that God had gone back on His promise. And that is a problem.

Though we have the luxury of hindsight in this case—we can see how God did fulfill His promise in King Jesus—many Christians over the years have found themselves in similar positions to that of the psalmist. Some have developed theological arguments to explain why we don't see God doing what the Scriptures would lead us to expect.

---

[163] Literally, "the flint of his sword."

Perhaps the most prominent point of tension concerns healing. The Scriptures tell us in very plain language that Jesus is both willing and able to heal whoever comes to Him. In Mark 1:40-45, a leper came to Jesus, pleading, "If you are willing, you can make me clean." Jesus' response was "I am willing. Be clean." And immediately the man was healed. Jesus sent out His disciples with "power and authority over all demons and to heal diseases" (Luke 9:1)— He first sent the twelve, then seventy-two others (Luke 10:1, 9), and finally He declared, "Truly, truly, I tell you, whoever trusts in me will do the same works that I do, and will do greater than these, because I am going to the Father" (John 14:12; see also Matt 28:18-20; Mark 16:17-18).

All of us, however, have prayed for sick people who didn't get healed. What do we do with that dissonance? One option is to devise a new theology to explain why God no longer needs to grant physical healings. But the Scriptures are too clear: Jesus told His followers to go out, proclaim the Kingdom of God, heal the sick, raise the dead, cast out demons, and cleanse lepers (Matt 10:7-8), and He commissioned them to keep at it until the end of the world (Matt 28:18-20). Paul told the church to seek gifts of healings and miracles (1 Cor 12:8-10; 14:1). What's more, we do still see *some* of the sick healed, some of the dead raised, some lepers cleansed, and some delivered of demons, through the ministry of believers all around the world. But if some, why not all?

When Jesus descended the mountain where He had been transfigured before Peter, James, and John, He found the other nine disciples with an epileptic boy they had tried and failed to heal (Matt 17:14-20; Mark 9:14-29; Luke 9:37-43). Did they reason that it wasn't God's will to heal the boy? No. Jesus came and healed him by delivering him from an evil spirit. Afterward, the disciples did something important: They came to Jesus and asked why they couldn't deliver the boy (Matt 17:19; Mark 9:28). And they received an answer.

We don't always know why some prayers seem to work while others seem not to. There could be many different reasons in different cases. But Jesus knows, and He invites you to pursue Him in the secret place of prayer until you see a breakthrough. Never forget the parable of the persistent widow (Luke 18:1-8). Do not give up. Our God is not an unjust judge, but "righteousness and justice are the foundation of [his] throne; loyalty and faithfulness are before [his] face" (v. 14). Will your faith rise up to meet Him?

What prayers have you given up on? Are you willing to press in until you have the mind of Christ on those matters?

Lesson Review

These last four psalms of Book 3 have all addressed God's messianic promises and their fulfillment. After being reintroduced to David in Psalm 86, we saw a preview in Psalm 87 of the adoption of heathen nations into the Kingdom, which would only be made possible through the death and resurrection of Jesus—the Son of David—making way for the new birth by His Spirit. Psalm 88 took us with Jesus to the depths of the pit as He bore our sins there. Finally, Psalm 89 pointed to something that the psalmist could not yet see but that has now been revealed: All of God's promises are fulfilled in Christ Jesus.

Final Thoughts

This study has covered Books 2 and 3 of the Psalms (Pss 42–89), which have taken us from the depths of depression (Pss 42–43) to joyful anticipation of the heavenly wedding banquet (Ps 45) and from the agonies of defeat (Ps 44) to the assurance of ultimate victory and an end to all wars (Ps 46)—and back to defeat (Pss 74, 79) and the brink of despair (Pss 88–89). While Book 2 (Pss 42–72) still spoke from David's life and experience with God, Book 3 (Pss 73–89) brought us forward to the destruction of the kingdoms of Israel and Judah generations later. From here, we eagerly await the coming of the new King who would fulfill all that God had spoken concerning His Anointed One, great David's greater Son.

From our vantage point as readers in the twenty-first century, we still await the return of our King who will come in glory to judge the living and the dead and bring the Kingdom—which has already been inaugurated—in all its fullness. We do not know when that day will come, but we can prepare for it by walking in holiness (2 Pet 3:11-12), by being filled with the Holy Spirit (Eph 5:18) as the wise bridesmaids of Jesus' parable kept their lamps filled with oil (Matt 25:1-13), and by proclaiming the gospel in all the earth (Matt 24:14).

Before you close this book, pray for God to rekindle your eager longing for the fullness of His Kingdom. Allow Him to speak to you about anything He would have you do to align yourself with His plans and to help your neighbors get ready for the day that draws ever nearer. Use the space below to record any closing reflections of your own.

PSALM SUMMARY CHART: PSALMS 42–89

Psalm	Psalm Summary	What It Reveals about God
42–43	A self-exhortation to hope in God when feeling depressed	God commands His loyalty and sends His light and truth to guide us
44	A cry for restoration when God's people seem abandoned to defeat	God sometimes hides His face for reasons we may not immediately understand
45	A wedding song for the King	God is righteous; defends truth, humility, and righteousness; and covets His bride's beauty
46	The celebration of an end to war; God is with us	God is readily available as our refuge, strength, and help in times of trouble
47	Let all the peoples of the earth praise Yahweh	God is awesome, the King over all the earth
48	A celebration of God's presence guarding the holy city	God is loyal to His people forever and frightening to His enemies
49	The wealthy and wise die like everyone else, but God redeems the upright	God is not impressed by worldly wealth or wisdom
50	A call to right worship, not just in form but in heart	God desires heartfelt acknowledgment and faithful obedience; He is not otherwise appeased
51	A sinner's prayer for forgiveness	God honors the sacrifice of a contrite heart
52	The righteous will mock the wicked in the end	God's loyalty continues all day long; He uproots the treacherous
53	Everyone has turned aside from God (a variation of Ps 14)	God actively looks for those who seek Him and scatters those who don't
54	A prayer for deliverance from enemies (strangers)	God is our Helper, Sustainer, and Judge; He gives justice to the faithful
55	A prayer for deliverance from enemies (personal betrayal)	God redeems in peace, however many enemies there may be
56	"The day I am afraid, I trust in you"	God keeps a record of our weeping; He is trustworthy to bring us through times of trouble
57	A plea for refuge from acute danger	God gets things done for His servant; His loyalty is as great as the heavens
58	God judges the unjust rulers and principalities who are over the world	God will have vengeance on His enemies
59	A prayer for rescue from unprovoked attack; may all the earth see God's justice	God is strong and loyal
60	A prayer for restoration in the face of military defeat; without God, we shall be ruined	God allows defeat as a form of judgment, but He "will trample down our adversaries"
61	"From the end of the earth I call to you while my heart is faint"	God hears the vows of the weary and draws in the faithful under His protection
62	Confident assurance in the face of adversaries	God is strong and loyal, and He rewards all people according to their deeds
63	An expression of wholehearted seeking after God	God's loyalty is better than life itself; He gives joy to those who swear by Him
64	A prayer for rescue from scheming liars, with a swift answer	God brings justice suddenly, giving joy to the upright in heart
65	A celebration of peace, rest, and abundance in God	God attends to the earth and crowns it with goodness

Psalm	Psalm Summary	What It Reveals about God
66	A call for all the earth, Israel, and the psalmist to praise God	God keeps watch on the nations, tests His people, and powerfully answers the righteous
67	A prayer for blessing on God's people and on the land	God judges people with equity and blesses His own with a good harvest
68	"God will arise, his enemies will be scattered"	God is "Father of the fatherless and Judge for the widows" as well as the all-powerful God
69	The prayer of a God-fearing person suffering persecution	God listens to the needy
70	Help me quickly!	God helps the lowly and needy
71	A testimony of lifelong trust in Yahweh, anticipating help once again	God works salvation throughout a lifetime, reviving those who have seen troubles
72	A prayer for David's son and successor	God alone does wonders; in King Jesus, He fulfills our hopes for the world
73	An honest expression of doubt, resolving into faith by a revelation of God	God is good to the pure in heart; He will sweep aside the wicked and establish the faithful
74	A lament over the ruin of the sanctuary and God's apparent absence	God has shown Himself in the past as a strong deliverer; He cannot have changed
75	Eager anticipation of God's vengeance and ultimate justice	God brings down the boastful and the wicked in wrath but lifts up the righteous
76	A vision of the Lion of Judah returning from having executed final judgment	God is majestic, holy, and fearsome
77	Wondering why God isn't acting now to rescue Israel as He did in the exodus from Egypt	God punishes apostasy, but He will restore those who return to Him wholeheartedly
78	An account of Israel's history, teaching future generations not to repeat the sins of the past	God is angered by rebellion yet persistent in shepherding a stubborn people toward the fulfillment of His purposes
79	An appeal for national revival for the sake of God's honor	God forgives and restores, for He is merciful
80	A prayer for revival in solidarity with the northern tribes	God desires unity among the faithful
81	A call to praise God and to obey His word	God longs for His people to listen and learn obedience
82	God judges the principalities who are over the world	God desires justice
83	A prayer for protection against the nations' schemes to eliminate Israel	God is Judge, "the Most High over all the earth"
84	A celebration of coming to God's house	God provides a home even for the birds; He "does not withhold good from those who walk in integrity"
85	A prayer for reconciliation between God and His people and the return of His blessing on the land	God speaks peace to His loyal ones; His salvation is near to those who fear Him
86	A Davidic prayer for salvation	God is "compassionate and gracious . . . slow to anger and abounding in loyalty and faithfulness"
87	A prophetic oracle of the Gentiles being declared children of Zion	God is Father of a people from every nation
88	A lament in the midst of raw suffering, almost without hope	God redefines suffering through the death and resurrection of Jesus
89	A prayer for when experience doesn't seem to align with what we know of God's promises	God is faithful, answering His promises in Christ Jesus

Appendix A: Does the Bible Say How Much I Should Pray?

by Matt Bennett (founder and CEO, Christian Union)

You were designed to live in regular, ongoing fellowship with your Creator and Lord. Without that continuous and deepening bond, you will never fulfill the destiny God has planned for you. Just like all your other relationships in life, your relationship with God will only be successfully maintained with active, purposeful thought, self-discipline, and intentionality.

God loves you and wants you to succeed in your walk with Him and in your life more generally. He knows even better than you do your need for His abiding influence and presence. In order that you would know how to live, He has made plain in the Scriptures how you are to commune with Him on a daily basis. The pattern He sets forth in the Scriptures, and which has been practiced by many through the years, is that of praying and reading the Bible two or three set times per day, either on your own or while gathered with fellow Christians. Unfortunately, this is not the pattern of the vast majority of Christians in the West, and the West is suffering for it. When Christians do not have a solid, continuous walk with the Lord, all of society experiences the effects.

It's important that you see from the Scriptures that two or three set times per day is what you need to thrive spiritually. But you will also find that as you put this pattern into practice, you will be convinced not only by the Scriptures but also by your experience. Even if people are not convinced by health experts that weightlifting and cardio exercise will change their bodies for the better, putting a regular exercise routine into practice will demonstrate that it does indeed benefit them enormously.

What is clear from the Scriptures and a historical analysis of the New Testament era is that both pious Jews and then Christians prayed and read (or recited from memory) the Bible two or three set times per day. It seems that some practiced this discipline three times per day and some two times per day. It is hard to know for sure which tradition was more prevalent among first-century Christians and Jews.

PRAYING TWICE DAILY: NIGHT AND DAY

The scriptural evidence for night-and-day prayer (and Bible reading/meditating) begins early in the Old Testament and runs through the New Testament. One of the most revered and recited passages in the Old Testament is Deuteronomy 6:4-9:

> Hear, Israel: Yahweh our God, Yahweh is one. And you shall love Yahweh your God with all your heart and with all your soul and with all your strength. And these things which I command you today shall be upon your heart. You shall ingrain them in your children and talk about them when you sit in your house and when you walk along the road, *when you lie down and when you arise.* You shall bind them as a sign on your hand, and they shall be as frontlets between your eyes. And you shall write them on the doorposts of your house, and on your gates.

Notice the admonition to talk about the commands of God when you lie down and when you get up. Devout Jews understood this to mean that, at a minimum, they must meditate on the Bible at the beginning of the day and at the end of the day. The next book in the Old Testament, Joshua, confirms the importance of meditating twice a day on the Scriptures: "This book of the Torah shall not depart from your mouth, but you shall *ruminate on it day and night,* that you may be attentive to do all that is written in it; for then you shall make your way successful and shall have understanding" (Josh 1:8). It was not enough for Joshua to have been appointed by God and promised victory in his campaign to take the Promised Land. In order to succeed, he needed to meditate on God's word twice a day, both during the day and at night.

There are numerous examples of godly men and women praying day and night in the Bible, fulfilling the commands to regularly seek God in this way. For example, when Nehemiah heard the news that the walls of Jerusalem were still down, symbolizing God's abandonment of Israel, he prayed night and day. Nehemiah 1:4-6 says:

> When I heard these things, I sat down and wept; I mourned for days, fasting and praying before the God of heaven. I said: "Please, Yahweh, God of heaven, God great and awesome, who keeps covenant and loyalty for those who love him and keep his commandments, let your ear be attentive and your eyes open to hear your servant's prayer, which I am praying before you today, *by day and by night* on behalf of the children of Israel, your servants. I acknowledge the sins of the children of Israel, which we have sinned against you, and that I and my father's house have sinned."

IN THE GOSPELS

The twice-a-day pattern continues into the New Testament with the Gospels. Anna the prophetess made it her regular practice to pray, worship, and fast night and day over the course of many decades. Luke 2:36-37 says:

> There was also Anna, a prophetess, daughter of Phanuel, from the tribe of Asher. She was very old, having lived with her husband seven years from when she was a virgin, and by herself as a widow for eighty-four years. She never left the Temple, but *with fasting and prayer worshiped night and day.*

Jesus emphasized the need to persevere in prayer, and by this He meant that Christians ought to pray at least two set times per day, during the day and at night. Notice in the following parable what Jesus says in the first verse: He tells the disciples how *they should always* pray.

> Then he told them a parable to show that they should always pray and not give up, saying: "There was a judge in a certain city who neither feared God nor respected man. And there was a widow in that city who kept coming to him, saying: 'Give me justice against my adversary.' He was unwilling for a while, but finally he said to himself, 'Though I neither fear God nor respect man, yet because this widow keeps hammering at me, I will grant her justice, lest in the end she should give me a black eye!'"
>
> And the Lord said, "Hear what the unjust judge says. And will not God give justice to his chosen ones who *cry out to him day and night*? Will he suffer long over them? I tell you that he will give them justice quickly. Only, when the Son of Man comes, will he find faith on the earth?" (Luke 18:1-8)

Jesus' words show God's desire that His chosen ones persevere in prayer by crying out to Him day and night. But the real question, the question that the parable ends on, is whether faith exists among God's people—that is, whether His chosen ones have the faith to believe Him that their prayers are effectual and that they ought indeed to persevere by praying day and night.

IN THE PAULINE EPISTLES

Paul, Silas, and Timothy are listed as the authors of the first letter to the Thessalonians (1 Thes 1:1), so whenever the text says *we*, it must refer to at least the three of them, if not more people. First Thessalonians 3:10 says, "*Night and day we pray* exceedingly that we may see you in person and remedy what is lacking in your faith." Therefore, it was the practice of at least Paul, Silas, and Timothy to pray a minimum of twice daily.

In the context of instructing Timothy about the circumstances in which the church should extend material support to widows, Paul provides a fascinating insight regarding godliness. Paul instructs Timothy that the church should financially help only those widows who are over sixty and who have been faithful to their husbands and well known for their good deeds (1 Tim 5:9-10). A few verses earlier, he makes plain the expectations of how a godly person should live: "The real widow, left all alone, has set her hope on God and continues in *supplication and prayer night and day*. But the self-indulgent widow is dead even while she lives" (1 Tim 5:5-6). Notice the contrast between the two halves of this passage. On the one hand is the godly woman who prays night and day; on the other hand is a woman who lives for pleasure and is dead even while she lives. The implication is that those who do not pray night and day are lovers of pleasure and are (spiritually) dead even while alive.

Paul also affirms in his second letter to Timothy what was most likely his normal pattern of praying at least twice per day: "I give thanks to God, whom I serve, as my forefathers did, with a clear conscience, as I constantly remember you in *my prayers night and day*" (2 Tim 1:3).

OTHER NEW TESTAMENT BOOKS

During the first century, persecution against Christians periodically intensified, prompting some Jewish Christians to consider returning to Judaism, which at the time was not experiencing persecution like Christianity. The letter to the Hebrews was written to such a group of Christians, urging them to stay faithful to Christ and explaining the reasons why it made no sense for them to return to Judaism. The author draws several comparisons between the old covenant and the new covenant, including in Hebrews 13:9-17, where a comparison is made between the twice-daily burnt offerings of the old covenant and the "sacrifices" that readers are now to make as Christians. The twice-daily animal sacrifices administered by the priest were a type of what was to come in Christ. Instead of offering animal sacrifices, Christians are to come before God twice a day and praise Him with their lips: "Through him, then, let us offer up a sacrifice of praise to God continually—that is, the fruit of lips confessing his name" (Heb 13:15). The ministry of animal sacrifice is to be replaced with the ministry of praise. In fact, the wording used to talk about the "sacrifice of praise" is similar to that used to explain the continual (twice-daily) burnt offerings recorded in Exodus 29:38-43.

Notice that Hebrews 13:15 is a command. We *must* "offer up a sacrifice of praise to God continually," and in the context of comparison with the daily burnt offerings, this meant twice daily—in the morning and at twilight.

The last example in this study of day-and-night prayer is found in the book of Revelation. Revelation 4:8 says, "And each of the four living creatures had six wings and was full of eyes all around and within. *Day and night* they say without ceasing: 'Holy, holy, holy is the Lord God, the Ruler of all, who was, and who is, and who is to come.'" In this context, "day and night" probably means "continuously." It is extraordinary that God has created living creatures that minister to Him around the clock, praising His glorious Name.

JEWISH PATTERN IN THE FIRST CENTURY AD

It is tempting to view the biblical commands to pray day and night hyperbolically and not literally. Many read the passages enjoining night-and-day prayer casually, assuming the passages mean simply "You should pray a lot" and leave it to each person in his or her own context to determine how much "a lot" should be. However, it is important to interpret Scripture within its historical context, answering the question, "What would the original hearers/readers have understood from these passages?" Given the historical context and practices, we can confidently say they would have understood the passages to mean that every Christian should literally pray at two set times per day, at a minimum.

We know from the Mishnah[164] and the Talmud[165] that the pattern of devout Jews during the first century AD was to pray two or three set times per day. Paul F. Bradshaw, professor emeritus of liturgy at the University of Notre Dame, provides historical context in his book *Daily Prayer in the Early Church: A Study of the Origin and Early Development of the Divine Office*:

> Although it is not strictly a prayer but rather a creed, the recitation of the *Shema'* (Deut. 6.4-9; 11.13-21; Num. 15.37-41) is well attested as the fundamental daily devotion of Jews in the first century, both in Palestine and in the Diaspora. The custom of reciting it twice a day, "when you lie down and when you rise" (Deut. 6.7; 11.19), according to the Mishnah in the morning between dawn and sunrise and in the evening after sunset, is first mentioned in the *Letter of Aristeas* (145–100 B.C.).[166]

The twice-daily recitation of the Shema was accompanied by prayer in the form of fixed benedictions and free-flowing prayer:

> According to the Mishnah the *Shema'* was to be accompanied by a series of fixed benedictions: "In the morning two benedictions are said before and one after; and in the evening two benedictions are said before and two after, the one long and the other short."[167]

PRAYING THREE TIMES A DAY

There is also ample evidence for patterns of praying at three set times per day, which is corroborated in the New Testament as a pattern adopted by first-century Christians:

> Alongside the twofold recitation of the *Shema'* we find in Rabbinic Judaism the quite different custom of praying three times a day—morning, afternoon, and evening, the first and last being in practice combined with the saying of the *Shema'*. The observance of the afternoon time of prayer is mentioned in the New Testament: Peter and John go up to the Temple "at the hour of prayer, the ninth hour" (Acts 3.1), and Cornelius the centurion keeps the ninth hour of prayer in his house (Acts 10.3, 30). The ninth hour, 3 p.m., appears to have been chosen for the afternoon prayer in order that it might coincide with the time of the offering of the evening sacrifice in the Herodian Temple.[168]

It is believed that the practice of threefold daily prayer came about because of the influence of two passages in the Old Testament. The first is from the book of Psalms: "Evening, morning, and noon I muse and murmur, and he hears my voice" (Ps 55:17). The second comes from the book of Daniel. Daniel's godly lifestyle confirms the significance of drawing close to God in prayer. He believed prayer was so important that he would not stop praying three times per day even under the threat of death. Daniel 6:10 records his mindset and practice: "When Daniel learned that the decree had been signed, he went into his house, with the windows opened for him in his roof-chamber facing Jerusalem. And three times a day he continued kneeling down, praying and offering thanks before his God, as he had done before." You may know the story of how he was arrested for this and thrown into the lions' den and yet was delivered by God and restored to his place at the side of the king. If Daniel felt it was worth risking death to keep praying three times per day, it's worth considering whether this should be the modern Christian's practice as well.

---

[164] The Mishnah is the oral tradition of the Jews compiled into written form around AD 200.

[165] The Talmud is a Jewish commentary on the Hebrew Scriptures compiled around AD 500.

[166] Paul F. Bradshaw, *Daily Prayer in the Early Church: A Study of the Origin and Early Development of the Divine Office* (Eugene, OR: Wipf & Stock, 1981), 1.

[167] Bradshaw, *Daily Prayer*, 1-2, citing *m. Berakhot* 1.4.

[168] Bradshaw, *Daily Prayer*, 2; see also Robert Taft, *The Liturgy of the Hours in East and West: The Origins of the Divine Office and Its Meaning for Today*, 2nd rev. ed. (Collegeville, MN: Liturgical Press, 1993), 3-11.

PRAYING CONTINUALLY

In addition to the scriptural injunctions and examples of praying two or three set times per day, there are numerous admonitions to pray all throughout the day, at all sorts of times and for all sorts of occasions. Paul instructs believers to "pray unceasingly" (1 Thes 5:17), and the Bible is full of examples of godly men and women practicing this sort of prayer. Praying at several set times per day does not take away the need to pray at other times as appropriate.

CONCLUSION

As we have seen, the scriptural and historical evidence for praying two or three set times per day is very strong, and because it is shockingly different from the typical practice and mindset of the twenty-first-century Western Christian, it can seem radical. It is always a jolt when we encounter God's divine truth in a way that shows us that our mindsets and lifestyles need to change significantly. For example, if you became a Christian later in life, the Scriptures undoubtedly were shocking to you in their expectations that you practice sexual integrity and that you forgive from the heart all who may have hurt you in the past. It is important that new knowledge, such as the knowledge of what your daily devotional life would look like if it were modeled on Scripture, does not remain simply an intellectual curiosity for you but is applied so that you can make all the necessary adjustments in your life. You will find that although there will be difficulty in getting your life to consistently reflect the biblical pattern, the reward will be astonishing. You will experience God's presence and fellowship like never before, and you will be in a much better place to fulfill God's purpose and destiny for your life.

Appendix B: Seven Principles of a Seeking-God Lifestyle

by Matt Bennett (founder and CEO, Christian Union)

It is the honor and privilege of every Christian to know God and to walk with Him on a daily basis. He is the one true and glorious God, who has created us and redeemed us so that we may walk with Him in this life and the next.

Though some Christians have known God for years since they first received the forgiveness of Jesus Christ, they may not be aware of what it means to truly seek God or what He expects of those called by His name. To be a Christian is to be a follower, an imitator, of Jesus Christ. We must pursue God, love Him, and serve Him the way our Lord and Savior has modeled for us.

Seeking after God isn't something to be undertaken primarily by non-Christians, but by Christians. It's common to call an interested non-Christian a "seeker," which isn't wrong. However, in about 90 percent of the instances Scripture speaks of people seeking after God, it refers to believers, not unbelievers. Seeking God is thus an *ongoing* mindset and lifestyle of those who desire to know, love, and follow God. Becoming a Christian is a step in the process of seeking God, but only the first step; the rest of one's life is to be spent drawing closer to Him.

When the Scriptures describe seeking God, they often use the image of attracting His presence: As we draw near to God, He draws near to us. As the prophet Azariah told King Asa in 2 Chronicles 15:2, "Yahweh is with you when you are with him. If you seek him, he will be found by you; but if you leave him, he will leave you." God's presence comes in the Person of the Holy Spirit. When we seek Him, He pours out His Holy Spirit into our lives individually and corporately. While in one sense God is everywhere—He is omnipresent—we also see in the Scriptures that He inhabits certain people or groups of people in special ways at discrete times. This is what we are to seek after—the very presence of God in our lives and communities. We want the presence of God to be on earth as it is in heaven.

What follows are seven principles that describe what it means to seek after God. These are activities we do that attract His supernatural presence in the outpouring of His Holy Spirit. God's sovereignty over all people and events does not nullify the responsibility of humanity to seek after Him. God ordains the end, but He also ordains the means. Just as a person must repent of his or her sins and believe the Good News to become a Christian, so a Christian must continue to actively pursue God. Understanding and practicing the following seven principles will help make you a seeker after God. This is what you were designed for, and it is what the Lord expects of you.

PRINCIPLE 1: HUMILITY AND FASTING

The very essence of following Christ is to imitate Him in His humility. Though He was God Himself, He set aside His power and glory to become part of the creation. He went still further and became willing to be treated like a criminal and to die on the cross for humanity's sins (Phil 2:5-11). Jesus exemplified a humble life, and every Christian is to emulate His humility.

Pride is the opposite of humility, and we know from the Scriptures that God judges and actively opposes the proud (Jas 4:6; 1 Pet 5:5). It's a terrifying reality to be opposed by the God of the universe, yet that is where many stand. And not only non-Christians but also proud Christians can expect the opposition of the God of heaven and earth. The admonitions to be humble in Philippians, James, and 1 Peter are all written to a Christian audience.

Meanwhile, God has made plain that He loves to support and dwell with the humble in heart. Isaiah 57:15 says, "For thus says the One who is high and lifted up, who inhabits eternity, and whose name is holy: 'I dwell in a high and holy place, and with the crushed and lowly in spirit, to revive the spirit of the lowly and to revive the heart of the crushed.'" Similarly, in Isaiah 66:2, the Lord says, "I will have regard for this one: the lowly and broken-spirited, who trembles at my word."

God commands us numerous times in the Scriptures to "humble ourselves." It is our own responsi-bility to humble ourselves, not something we passively wait for and hope happens at some point. It's a command that we must obey, and God has given us a tool to help us: fasting. Fasting is not the only such tool; among other ways of developing humility, there is also confessing sins as well as meditating on the life and example of Christ. However, fasting is an important tool and one that has often been neglected in the Western church. It is important not to take fasting too far in thinking that it is the sine qua non of the Christian life. The Pharisees in the New Testament showed that a person can fast regularly and still be self-righteous, proud, and greedy. It is not the answer to all spiritual problems in a person's life. But the practice is in the Scriptures for a reason. It is indeed important and should be practiced regularly. While it is not a spiritual panacea, neglecting one of the most potent tools for generating humility is a failure to take advantage of a God-intended means for spiritual growth. After all, Jesus said to His disciples, "*When* you fast . . ." (Matt 6:16).

And fasting isn't something that developed only during the first century; it had existed among God's people for centuries. For example, Moses, Elijah, David, Daniel, Nehemiah, and Mordecai all fasted. Sometimes people fasted for a day and sometimes for as long as 70 days (Mordecai and all the Jews in the Persian Empire) or 120 days (Nehemiah). (Commentators generally believe that for long fasts, those fasting ate one meal per day unless stated otherwise.)

After Jesus died and rose from the dead, it was assumed that fasting would be part of the Christian life. There was no need to fast when Christ was present because there was no need to mourn over the absence of God, but once He ascended to the Father, the practice of fasting returned for the people of God (see Matt 9:14-15). We know from early church documents like the *Didache* that it was the practice of Christians in the first century to fast every Wednesday and Friday until 3:00 p.m.[169] They would have a meal in the evening, which would be all the food they took in for those days. There would also be special times of extended fasting just as there were before Christ came. Different circumstances require different lengths of fasting. For the Christian seeking to be humble before God, fasting must be a regular part of life.

Takeaway:
Christians are to continually cultivate humility, making use of the discipline of fasting regularly as well as episodically. The first-century church fasted every Wednesday and Friday until 3:00 p.m.[170]

PRINCIPLE 2: FERVENT AND FREQUENT PRAYER

The typical prayer life of the first-century Christian and the average Christian in Asia or Africa is mark-edly different from that of the average Christian in America and Europe. Of course, there are exceptions, but by and large there is little to no dedication to regular prayer among Christians in the West. Yet the Scriptures admonish us to pray on all occasions with all kinds of prayers and requests. The example of Epaphras, one of Paul's associates, suggests that consistent, dedicated prayer can make a significant differ-ence in the lives of our loved ones and in the world at large (Col 4:12-13).

Many Christians lift up prayers during the day as they go about their business, which is a good thing and is modeled in the Scriptures (e.g., the book of Nehemiah). However, the biblical pattern suggests

---

[169] *Didache* 8.1; Tertullian, *On Fasting. In Opposition to the Psychics*, 10.
[170] The "Takeaway" given at the end of each principle is designed to give practical ideas for living out the principles.

doing more than that.[171] Repeatedly in the Scriptures, we are told to pray night and day. Luke 18:1-8 (the parable of the persistent widow) encourages this practice. We see in 1 Timothy 5 that widows who prayed night and day demonstrated that they had set their hope on God and were not lovers of pleasure who were undeserving of financial help from the church. Hebrews 13:9-17 suggests that the twice-daily burnt offerings at the Temple were a "type" of the twice-or-more daily prayer offerings that Christians are to give to the Lord. Some of these set times of prayer are described as the "hour of prayer" (e.g., Acts 3:1), which may give us a sense of their length. This indicates a situation in which the practice of praying two or three times a day, combined with Bible reading, could total a couple of hours over the course of the day. This practice of prayer can be done on one's own or in a gathering with other Christians.

Takeaway:
Christians are to pray fervently two or three set times per day (note: Worship and praise are types of prayer). This is in addition to praying throughout the day as God leads.

PRINCIPLE 3: TAKING IN THE WORD
Similar to the discipline of praying two or three times a day is the discipline of taking in the Word of God. The Scriptures are to be read, heard, or meditated upon two or more times per day (Deut 6:4-9; Josh 1:8) so that we can know and do the will of God. Every day, pious Jews in the first century would recite from memory the Shema (from Deut 6:4-5) along with accompanying blessings (from Numbers and Deuteronomy).[172] They would also read or hear the Scriptures together, recite from memory various other passages, and regularly meditate on the Word of God. This became the practice of the early Christians as well.

In the Bible, "word of God" can refer to the Scriptures, but not exclusively so. The word of God also comes in other ways. If God speaks to you through a prophetic message, dream, angelic visitation, or any other means, then you have heard the word of God, and you must obey and follow the Lord. These revelations certainly need to be weighed against the Scriptures and talked over with godly friends so that you can accurately sense what God has said. But if God has spoken to you, then you must obey Him. Unfortunately, some of these other means of receiving God's revelation are not known or considered legitimate among most Western-educated Christians. Some wrongly believe that celebrating and practicing spiritual gifts like prophecy and the "word of knowledge" (see 1 Cor 12:8) take away from the authority of Scripture, but it is the Scriptures themselves that authenticate the legitimacy of hearing from God in these ways. We must have the courage to obey the Scriptures in these areas even if their testimony does not match our prior experience. As with anything else unfamiliar, there is much to learn and there will be many growing pains, but by actively cultivating the art of hearing God, you will be able to know His will and be able to seek Him much more specifically and wholeheartedly.

Takeaway:
Christians are to pray and read the Bible on their own or with others two or three set times per day. This will likely total about one to three hours per day and may include weekly church services, Bible studies, daily devotions, prayer meetings, Wednesday night church gatherings, accountability groups, and so on.

PRINCIPLE 4: REPENTANCE
The Lord loves and draws near to all who repent of their sins, because repentance delights God's heart like little else. Luke tells us that there is extraordinary joy in heaven when sinners repent and turn to God (Luke 15:10). God yearns and deeply desires to show mercy and give blessing, but often He will do so only when He sees genuine repentance in people's lives. Ezekiel 18:31-32 says, "Cast off from yourselves all the transgressions you have committed, and get yourselves a new heart and a new spirit. For why should you die, house of Israel? For I take no pleasure in the death of the one who dies,' declares my Lord Yahweh. 'Turn back and live!'"

---

171 According to Paul F. Bradshaw, the pattern for pious Jews and Christians in the first century was to pray two or three set times per day, in addition to praying continuously throughout the day (see Bradshaw, *Daily Prayer*, 2).

172 Bradshaw, *Daily Prayer*, 1, 9, 23-26.

There is an extraordinary story of King Ahab, who was an exceedingly wicked king of Israel. He repeatedly rebelled against God and supported the murderous actions of his wife Jezebel. God sent Elijah to pronounce judgment on him, warning him of impending disaster. Yet Ahab humbled himself and repented of his sins, moving God to relent in sending punishment. God said to Elijah in 1 Kings 21:29, "Have you seen how Ahab has humbled himself before me? Because he has humbled himself before me, I will not bring this disaster in his days, but in the days of his son will I bring disaster on his house." If even wicked Ahab could obtain mercy through repentance, surely we should be encouraged to repent of our own sins.

At another time in Israel's history, the people were being faithful to keep regular times of prayer and fasting yet were rebellious against God. This hypocrisy angered God, who rebuked them in Joel 2:12-13: "'Even now,' declares Yahweh, 'return to me with all your heart, with fasting and weeping and mourning. And tear your heart, not your garments. Return to Yahweh your God, for he is gracious and compassionate, slow to anger and abounding in loyalty, and he will change his mind about sending calamity.'" The people were hypocritical for going through the motions of fasting and rending their garments while not genuinely repenting ("tearing their hearts") before God for the evil they had done.

Takeaway:
Christians are to repent regularly when seeking after God. All areas of life are to be examined, and any doubtful habit that may be displeasing to God should be eliminated.

PRINCIPLE 5: OBEDIENCE
The flip side of repentance is obedience, and authentic repentance always leads to obedience. Repentance is looking at past sins and acknowledging what needs to change before God. Obedience is daily walking in holiness and surrendering to Jesus Christ as Lord. God delights in and draws close to those who live righteously.

Every culture has characteristics that reinforce and commend the eternal commands of God—things a society values that God also values. However, every culture also has values that are contrary to the will of God, out of alignment with Him. In such cases, it is the duty of Christians to reject cultural norms and faithfully adopt God's values. Faithfully walking with God even when this brings one in conflict with the surrounding culture exemplifies a righteous and holy life, pleasing to God.

As an example, in America, society has strayed far away from the biblical norms regarding sexual integrity that it once largely embraced. Fornication, pornography, homosexuality, adultery, and divorce are all common in the United States—in both Christian and non-Christian culture—undoubtedly bringing great grief to the heart of God. These forms of sexual immorality often result in abortion, which has claimed tens of millions of lives in the last fifty years, amounting to a death toll much higher than the Holocaust of World War II or the combined casualties in all American wars. God forgives when there is genuine repentance, and America—including American Christians—has much to repent of in this area.

Another American cultural norm that surely grieves the heart of God is materialism and greed. Although America is the richest country in the history of the world, American Christians give away just 2.5 percent of their income.[173] Giving away 10 percent of one's income was the norm for pious Jews and Christians in the first century, such that people were considered generous only if they gave considerably more than 10 percent. Now it is often considered remarkable if Christians give away just 10 percent. How has our thinking been so altered that we are so wealthy yet so stingy at the same time? Throughout Scripture, we can see God's heart for generosity, especially in His concern for the poor and oppressed. Every Christian must break free from the demonic stronghold of materialism and greed and learn to live generously.

Takeaway:
Christians are to obey all the Lord's commands, including the commands to love Him with one's whole heart and to love others. They are to resolve to live righteous lives, obeying the Lord moment by moment.

---

[173] John Lee, "Who Are the Most Generous? Not Who You'd Expect," *Christianity Today*, August 13, 2020, https://www.christianitytoday.com/ct/2020/august-web-only/most-generous-not-who-you-expect-vertical-generosity.html.

PRINCIPLE 6: COMMUNITY

Seeking after God isn't just an individual pursuit but also a corporate one. Jonathan Edwards, perhaps the most respected theologian on the subject of revival, wrote that the best biblical passage on the topic is Zechariah 8:20-23,[174] which states:

> Thus says Yahweh of Hosts: "Yet again, peoples and the inhabitants of many cities shall come, and the inhabitants of one city will go to another and say, 'Let us go without delay to entreat Yahweh, to seek Yahweh of Hosts. I myself am resolved to go.' And many peoples and great nations will come to seek Yahweh of Hosts in Jerusalem and to entreat him."
>
> Thus says Yahweh of Hosts: "In those days ten men of all languages and nations will seize a Judean man by the hem of his garment, saying, 'Let us go with you, for we have heard that God is with you.'"

Notice the zeal of those seeking after the Lord. It was not enough that they themselves were seeking after God, but they were compelled to encourage others to seek God as well.

Not only is the gathering *of* others important in seeking God, but gathering *with* others is also critical. It is important that Christians gather with others on a weekly (if not daily) basis to encourage each other in the faith, to remain strong in the Lord, and to minister to each other, building up the body of Christ. Christians should be regular participants in churches, small groups, and other large and small group gatherings in order to stimulate one another to love and good deeds.

Moreover, there is value in gathering for longer periods (such as multiday Christian conferences) several times per year for the purpose of deepening love for and devotion to God. This sort of practice has biblical precedent. The ancient Israelites were told to keep various feasts (or festivals) throughout the year, including the weeklong Feast of Unleavened Bread, the weekend Feast of Pentecost, and the weeklong Feast of Booths. During these times, there was celebration, public reading of the Bible, teaching, praise and worship, and confession of sin (see Exod 23:14-19; 2 Chr 30; Neh 8). Every man in the nation of Israel was required to gather for these three annual feasts (women and children likely often accompanied them) so that they would be strengthened in their love for God, ready and able to serve Him and walk with Him all year long. Unfortunately, the Israelites did not always keep these feasts, and their hearts strayed away from the Lord. However, over the years, they would periodically repent, return to God, and hold these feasts—with spectacular results! (As examples, read Nehemiah 8 and 2 Chronicles 30, and notice the extraordinary joy and zeal for God that would develop during these feasts.)

The same pattern should be true of those who seek after God in our current age. People remain strong and devoted to God when they have regular (preferably multiday) experiences of teaching, encouragement, worship, confession, and prayer. For Christians seeking after God, the question should not be *whether* they will attend a few multiday Christian conferences in the upcoming year, but rather *when*, and which ones, they will attend.

Takeaway:

Christians are to join with others for multiday Christian conferences for strengthening and devotion. Moreover, they are to urge fellow Christians to seek God wholeheartedly.

PRINCIPLE 7: PERSEVERANCE

Seeking God is a way of life and not something to be done solely in times of desperate need. God's presence and favor are worth pursuing diligently day by day. Just as we may show diligence in pursuing education for many hours a day, striving for athletic excellence through many hours of practice, or devoting significant effort to a worthy cause, we should show the same kind of dedication to pleasing and following the one true God. As the Scriptures say in 1 Timothy 4:8, "Bodily training is of some benefit, but godliness is all-beneficial, holding promise both in the present life and in the life to come."

---

[174] See Jonathan Edwards, "An Humble Attempt to Promote Explicit Agreement and Visible Union of God's People in Extraordinary Prayer, for the Revival of Religion and the Advancement of Christ's Kingdom on Earth, pursuant to Scripture-Promises and Prophecies concerning the Last Time" (1747), which takes Zechariah 8:20-22 as its theme text.

It is extraordinary to notice the hard work and persistence that some Christians apply to certain aspects of their lives, be it education, athletics, or hobbies. However, many of these same Christians exhibit extraordinarily low prioritization of their walk with Jesus Christ. And then they wonder why they do not have the Lord's presence and power in their lives. Those who are out of shape physically usually know why they are out of shape: They don't exercise enough. Those who do not perform well on tests know that the reason is often that they have not studied. Yet while many Christians have little victory and power in their lives, they often have no idea why. But they have not been praying and reading the Scriptures diligently, fasting, humbling themselves, repenting of their sins, and practicing consistent obedience to God. God can be displeased with and perhaps even "opposing" us (see Jas 4:6; 1 Pet 5:5) while we are completely ignorant of it.

Notice the single-minded zeal of the apostle Paul in Philippians 3:12-14:

> Not that I have already laid hold of these things or have already been perfected, but I press on to take hold of that for which Christ Jesus took hold of me. Brothers, I do not consider myself as having taken hold of it, but I have one thought: Forgetting what lies behind and reaching out toward what lies ahead, I press on toward the goal for the prize of the upward calling of God in Christ Jesus.

It is this perspective that must be the mindset of every person who seeks after God diligently. We must fiercely pursue God, never being satisfied with anything less than His divine blessing and presence in our lives.

Takeaway:

Christians are to diligently persevere in their efforts to seek God day after day, month after month, and year after year.

OBSTACLES TO SEEKING GOD

There are two significant obstacles to adopting a Seeking-God Lifestyle that need to be briefly addressed: a wrong theological understanding of legalism and the notion of "busyness."

There are few concepts in American Christian culture more misunderstood than legalism. To the average American Christian, "legalism" refers to having to do something in the Christian life that one does not want to do. This is very different from the biblical attitude toward following the commands of God. All the principles in the foregoing essay on seeking God have nothing to do with legalism and everything to do with fulfilling God's commands and living as a Christian. Legalism, rightly understood, refers to three possibilities:

First, it can be legalistic to believe that a person has to perform a work in order to be saved instead of relying on God's grace given through repentance and faith in Jesus Christ. For example, if a person believes you must attend church services a certain number of times before you can become a Christian, that is an inaccurate and legalistic understanding of the gospel. Any requirement added to the gospel message of salvation is unacceptable.

Second, it can be legalistic to add undue requirements to what it means biblically to live a God-fearing life. For example, the Pharisees decided—based on their interpretation of the Law—that it was a violation of the Sabbath for Jesus or anyone else to perform a healing on the Sabbath. Jesus rebuked them, pointing out that every single one of them would rescue one of their prized animals if it fell into a pit on a Sabbath. So how could it be impermissible to heal a person on the Sabbath? The Pharisees added numerous requirements to God's commands, depending on their own traditions instead of God's desires. An example in our context would be telling someone that they must pray at exactly 6:00 a.m. every single day or they are being disobedient to God. The Scriptures do indeed teach us to pray and read the Bible two or three times per day, but never is it stated at exactly what time that should be done. Nor is it wrong to set 6:00 a.m. as a time of prayer for ourselves individually or for a gathering of believers. But this becomes problematic when we suggest that people are disobedient to God if they don't do it at that time.

Third, it can be legalistic to hypocritically emphasize less important commands of God while neglecting more important ones. Jesus emphasized this in a rebuke to the Pharisees: "Woe to you, scribes and Pharisees, hypocrites! For you tithe mint and dill and cumin, and you have neglected the weighty matters of the law—justice and mercy and faith. But you ought to have done these things without neglecting the other" (Matt 23:23). Note that Jesus explicitly stated that they were indeed right not to neglect the "less weighty matter" (tithing). The problem was that while they were extremely fastidious about their tithing, even making sure they tithed the increase in their plants, they were neglecting even more important commands, including those pertaining to justice, mercy, and faith. A parallel example today would be for a person to meticulously pray and read the Bible regularly three times per day yet commit sexual immorality and think nothing of it. The solution is not to neglect regular, daily prayer, but to remember to be faithful to God in all matters. It would be much better to miss prayer once in a while and have sexual integrity than to be extremely fastidious about set prayer times while living in sexual immorality.

A wrong understanding of legalism has kept many from following God with the diligence and wholeheartedness that He is owed. The seven principles listed in the foregoing essay are not legalistic burdens but an explanation of what the Scriptures teach about how to seek after God. These means are designed for our benefit—to bring blessing and growth in one's relationship with God. Take a close look yourself and see what the Scriptures are teaching on what it means to seek God, and then be faithful to those principles.

A second common obstacle in seeking God is "busyness." Many Christians do not want to spend the time that seeking after God requires because they are too busy. Perhaps their love for God has grown so cold that even when it becomes clear to them from the Scriptures how they ought to spend their time, they will not make God their priority. They will rarely state it so starkly but instead will point to their responsibilities at work, at church, in their studies, in driving their kids to events—and the list goes on and on.

When students decide they want to play sports at the college level, it means they will need to spend time getting in shape and practicing, and this means that other activities will be left behind. By necessity, the student-athlete will not have as much time for other organized campus events or for entertainment, like movies, TV, video games, and surfing the internet. College athletes know that their time in athletic training must be prioritized if they are going to succeed.

Similarly, adopting the Christian lifestyle as described in the Bible will mean making sacrifices in other areas. What can make this especially difficult is that some Christians have lived for years without making God a priority, so when they are confronted with the explicit expectations of God in the Bible, they do not want to change their priorities. Other activities, as good as they may be, can become idols and fill the place of the Christian's first love instead of Jesus Himself. Righting oneself and making changes to one's schedule and priorities is a difficult and sometimes even a grief-filled process. We naturally grieve when we lose things we love, and unfortunately, for many Christians their first love is actually the other pursuits in their lives instead of the desire to please and serve God Himself.

As you put these seven principles into regular practice, you will notice significant changes in your life. Your decision-making will be more consistent with God's plans, you will have greater power over sin, you will hear the voice of God more often, and you will experience fillings of the Holy Spirit. It's the life that God has planned for you, and doing any less may mean that you will miss out on God's specific purposes and calling on your life.